"FEMINISM IS NOT THE STORY OF MY LIFE"

"FEMINISM

How Today's Feminist Elite

IS NOT

Has Lost Touch with the

THE STORY

Real Concerns of Women

OF MY LIFE"

ELIZABETH FOX-GENOVESE

Anchor Books

Doubleday

New York London Toronto Sydney Auckland

An Anchor Book

PUBLISHED BY DOUBLEDAY
a division of Bantam Doubleday Dell Publishing Group, Inc.
1540 Broadway, New York, New York 10036

ANCHOR BOOKS, DOUBLEDAY, and the portrayal of an anchor are
trademarks of Doubleday, a division of Bantam Doubleday Dell
Publishing Group, Inc.

"Feminism Is Not the Story of My Life"
was originally published in hardcover
by Nan A. Talese/Doubleday in 1996. The Anchor Books edition
is published by arrangement with Nan A. Talese/Doubleday.

Book design by Chris Welch

The Library of Congress has cataloged the Nan A. Talese/Doubleday
hardcover edition of this work as follows:

Fox-Genovese, Elizabeth, 1941–
"Feminism is not the story of my life": how today's feminist elite has lost
touch with the real concerns of women / Elizabeth Fox-Genovese.
—1st ed.
p.   cm.
Includes index.
1. Feminism—United States.   2. Women—United States—Social
conditions.   I. Title.
HQ1421.F69   1996
305.42′0973—dc20   95–31602
CIP

ISBN 0-385-46791-5

Copyright © 1996 by Elizabeth Fox-Genovese

All Rights Reserved

Printed in the United States of America

First Anchor Books Trade Paperback Edition: January 1997
1   3   5   7   9   10   8   6   4   2

FOR

BETTY FOX

JO GENOVESE

ANNIE FASULO

KATIE FASULO

ACKNOWLEDGMENTS

E ven more than most, this book could never have been written without the generous assistance of countless people. Without the many women and men who have spoken with me of their lives or consented to be interviewed, there would literally have been no book—or at least not this book. And although, even now, I cannot name them, I trust they will know that I am grateful beyond words and have tried to honor their trust.

John Shelton Reed generously opened the polling resources of the Institute for Research in Social Science to me. Kathy Braxton helped to analyze the polls, and although I ultimately edited out many of the fascinating variations in people's attitudes by income, education, age, region, race, ethnicity, and religion, I could never have written with confidence if she had not done so. Kimberley Beakley patiently endured and supplied the vagaries of my research requests, and she lived so closely with the initial stages of the book that she was able to conduct a few of the interviews for me. Our continuing conversations about the issues and women's lives proved a touchstone for me as well as a bridge to the thinking of a new generation.

During the years I have been working on this book, I have benefited from the opportunity to present versions of the arguments to a range of groups and have always profited from the ensuing discussions. My warm thanks for especially valuable discussions are due to the American Education Research Association, the American Enterprise Institute, Berry College, the Center for Adult Life and Learning at the 92nd Street YMCA in New York City, the Council for Women in Independent Schools in Philadelphia, the Annual Faye Goosetree Women's Symposium at Texas Wesleyan University, Franklin and Marshall College, the German Historical Institute in Washington, D.C., the New School for Social Research, Oglethorpe University, the Queens University in Belfast, Austen Peay State University, Providence College, and the First Unitarian Church of Memphis.

Many of the people to whom I am most directly beholden are quoted at some point in the book. In each case, except for Nancy Wilson, the name has been changed and the location or occupation or both disguised. Even so, I am loathe to thank them by name. So, I can only hope that the many students and friends who have been generous beyond measure in their interest, support, and tolerance of my developing ideas will know that I recognize and cherish their contributions. And it is my great pleasure to thank by name others, who are not quoted. Stacey Horstmann's exceptional research skills have come to my rescue more times than I care to remember. Stacey, Laura Crawley, Naomi Nelson, Sheila O'Connor, and Isa Williams took time to read the entire manuscript, discussed the issues at length, and frequently challenged me to rethink. Dale Reed read parts of the earliest draft, and her questions helped me to frame later ones. Anne Hartle, Allan Kulikoff, and Loraine Smith Pangle all read the entire manuscript with extraordinary care, and I only hope that the final version justifies the attention they gave.

Lou Ferleger and Bob Paquette have, by now, lived with my work and ideas for years, and I still marvel at their continuing tolerance for both—not to mention for me. For the past two years, Bob has tirelessly discussed aspects of the book, frequently faxing articles I might have missed or suggesting fresh perspectives, and, at the end, he read the entire manuscript with exemplary care. Lou has "grannied" this book from the start, sharing his vast knowledge of public policy and economics, reading every draft, and, above all, always urging me on.

Kim Witherspoon, my agent, has dexterously and delicately shepherded me through proposal, contract, and final revisions. In the process, she has become a friend. Among the many things for which I owe her thanks, finding a home for this book at Doubleday ranks high on the list. Nan Talese recognized the possibilities from the start, graciously put up with the delays as the book evolved from one conception to another, read the manuscript with that rare combination of appreciation and criticism for which authors proverbially bless good editors, and has shown a confidence I may not have merited, but deeply value. And, in the final stages, Judith Riven provided an exceptionally sensitive and exacting editorial guidance for which I am not merely indebted but grateful.

Much of this book concerns women's webs of friendship and connection with other women, and, in many respects, might be seen as an extension of my continuing conversations with the women who figure at the center of my own life. My sister, Rebecca Fox, and I have discussed these issues almost since the days she could first talk, and this time she spent hours discussing them further and filling in with examples from her own special knowledge of young women's dreams and nightmares. A rich, unending conversation has bound me and my friend Nancy Wilson since our first days at college, and the recurring topics of that conversation continue to weave through this book. In addition to talking and retalking everything, Nan read the entire manuscript and, throughout, offered the extraordinary combination of tough criticism and warm appreciation that sustains, deepens, and defines a friendship that has lasted for thirty-five years.

And it seems a fitting tribute to those abiding ties that her daughter, Elizabeth Wilson, joined the conversation, adding the perspective of the next generation.

Much of this book also concerns marriage and family, especially their centrality to most women's lives. Here, my views do, unapologetically, reflect my own experience, for I have been fortunate in parents who have followed my efforts with interest and love. Personal experience has also convinced me that if marriage necessarily limits anyone's freedom, a good marriage nurtures a woman's independence. As usual, Gene has read every draft, encouraging, chiding, and even enjoying. This book and I have immeasurably benefited from his peerless gifts as editor and reader, and, especially, the sustaining companionship that binds our lives and work.

CONTENTS

Acknowledgments   V I I

Preface   1

O n e   WHAT'S FEMINISM GOT TO DO WITH IT?   9

T w o   GROWING UP FEMININE   3 5

T h r e e   SEXUAL REVOLUTION   5 8

F o u r   LIVING WITH SEXUAL LIBERATION   8 3

F i v e   ECONOMIC REVOLUTION   1 1 0

S i x   WE ARE ALSO OUR MOTHERS' DAUGHTERS   1 4 0

S e v e n   WORK AND FAMILY   1 7 2

E i g h t   WHAT MOMMY TRACK?   1 9 9

N i n e   WOMEN IN THE CULTURAL WAR   2 2 7

Selected Bibliography   2 6 1

Index   2 6 5

PREFACE

I n the fall of 1991, a young woman reporter from a large metropol-
itan newspaper called to interview me about my recent book,
Feminism Without Illusions. Toward the end of a long and cordial conversation, we started to talk about children as a priority for
society. Suddenly, she startled me, saying, "You know, last week I
attended the NOW convention and, out of hundreds of sessions,
only one focused on children—and it was on lesbian mothers." She
added softly, "I am seven months pregnant." Long after she hung
up, the conversation haunted me. Here was a young woman of
about thirty who was successfully pursuing a career and loving it and
about to have a child she expected to love. Where did she turn for a
story that would capture her life and help her to live it more easily?
As I replayed our conversation in my head, other conversations re-
surfaced. Since the appearance of *Feminism Without Illusions,* I have

spoken with a large number of young professional women, in business, law, and the media, all accomplished, successful, engaging, many planning to become or already mothers. Those conversations had an implicit refrain: Feminism is not talking about my life. And gradually, it struck me that those conversations echoed the words of the many women of all classes and races who regularly tell reporters and pollsters, "I am not a feminist, but . . ."

My mind kept returning to those conversations, and I found myself listening carefully to the many women I met on my own campus, Emory University, around Atlanta, and on my travels around the country. Those conversations spurred my desire to understand what women wanted for their lives. By the spring of 1992, I knew I was going to write a book. I started taping interviews, studying polling data, and doing systematic research. The work itself went rapidly, but I needed time to live with the stories I was hearing. In the end, it took two years for this book to take shape. For a long time, I kept wrestling with the problem of why so many women who fiercely value independence refused to identify with feminism.

For several decades, I have called myself a feminist and, like many women of my generation, have been puzzled that so many women reject the term even though they have benefited from the feminist gains of the past thirty years. Hard experience has also taught me that the "official" feminist movement does not have much patience for women who do not support every plank in its increasingly radical platform. And it gradually dawned on me that even when the women whom I interviewed and with whom I had been speaking informally knew little or nothing about feminist positions, they had a gut sense that feminism was not talking about their lives. Worse, they had a sneaking suspicion that feminists do not think that their lives are important.

Day by day, my work on this book reminded me of how important women's lives are—important to the women who live them but no less important to families and to our society. Today, women's lives are more important to society and more complicated than ever. The media bombard us with images of women who dash from job to children to kitchen, juggling the conflicting demands with cool grace. Most women do not find the juggling easy, especially when the pulls take the form of demanding employers and sick or unhappy children. Many women want rewarding work even as they continue to cherish traditional family values. Many want to be respected as competent workers even as they continue to enjoy the pleasures of femininity. Most cherish their independence even as they want binding ties to a man and children. The women to whom I have been listening do not want to sacrifice one side of their lives to another, but living with the tensions has taught them that no one can "have it all." So, like the rest of us, they make the best compromises they can.

As the young woman who interviewed me complained, feminists normally minimize the importance women attach to the bearing and rearing of children on the grounds that women, like men, should be free to work as hard as they choose. Yet most women see their children as central to their lives. Of course the bearing and rearing of children cost women heavily. Of course it is not "fair" that family responsibilities usually fall more heavily on women than on men. Of course women who take time away from careers or jobs to care for children may never achieve "equality" with men who do not. Yet women would not feel such tension between work and children if their self-image as good mothers did not matter so much to them and if they did not find their children an inestimable source of love and personal satisfaction.

Much of my evidence for the ways women think about their lives, feminism, and women's issues comes from the many extended formal interviews that I have conducted with them, buttressed by hundreds of informal conversations and opportunities to hear women express their views. I make no pretense to have constructed a scientific sample, although I have made every effort to include women of different backgrounds, generations, and parts of the country. Living in Georgia, I do not have to be told that New York is hardly representative of America. But I was especially fortunate to be able to talk at length with a group of women and one man in a general equivalency diploma class at Lehman College in New York City and a group of girls who attend a private school, also in New York. Many long interviews with the woman I call Gloria Patterson, as well as shorter interviews with her friends and women in her church, gave me a valuable introduction to the beliefs and concerns of Southern-born African-American women.

In addition to these formal interviews, I have, during the past two years, kept notes of the many conversations I have had with women about their lives, here in Atlanta, throughout the South, and across the country. Few of the women I interviewed or spoke with are directly quoted in the book, but their thoughtful responses to the issues has informed and sustained my general arguments. Throughout, I have used first names for those I have spoken with, not out of disrespect, but because I could devise no better way to capture something of the quality of the conversations and the immediacy of their concerns.

I have drawn heavily upon public opinion polls, especially two series conducted by George Gallup and Louis Harris organizations from the 1960s through the early 1990s, and have relied upon published statistics, notably from the Bureau of the Census and the Department of Labor. Yes, I know: We all instinctively feel that no pollster captures our own views, and there are scholarly as well as intuitive reasons to doubt the accuracy of some of their findings. But, for better or worse, they remain our best source for general opinion on a range of issues over time, and I have tried to use them with great caution and care. In most instances, notably the chapters on changing views during the economic and sexual revolutions, I broke down and analyzed the "average" response to determine variations by sex, income, education, and race or ethnicity. In the end, I deleted most of the specific numbers from the text, but working through them permitted me to construct general arguments.

In the interests of writing as readable a book as possible, I have kept scholarly references to a minimum, citing only those works from which I quote directly or upon whose evidence I specifically draw. In *Feminism Without Illusions: A Critique of Individualism*, I explored some of the theoretical issues, making clear my own point of view, and I added an extensive bibliography that indicates some of the influences on my thought. *"Feminism Is Not the Story of My Life"* is also grounded in, and could not have been written without, a vast literature that has engaged the topics upon which it touches, notably contemporary debates over public policy. Some of the most directly relevant of these sources are listed in the bibliography as a guide for those who wish to pursue further reading. Through the years, I have also learned immeasurably from the work of other women scholars who write about women's issues and may or may not call themselves feminists. I only hope that they recognize the ways in which their thinking has helped to shape my own, even where we do not agree: Jean Bethke Elshtain, Susan Estrich, Mary Ann Glendon, Claudia Goldin, Linda Gordon, Susan Reverby, Elizabeth Wolgast.

It would be presumptuous to argue that either my scholarly training or my personal experience better qualify me than others to write of the views of women for whom feminist scholars do not normally speak. My convictions about the importance of motherhood to feminism do not directly derive from my personal experience. Although my husband and I wanted children, we were not blessed with them. So my knowledge of the pulls that most women suffer between work and children derives from observation and listening rather than from personal experience. Indeed, my own life has, in most respects, typified that of the upscale professional woman who derives tremendous satisfaction and personal gratification from a demanding and time-consuming career. Personal experience has, nonetheless, taught me something of the pulls between career and family. Having married before my career was firmly launched—before I even fully believed I would have a career—I have always felt that my marriage has provided the foundation for my professional independence. Facing a world even less friendly to women than the professional world of today, I was never tempted to underestimate the value of having a secure refuge, the value of having my sexuality "spoken for," the miraculous value of living with someone who delighted in my ac-

complishments. I have always known that, faced with a choice, my
marriage would come before my career. Happily, one of the great
pleasures of a good marriage is that those choices do not have to
arise every day, and as time goes by and the marriage gets stronger,
they arise ever less frequently. But then, my husband and I both
recognize that marriage, like all close human relations, takes time
that might otherwise be devoted to work or professional networking.
I think, or at least hope, that our inability to have children has made
me more, not less, conscious of the problems of most women.

Personal experience has also taught me something of what mothering can mean to children. Throughout the writing of this book, I
have become increasingly conscious of what my own mother's mothering meant to me. Like many daughters, perhaps especially oldest
daughters, I had my moments of adolescent and young adult rebellion and was fiercely determined to define my own identity as separate from hers. As I became more confident in that independence, I
found it easier to recognize aspects of her in myself. Today, I am
above all conscious of the ways in which she nourished my mind.
The jingles and songs, like the poetry and Bible verses, that are most
firmly etched in my mind are the ones I first sang or read with her.
All the trips of my childhood were made in her company, and my
memories of them are laden with echoes of her memories of trips
she made when she was a girl. And I now know, although I did not
know it at the time, that from her I learned much about fear and
courage—especially courage. One of my favorite images of her actually dates from the time when I was already an adult. On one of
those dazzlingly clear and ferociously windy fall days that you occasionally see in upstate New York, I went to meet her at the airport.
As I waited for the small plane, I could not help but think of how
turbulent the flight must have been and, being myself something of
a coward about adventurous flights, I wondered if she would arrive
shaken. Suddenly, there she was, more than sixty at the time, walking gallantly across the tarmac, head high, eyes sparkling. Cautiously, I inquired about the flight. "Oh," she said, "it was exhilarat-

ing." How nice, I thought, knowing that in her place I would have been shaking and reaching for a shot of vodka.

Too frequently, we do not see our mothers—or do not see them clearly. In *Where the Girls Are*, Susan Douglas suggests that the internal struggles for women of her baby boomer generation began, consciously or not, in their visceral rejection of their mothers' roles. Even before Douglas fully understood the category of woman that her mother represented, she had determined that she wanted no part of it. Who would want to be "torn in a million directions and be ridiculed as dumb yet overbearing, incompetent yet scheming, and frivolous yet dangerous?"[1] What Douglas does not say is that children's own perceptions help to create those roles. Children want mothers to be there, like the air they breathe. More often than not, the mother they first recognize as an independent being is the mother they are defining themselves against. But with luck, as we get older, we begin to see our mothers as women. On that windy day, I caught one such glimpse of mine. Since then, a fuller picture has come into focus. Now in her eighties, she provides my sister and me with a model of how to cope with the infirmities of aging—a model of pride and dignity combined with realism, good sense, and a generous spirit.

Whatever my personal feelings about the ways in which motherhood shapes most women's lives, I remain very much a member of a professional elite that is more likely to write about people than converse with them. I know that my personal history is anything but typical. And by way of confirming the worst so we can get on with it, let me confess that the first movie I saw was Shakespeare's *Henry V*, that I did not see it until I was eight years old, and that, even then, I had to stay home from school in the afternoon to have a nap since the movie began at 7:00 P.M., by which time I was supposed to be in bed. This was not a background that favored long hours listening to pop records, much less watching television. What nonetheless bound me to the world of women was a web of lore, stories, shopping, and all the things that women across generations do. Normally, we do these things with women of similar background, which may lead us to forget that women of different backgrounds frequently do the same things with their mothers, sisters, and friends.

Through the years, I have been privileged to be introduced to other webs of female connection, from the most serious matters of life and death to the most casual. This book is written out of the conviction that those webs help to define us and ground our identities. Some feminists have seen them as a trap—even a prison. As we confront new possibilities and new dangers, I see those webs as a fund of strength that helps us to remember how we became who we are. I am strengthened in my belief by my relations with the women of my husband's family, who have, through the years, become my family and my friends. On the surface, the old working-class and lower-middle-class neighborhood in Brooklyn—Bensonhurst, to be precise—could not differ more from the neighborhoods in which I grew up. And yet the women of my Italian-American family and I settle into conversation as if we had grown up together. Talking to my sister-in-law, Jo, and her daughter, Annie, I relax into the companionship of women who see a telltale mark on another woman's arm and knowingly ask, "The oven?" And the three of us talk over the head of Katie, who alternates between play and darting over to the men for the indulgent adoration little girls so easily evoke. Feeling so close to them, with a burst of warm familiarity, I suddenly remember my own mother. This book is dedicated to them and to the ties among women across generations.

NOTES

[1]Susan Douglas, *Where the Girls Are: Growing Up Female With the Mass Media* (New York: Times Books, 1994), 54.

One

WHAT'S FEMINISM GOT TO DO WITH IT?

None of the women in the Alternative GED Program at Lehman College in New York City calls herself a feminist and the three men in the program regard the word with downright suspicion. Yet Maria Ramirez, a happily married mother of three, seized upon my question, "What do we want for our daughters?" She opened the discussion with, "That's good, what do we want for our daughters?" And unhesitatingly answered: "Independence." As the general murmur of agreement subsided, she elaborated, "Not having to count on a man." And again Maria clarified her own meaning: "I'm forty-three years old and I'm still where I depend on my husband." The other adult students, many of whom were divorced or had never married, responded sympathetically. All eighteen, including the three men, wanted their daughters to be able to support themselves—and to take satisfaction in doing so. All, like Maria, who loves her husband, her children, and her life, also wanted their own daughters "to have a happy marriage."

Yet despite their mistrust of feminism, all of them have absorbed ideas that many people associate with it. Above all, they agree that women must be able to take care of themselves and their children in case a marriage fails or never occurs. And agreeing on women's need for economic independence, they also agree that if women do the same work as men, they should receive equal pay. They all regard sexual harassment, to say nothing of rape, as intolerable; they all believe that their daughters should have the same employment opportunities as their sons. And although many have come to fear unlimited sexual freedom, they all want young women to be free to shape their own sexual lives.

So why do these women and men mistrust feminism? The short answer is that they do not see feminism as a story about their lives. For some, it is a story about rich women's lives, or white women's lives, or career women's lives. For the Catholics among them, it stands for a defense of abortion, which they cannot accept. For many of the women, as well as the men, it stands for an attack on men that threatens them directly or threatens their husbands, boyfriends, or sons. For most, it is simply irrelevant to the pressing problems of managing life from day to day.

Everyday life, not intellectual abstraction, lies at the heart of women's concerns. Yes, countless women regularly encounter discrimination and large and small injustices that complicate their lives. And feminism has helped to strengthen their determination to strike out against the unfairness that still affects all women simply because they are women. But beyond the discrimination and the injustices lies the complex fabric of lives that include relations with men, children, and other women. Women, like men, try to negotiate these relations with a mixture of love and impatience that cannot fit neatly into official programs and slogans. You give a little here and demand a little there. Above all, you try to keep going and save serious confrontations for the rare occasions in which you can no longer give in and retain your self-respect. Working mothers, who are now the majority of American working women, are especially conscious of the complexities—and of the inadequacy—of any simplistic solutions. They, more than others, know that children's demands are frequently nonnegotiable. And, more often than not, they know that those demands should be met, even at the (temporary) expense of women's freedom. Feminism, as they perceive it, simply does not provide an adequate response to the problems and challenges that shape their lives. Many women are therefore hostile to feminism, but most simply regard it as beside the point.

This mistrust of feminism angers many feminists, who, with good reason, argue that their movement has opened new opportunities for women. It saddens other women, who would like to think of themselves as feminists, even if they could not give you a precise definition of what feminism stands for. For them, feminism should represent a defense of women's independence—what Maria wants for her daughter. And they assume that feminism is a broad, generous movement that has room for all kinds of women and that it tolerates a variety of views on difficult topics. Even in this age of homogenized, mass culture, feminism means radically different things to different people.

As I worked on this book, these differences became increasingly clear, and the reasons for them increasingly confusing. My oldest friend, Nancy Wilson, who has successfully juggled a rewarding marriage, three children, and work as a teacher and writer, unhesitatingly thinks of herself as a feminist and remains puzzled that others do not understand the word as she does. But then, as she constantly reminds me, she has always worked part-time and does not count as one who has really "done it all." For her, feminism primarily means enlightened social policies that help women to meet their responsibilities to themselves and their families. Although strongly prochoice on abortion, she believes that feminism should include women who do not share her views.

Many feminists encourage the belief that their movement speaks for all women, but for them that is more likely to mean that all

women must support their positions than that they should respect
the positions of others. For most Americans, feminism refers to such
visible groups as the National Organization for Women (NOW), the
National Abortion Rights Action League (NARAL), the Fund for a
Feminist Majority, the Ms. Foundation, and the National Women's
Political Caucus. Although these groups differ somewhat in membership and purpose, their memberships overlap and they agree on
essentials. Together, they define a public "feminist" agenda that
supports specific policies and goals. And I strongly suspect that
many of the women who wish feminism well do not know what they
are supporting any more than those who oppose feminism know
precisely what they are opposing. Many who call themselves feminists will read my criticisms of feminism and say, "But that is not
what I believe." More often than not, they will be right. But they
have chosen to identify with a movement the ideology, public presence, and consequences of which they do not control. However
bravely and honestly they are wrestling with difficult issues, they
tacitly allow others to speak in their name.

Many, if not most, of the women who see feminism as a broad
movement that respects differences among women readily support
the pro-choice position on abortion. More than any other single issue, support for a woman's right to choose to have an abortion has
become the litmus test of feminism. Feminists must, by definition,
support that right, and, according to feminists, anti-feminists oppose it. But then, how do we explain that many who do not call
themselves feminists also support the right to abortion while at least
some who would like to call themselves feminists do not? Do feminists believe that feminism has no room for pro-life women even if
they support equal pay for equal work and related women's issues?
Apparently it does.

In 1991, feminist groups in Rochester, New York, were planning a
month of programs to protest violence against women. The leaders
of this project, however, refused to allow the group Feminists for
Life to participate on the grounds that denial of abortion constitutes
the single greatest form of violence against women. So much for

feminism's tolerance of a wide range of views! But then, how many of those who support the feminist campaign to protect abortion rights really know how feminists define those rights? At the moment, official feminism insists that a woman's right to choose means that it is wrong to save the life of a child who survives the abortion, for saving that life impinges upon the mother's "rights."[1] The defense of women's independence requires that a twenty-day-old child be killed—or allowed to die from lack of medical attention. It is hard to believe that most women see the sacrifice of a living baby as part of the story of their life. And even if they do not know that feminism defends that sacrifice, they do sense that feminism stands for things they cannot identify with.

During the past thirty years, feminism has decisively contributed to the revolution that has transformed women's lives and has helped to reshape the ways in which we think about what it means to be a woman. But it has still not convinced the majority of American women that it offers an adequate story of their lives. And the story it offers does matter, for, as the Baptist theologian James McClendon, himself a man of the Left, writes, "Society may take many forms, but it *must* be narrative to be a society. The stories a people tell, the memories and traditions they share, the history that they receive and modify by their own lives and pass on to their children—these are the carriers of social value."[2]

In the following pages, I will be drawing upon lengthy conversations with a wide variety of women. Separately and together, these conversations capture a sense of the stories that women construct to explain and find meaning in their lives. The conversations strikingly confirm both the differences among women's experiences and the persistence of common themes. Some of the women with whom I have spoken or whom I have interviewed appear only occasionally, as their words capture specific points. Others, notably Gloria Patterson, Aprill Ravenel, Gabriella Ortiz, and Linda Maldonado, appear more frequently. In this sense, they emerge as central characters in my account of women's relation to feminism. Much of their experience is representative of the experience of countless other women like them, and each of them has a special talent for capturing her thoughts and responses in words. Each has the gift of bringing to life the goals and values of resilient, independent women who do not fit easily into the story of upscale feminism.

To trace that story, I vividly recall that the word "feminist" was not yet in vogue when I graduated from college in 1963, but I vaguely assumed that I was one. Bryn Mawr College had long produced independent, accomplished women, and as undergraduates my friends and I, with a mixture of mirth and anxiety, would repeat to each other the college's reputed unofficial motto, "Only our failures marry." We feared being something of a disappointment to our professors because most of us were indeed hoping to become "failures," and a large number of us were engaged to be married at graduation. The vast majority did go on to successful careers, but at the time we were preparing to follow the pattern of our educated, middle-class mothers, most of whom had devoted their lives to husbands, children, and volunteerism.

Betty Friedan's *The Feminine Mystique* fired our imaginations and made us wonder about burying our talents in the suburbs, but it did not immediately alter our vision or plans for our lives. Most of us had reflected barely, if at all, about the issues that would emerge as pressing feminist issues within a few years. I do not think it had occurred to me that a married woman might have trouble getting credit in her own name. None of my newly married friends kept her maiden name or thought about the difficulty of trying to do so. We did not discuss, and may not have noticed, that women could be paid less than men for the same work. Strange to say, few of us expected to do precisely the same kind of work as the men of our social class, yet we had no doubt that we had received a better education than they. Many of us went to graduate school, but few, if any, into law, medicine, or business. Only a few expected to earn their own livings.

Most of us became enthusiastic supporters of the feminist movement that emerged during the years after our graduation. We knew we favored equal rights for women. Feminism rapidly helped us to understand how much farther we were from "equality" than we had naively assumed, even if we reflected little on the possible meanings of "equality." By the end of the 1960s, we worked for the passage of the Equal Rights Amendment. By the early 1970s, most of us supported a woman's right to have an abortion, equal pay for equal work, a married woman's right to keep her name, women's equal access to credit, and no-fault divorce. We delighted in such small new opportunities as going out to dinner together without feeling awkward and ordering drinks or a bottle of wine. Unlike our mothers, we stopped worrying about inviting a single woman to a dinner party, even when there was no "extra" man to pair her with.

During the early 1970s, my friend Michele and I organized a consciousness raising group for a few women in Rochester, New York. Alive with the enthusiasm of discovery, we met faithfully once a week for more than a year to explore our feelings and talk about our lives. Ranging in age from twenty-five to fifty, we were all white and married. Michele, who was married to a graduate student in English, was working as a secretary to put him through school. Constance, married to a doctor and to us a model of fragile beauty and enviable serenity, was, at fifty, our beacon of the hope that we, too, might someday grow up. Beth and Lucinda, both married to assistant professors, were struggling to raise babies on small budgets and with little help from their husbands. One night, the painfully reserved Beth broke out in a tirade. "Men," she exploded, "men! He just can't deal with shit!" Her husband, we learned as she simmered down, would never help to change the baby's diapers. Literally, he refused to deal with shit.

Together we read books, sipped coffee or wine, and nibbled cookies. At the time, claiming an evening a week for ourselves seemed almost radical. For that one evening Beth's husband had to cope with the shit, while the rest of our husbands coped with dishes, which by then some were doing anyway. Even at the time, we recognized our version of feminism as mild, but we never doubted that we and women like us were firm supporters of women's rights and, especially, women's expanding opportunities. Like characters out of such novels as Alix Kates Shulman's *Memoirs of an Ex-Prom Queen* or Anne Roiphe's *Up the Sand Box*, we combed our previous experience to identify the stereotypes and myths with which we had been raised. At first cautiously and then more boldly, we tried to help each other to become strong, independent women. We were encouraged to take these baby steps toward feminism by the knowledge that informal groups like ours were springing up all over America. Paltry as our effort might have seemed or in fact been, to us it represented the substance and promise of feminism.

No one, in 1963, could have predicted the impact that feminism was about to have on American society, but it did not take long to understand that it was rewriting the story of what it meant to be a woman in the United States. And from the start, that feminist story divided women by race, class, and religion. Through the late 1970s and early 1980s the emergence of new issues complicated things further: the Equal Rights Amendment (ERA), pornography, affirmative action, comparable worth, day care, surrogate motherhood, acquaintance rape, and sexual harassment.[3] As some pushed for greater rights and opportunities, others worried about losing their traditional roles as wives and mothers. But even as the struggles over the meaning of feminism escalated, the majority of American women (and men) came to accept such feminist goals as equality at work and even the more controversial right to choose to have an abortion. Today, most people see "women's issues" as legitimate, but many remain uneasy about feminism as the story of a woman's life.

The story of a woman's life lies at the core of the discomfort with feminism, because most women still hope to fit their new gains at work and in the public world into some version of the story of marriage and family that they have inherited from their mothers. Thus, many women who shudder at the mounting reports of sexual abuse and violence against women favor a strengthening of marriage and family rather than an increase in sexual permissiveness. And the growing numbers of working mothers especially worry about what is happening to children in a world in which most mothers work out-side the home. Women who still see marriage and children as central to their sense of themselves have retreated from feminism because they do not believe that feminists care about the problems that most concern them or because they believe that feminists favor policies they cannot support, such as abortion, affirmative action, or women in combat.

Brooke Mason, a Southern-born, thirty-year-old white woman, whom her employer describes as the "best mind" in a growing engineering firm, knows that neither she nor her friends would call themselves feminists. Brooke believes that feminism "has some connotations to it that not a lot of my friends agree with. To be honest, it's got a bad rap." When she hears the word "feminist," "I tend to think of the feminist radicals that support a lot of things that I don't support," especially abortion and affirmative action. Like so many other middle-class Southern white women, Brooke has moved into the world of work without abandoning the traditional religious and family values in which she was raised. She and her husband are happily living a modern version of the life that their parents lived before them. Brooke has "trouble believing that all women are harassed and suppressed." She knows full well that women face serious problems, including sexual harassment, and she is passionate about wanting "fair and equal" treatment on the job. Her problem with feminism is that she thinks feminists want women to receive "superior treatment," and she hates the idea of quotas for any group. She also associates feminists with the movement for abortion rights and "personally, I'm opposed to abortion so I wouldn't call myself a feminist and a lot of my friends wouldn't."

Sometimes I think that those of us who, for the past three decades, have thought of ourselves as feminists do not begin to imagine what the word means to others. But then I remind myself that the heady innocence of the early years of the women's movement has evaporated in the jaded cynicism and violence that have engulfed so much of our culture in recent years. It has become easy for feminists to assume that those who respond to feminism angrily or contemptuously are reactionary bigots—your typical pickup-driving, rifle-toting, beer-drinking, pinup-posting, sexist slobs. For surely, no honest person could possibly oppose the feminist movement's policies unless he—or, heaven forbid, she—favored women's subordination.

As it happens, most Americans no longer believe that feminism offers the best way to improve women's position. How else can we explain that an American public that has faithfully followed such television series as *Reasonable Doubts*, *Murphy Brown*, *thirtysomething*, and *China Beach* continues to regard feminism with suspicion? Our visual culture abounds with stories of women who are pursuing careers, struggling to raise children alone, suffering the indignities of sexual harassment or the horror of rape—and frequently enjoying independence and professional success. The women whose lives so many Americans follow are doctors, lawyers, reporters, police officers, soldiers. Few if any stay home with the kids; even fewer wear aprons. If these stories and others like them have anything to do with our culture, we have, willy-nilly, come a very long way in a very short time. If Americans could accept Tess Kaufman and Maggie Zombrow of *Reasonable Doubts*, then why do they not accept feminism? Or, to put it differently, why are Tess and Maggie not enough for feminism? The problem seems to lie in what feminists believe women should want.

Patricia Sanders grew up in Raleigh, North Carolina, as the fourth child in an African-American family of five girls and three boys in which everyone struggled to make ends meet. Now, she is happily married to a successful real estate developer, works full-time, and keeps her own bank account for clothing and other personal expenses. Comfortably settled in the new black middle-class, she enjoys a material comfort she could not have imagined when she was a child. And she has an independence of spirit that should have made her a natural supporter of feminism. Yet, she told me, "I don't think I could really call myself a feminist." Patricia's friends would not dream of calling themselves feminists. She would not swear that they see feminism exclusively as a white women's agenda, although many African-American women do. But she also doubts that they "really see it as a political issue." Most of her friends and acquaintances are simply turned off by the language of feminism and do not connect it in any way with the women's issues that matter to them. And like so many less affluent African-American women, they worry that white women's issues will hurt the prospects of black men.

Unlike Patricia, Mary Caggiano was born with all the advantages of wealth, class, and education that would seem to make her a natural candidate for membership in the feminist elite. As the firmly established vice president of a major branch of Citibank, Mary has amply demonstrated her ability to compete in a tough man's world, while she sustains her marriage and raises a child. Her choice of career, like her marriage to an Italian-American, clearly proclaim her willingness to break with tradition. Her father, who came out of the WASP elite and has spent his life working in the upper echelons of the military, the CIA, and the oil business, has nothing but admiration for her ambition and determination. Recently, in a manifestation of support, he told her that he had just made a generous contribution to NOW. "NOW?" she queried disbelievingly. "I would not give them a dime." Mary understood that her father was simply making a gesture of support for what he misunderstood to be her interests. But she believes that the only thing that will really help women is for them to do their jobs and pave the way for those who come after.

Many women like Brooke Mason and Mary Caggiano reject feminism because of what they perceive as its radical social and economic agenda. Brooke and Mary do not approve of affirmative action for anyone. Nancy Wilson, in contrast, accepts affirmative action for disadvantaged groups, even though she understands it may complicate life for her own sons. For Patricia Sanders, the issues are more complicated. As an African-American, Patricia understands firsthand the desperate need for social programs. Following a divorce, Debby, Patricia's younger sister, was left with full responsibility for her daughter and no help from her ex-husband. Unable to afford day care, she turned to Aid to Families with Dependent Children (AFDC). Patricia knows that day care, health care, and part-time work with benefits would have made all the difference to Debby, whom she calls "a real go-getter." Patricia suspects that Debby, who is "very, very independent," divorced, and does a lot of things with her many women friends, would not have a problem in calling herself a feminist, "although I've never heard her use the term." But Patricia herself does not believe that feminism really speaks for Debby or women like her.

Patricia grew up without Brooke's advantages but with the same ethic of individual initiative. As a child, she watched her father, the custodian for a local school, struggle to provide for his children, while her mother, who before the children came had worked as a cook, stayed home to take care of them. Loathing his own work, Patricia's father pushed his children to get an education. Even as Patricia continues to work as a secretary in a law firm, she is taking courses so that she may become the teacher she has always wanted to be. Her life exemplifies the black middle-class respectability that incenses so many black and white radicals. But it is hardly the story of a woman's turning her back on her own people. In college, Patricia has specialized in African-American women's literature because of her deep attachment to the sufferings and accomplishments of the women of her people. She treasures the stories black women have written about their own lives and draws from them inspiration and a model of courage for herself. But she does not believe they have anything to do with feminism.

Coming from a highly privileged background, Mary Caggiano might have seen feminism as a plausible story about her own life. She knows how hard it can be for even the most talented woman to establish a career and earn promotions. But Mary's impressive talents have not guaranteed her the respect and support of other women, who often respond with jealousy and resentment. Like Patricia, Mary gets more support and appreciation from her husband than she does from most of the women she knows. And Mary, like Patricia, thinks that poor women need strong families and the opportunity to stay home while their children are young more than they need sexual freedom.

All of these women seem to fit neatly into the upscale feminist mold. All between thirty and fifty-five years of age, they lead comfortably middle-class, even conventional, lives. All are married, and all work, although not all have worked full-time throughout their adult lives. All but one have children. Their lives resemble those of millions of other accomplished and well-educated American women who are struggling to combine work and family. Each, in her own way, has a strong sense of social responsibility to those less fortunate than herself. Each cares deeply about offering younger women expanded opportunities to become all that they may be. All, through work, friends, and family connections, know women who are in desperate need of social policies to help them cope with their lives and, especially, to raise their children.

Yet three of these four women do not call themselves feminists, and Nancy, the exception, calls herself a feminist primarily because she views feminism as an integral part of a larger program for greater social and economic equality for the American people in general. Nancy, no less than the others, continues to cherish a complex story of the many things it means to be a woman and, especially, the many stories of how women grow up to be themselves. No more than the others does she recognize herself in the feminist stories of heterosexuality as a male conspiracy to keep women in their place.[4] As women who enjoy men and love the fathers, brothers, husbands, and sons in their lives, they do not see men as The Enemy.

If many women who fit the typical upscale feminist profile are uncomfortable with the feminist label, what about the countless other women who do not fit the profile at all? What about Verna, who pumps gas at a Chevron station in Atlanta? Between ringing up her customers' change, Verna watches the talk shows. One day she exploded to Michael Skube of the *Atlanta Journal and Constitution* about the women who had been complaining about "patriarchy" and "gender" on the *Geraldo* show. "Some of them people got to get them a life," she informed Skube, before asking him if his wife was one of "them." And when he asked whom she meant by "them," she responded with a burst of laughter. "You know, one of them *nuts*"—her word for feminists.[5]

Maggie Richards, now in her mid-forties, grew up in urban middle-class comfort, but her marriage to a rancher led her to the wild, arresting country of northeastern New Mexico. Tough, independent, and strikingly beautiful with a mane of fiery red hair, Maggie initially found the transition to rancher's wife more than she had bargained for. In the small community in which the Richards live, everyone ranches, and, as in other farming communities, men's and women's roles remain close to the traditional division of labor that took men to the fields and left women in the kitchen.

Maggie had not come to New Mexico to be left in the kitchen, and, after a brief attempt to adjust to local customs, she tried to explain her feelings about them to her husband. It was not the work of housekeeping that she objected to, she told him, but the pointlessness. How, she asked, would he feel "if you put up a fence, and during the night it was torn down, and the next day you had to put it up all over again? If day after day, all you ever did was to rebuild the same fence?" He got the point. Since then, Maggie has ranched with the men, riding long hours in the saddle. It took the men longer than it took her husband to get the point. And, as he gradually turned more and more of the running of the ranch over to her, the men responded with mutterings and covert challenges. She held her ground, and they learned to accept her as boss. But Maggie scoffs at the idea that she might call herself a feminist. As far as she is concerned, feminism has nothing to do with her life, and feminists, whom she views as soft as well as softheaded liberals, would not last two days on her ranch.

Gloria Patterson grew up in a large African-American family of eleven children in low-country Georgia. Restive under the watchful eyes of her father, a Methodist minister, as soon as she finished high school she took off for New York with her boyfriend, Bobby, to taste the freedom of city life. It would be hard to identify a woman's issue about which Gloria does not have direct or indirect experience. After she and Bobby, who had become a policeman, married and had a child, he increasingly succumbed to the city's lurking temptations, especially women and drugs. Having a baby to care for, Gloria determined to put up with as much as she could. She hated the infidelity, resented his addiction to expensive clothes, and worried that his dabbling in drugs and gambling would lead to serious trouble. Many of the guys back home in Savannah did not behave much better than her husband, and she knew plenty of women who had survived worse. Then one day, Bobby hit her. That, she told him, she would not tolerate. He knew she meant what she said, and life returned to normal. But, as she tells it, the strain of the job and perhaps some lingering guilt about cheating on her got to him, and a couple of months later he hit her again. She waited until he had gone out, gathered up the baby, and left. She knew then that the marriage was over, although not until two years later did she get a formal divorce.

Not being able to support herself and the baby on her own wages, much less afford day care, Gloria went home to Georgia, where she lived for a time with her parents and eventually married an old childhood sweetheart. Her second marriage has been happy, but she has seen her female relatives and friends subjected to more than enough sexual brutality and abuse to last a lifetime. Gloria's account of her marriage strongly resembles that of many other African-American women with whom I have spoken, although the specifics vary from woman to woman. Many of the others, however, have not been as fortunate as she in making a happy second marriage, and as black men are having an increasingly difficult time finding secure employment, more and more black women are not remarrying or are never marrying at all.

Gloria wonders whether she would call herself a feminist. Like most of her sisters, sisters-in-law, and friends, she works. That is nothing new for African-American women, even when happily married. They have always had to be strong and independent. Gloria knows that many women need some social supports to help sustain

themselves and their children, but she sees no help for them in
feminism. In fact, as she has repeatedly told me, most of the women
she knows would never suspect that rich white women who do politics and write books even know they exist, much less that the needs
of black women may differ from those of white women. And on
more than one occasion, she has asked me if she might take copies
of essays I had written on African-American women, on abortion,
and on women and families to her church group, because she felt I
had gotten the issues right. I could not imagine, she told me, how
much it would mean to her friends to know that some white women
are listening and caring. I assured her that quite a few do, or at least
try to.

To illustrate the point, she told me of how one day two of the
younger women who belong to her church saw my book on feminism on the backseat of her car. "Lord, Ms. Stanton," they giggled,
"what you doin' with that feminism stuff?" And what, she retorted,
did they have against feminism? "Oh," they immediately replied,
"feminism ain't for black folks. Feminism means you got to shave
your legs and straighten your hair."

Gloria's young friends clearly see feminism as little more than a
matter of style—and as a white women's agenda. Clearly, they have
never heard of Naomi Wolf's book *The Beauty Myth*, with its sharp
critique of artificial standards of female beauty. But even if they
had, they would not think it had anything to do with them. They
know women want to be attractive to men. They simply reject what
they see as white standards of attractiveness. Young black women in
the dangerous Dorchester section of Boston do not feel much differently, although they do not even talk of feminism.

In Dorchester, Massachusetts, sex is cheap and life dangerous.
The impressive, well-educated, selfless women in the Azusa Christian Community, who run frightening risks in their everyday efforts
to rescue one person at a time from degradation and death, do not
talk about feminism either. They know all about it, from its political
programs to its high theory. They do not talk about it for the same
reason they do not talk much about other things that have no bear-

ing on their lives and work. Worse, to the extent that they are compelled to notice feminism, they see it as an attack on their own faith
and on the family life they are struggling to re-create as the sine qua
non of community survival.

Women, caught in the tentacles of the violent, and too frequently
deadly, street life of the inner city, have learned from their mothers
and the world around them that their primary, perhaps their only,
asset is their ability to attract a man. These are not women whom
feminists recognize, not the women the feminist agenda addresses.
Young women in Dorchester grow up knowing everything about
women's independence, which they primarily associate with brutality and abandonment. From the start, their lives unfold amid drugs,
guns, and prostitution—much as if they were living in the world of
the film *New Jack City*. What meaning has sexual liberation in such
neighborhoods, in which most women ask little more than to hold
their man and, even if he is brutal, get him out of jail?

Growing up in Dorchester makes girls tough—the condition of
survival. One of the girls' gangs, which are becoming common in the
neighborhood, requires that new members prove their toughness by
having had two abortions. In the same neighborhood, others get
pregnant because they want the babies. Many hope against all reason that the baby will lead their boyfriend to marry them, but even
when he predictably does not, many find that having the baby at
least gains them more love and attention from their own mothers.
Above all, they believe that the baby itself will be someone to love
them. As Dora Hooper, a teenage black mother in a poor section of
Pittsburgh said of her baby, Shawna, "I'm never sad anymore, because she's always there to make me happy." For Dora, her baby was
"one person that will always care about me and love me and I'll
never have to worry about her not loving me."[6]

The divisions between those who want babies and those who view
abortion as a sign of independence provide a sinister parody of the
divisions between the pro-choice and pro-life women of the middle
class. But in neither case does feminism have anything to do with
the lives of the girls and women of the inner city. Mara Carmichael

and Lisa Evans, who work with a group of militantly devoted black Pentecostals of the Azusa Christian Community, try not to despair of what they see each day. "It takes it out of you," Lisa admits with a sigh. Mara and Lisa dream of helping even a few of the girls to stay in school long enough to understand what it might mean to hold a job, but they are realistic about their poor prospects for success. Meanwhile, they struggle to persuade the girls to wear skirts that at least cover their upper thighs, knowing all the time that sex objects is what their young friends aspire to be.

For these women, as for others, the story of a woman's life has expanded dramatically during the past three decades—although not always in positive ways. Young African-American women, whether in New York, Dorchester, or low-country Georgia, are living through the breakdown of communities that were fragile enough to begin with. Ironically, the biggest change in their lives may well be the increased freedom of men to desert the women they get pregnant. Their opportunities for education, employment, and stable families appear to have decreased, and their opportunities for marriage assuredly have. The expansion of their opportunities for personal freedom has gone hand in glove with the contraction of their prospects for stable lives. They are pretty much free to do as they choose, but they have almost nothing to choose that is likely to improve their social and economic situation, much less that of their children. Like affluent women, many of these young women are doing things and enjoying an independence that their mothers and grandmothers could not have imagined. Perhaps even more than affluent women, they are likely to hear their mothers' and grandmothers' voices in their heads, knowing that however rapidly some things change, others seem barely to change at all.

Modern feminism has taken shape during a period of rapid, dizzying social change, and the most significant changes in women's lives are probably irreversible. It is hard to foresee a time at which most women will not need or want to participate in the labor force during most, if not all, of their adult lives. These changes directly affect marriages and the raising of children—the quality and stability of the lives of families and women's roles within them. For women, as for men, it is "the economy, stupid." But for women, no more than for men, is it only the economy.

Women do divide according to social and economic position, and those divisions are growing. They also divide according to political philosophy—a philosophy only a few articulate and most express only through their actions. As a rule, women are more sympathetic than men to spending on social programs. But as increasing numbers move into the upper echelons of business, government, and the professions, they are acquiring a deeper commitment to the protection of what they have earned. As some women become affluent by virtue of their own efforts, they may not be significantly more generous about social spending than the men whose ranks they are joining. It would be heartwarming to believe that a woman CEO of Dow Pharmaceuticals would welcome the opportunity to provide free measles vaccines to every child in the country, but let's not count on it. A woman, like a man, who did not put the company's bottom-line first would not last long as a CEO.

The economic changes of recent years have not been evenhanded. Some women have prospered but many have not. And although feminists still complain that women share the experience of economic deprivation, their slogans no longer ring true. Nor is the story of women's economic deprivation likely to strike large numbers of young women as an appealing story about their lives. The anxieties of young women about their own prospects for employment may help to explain why modern feminism seems reluctant to face the economic issues squarely. But whatever the reasons, we have had little candor about which economic policies benefit which groups of women and why.

In the debates over welfare, for example, feminists have uncompromisingly insisted that "compassion" requires support for existing federal programs, including AFDC. Their rhetoric suggests that if you do not agree with them you are declaring war on women and children. Yet it is not clear that unlimited federal welfare programs are the only, or even the best, way to improve poor women's conditions. What is clear is that the feminists are, above all, defending women's right to have children outside of marriage, which they claim is necessary to protect women's sexual freedom. If you believe their claims, you would never suspect that many intelligent, compassionate people might honestly believe that women would derive more benefit from marriage than welfare and from the strengthening of local communities and families than from the expansion of federal programs.

The most serious feminist failure, however, does not lie in the economic analysis of specific policies, about which there is much room for honest disagreement. That failure lies in many feminists' preference to consider women as independent agents rather than as members of families. Not for nothing do Patricia Sanders, Brooke Mason, and Mary Caggiano—not to mention Lisa Evans and Mara Carmichael in Dorchester—refuse to identify with feminism. They, and countless women like them, worry that feminist solutions are contributing to the disintegration of families rather than helping to reconstruct them. They believe, in other words, that what they see as problems, feminists see as ideals. Brooke would be the first to feel compassion for a single mother but could never accept single motherhood as a positive alternate way of life. Like Patricia, Mary, and even Nancy, Brooke believes that a woman's life should be grounded in her family and cooperation with men.

Feminist indifference, if not hostility, to men and families encourages Brooke and Mary and women like them to underestimate the crying needs of many poor women. For it permits them to argue, however unrealistically, that poor women should begin by respecting marriage and postponing children until they have a husband. They do not believe that poor women need or want the things that feminists advocate for them, and they fear that feminists are encouraging poor women to behave irresponsibly. And although the black women in Dorchester would say it differently, they basically agree. Furthermore, Brooke and Mary assume that support for women's issues as feminists define them will promote the careers and influence of feminist activists, whose policies will make poor women's lives only more difficult than they already are. For Brooke, a vote for a feminist politician means a vote for abortion, which she opposes on moral grounds. For Mary, a contribution to NOW means endorsement of Patricia Ireland's public celebration not only of bisexuality but of open marital infidelity, and it means an uncritical acceptance of the story of Anita Hill. For Patricia, support for feminism more likely than not means condemning black men as brutes and rapists. However unfair these increasingly widespread perceptions are judged, each contains too much truth to be turned aside.

Feminists have their own explanations for these attitudes, which they reject as outright bigotry, backlash, or mere stupidity. As the early feminist goals have been realized, feminists have discovered that even outstanding gains for women have failed to produce the "equality" they longed for. Impatient and frustrated, they have formulated a story of women's persisting disadvantages at home and work. Women are not just doing more than their share of the dishes and child care, they are battered, raped, and dying of eating disorders in alarming numbers. By the beginning of the 1990s, just when women's position seemed to be improving decisively, the feminist elite was sounding dire alarms. Naomi Wolf warned women that they are prisoners of a "beauty myth" that warps their minds and encourages them to hate their bodies. Susan Faludi warned them that they are victims of a "backlash" that is eroding whatever modest, fragile gains they have made.[7]

Faludi claims to be writing for all women, but she focuses on the experience of those young single women in business and the professions who earn enough to support themselves in at least modest comfort and lead the lives they choose. She is not talking about women who can barely earn enough to support themselves, much less provide for children. Inadvertently, she leaves by the wayside women who might prefer—or feel a responsibility—to stay home while their children are young. What, we may ask, of the lives of the majority of women—who are outside the ranks of business, the academy, and the professions?

Frustrated by divisions within the feminist ranks, the more radical leaders have increasingly insisted that anyone who rejects their views is "anti-woman." And anyone who speaks of family values is necessarily defending the religious right. In *The Second Stage*, Betty Friedan made a valiant attempt to reintroduce the family at the heart of feminist programs, but, resoundingly, she failed to convert radical feminists. Ellen Willis, speaking for the radicals, announced that "the family is a dying beast" and denounced pro-family feminists as no feminists at all.[8] For Willis, it is time for women to look out for themselves and let the devil take the hindmost. Yet most women, for good reasons as well as bad ones, see their connections to others as a central part of their own identity and are unwilling to enlist in a feminism that declares war on the family.

Feminists accuse the religious right of trying to dictate what a woman should be and how she should think about a vast array of complicated problems. Meanwhile these same feminists practice the very thing they preach against. Feminist evocations of diversity by gender, race, and class rarely acknowledge the real differences in women's lives and needs, much less deep-seated differences of political philosophy or religious and moral values. Thus, feminist diversity does not embrace women who oppose abortion, do not view heterosexual encounter as rape, prefer to stay home with young children, see some value in single-sex education, or do not want every workplace flirtation to be punished as sexual harassment. As a result, many women, including no small number who have benefited from feminist gains, find no place in feminism for themselves.

Some feminists, like Katie Roiphe and Naomi Wolf, are now challenging feminist correctness from the inside.[9] Roiphe and Wolf worry that feminist campaigns to impose "correct" thought and behavior will curtail the freedoms, including sexual freedom, feminists have been fighting for. They offer a refreshing corrective on the feminists who would program and regulate us all into compliance, but their feminist story has no more to do with the lives of ordinary women than the story they reject. For, like their opponents, they focus exclusively on the hopes and needs of young elite women like themselves without considering that their experience may be atypical. And even so, Katie Roiphe has come under attack from Susan Faludi, who condemns Roiphe and various others who do not share Faludi's views as "faux feminists."[10]

As a white middle-class professional from a professional family, I have considerable sympathy with the hopes and fears of such young women, among whom are students to whom I am deeply committed. But I also know that our lives interlock with the lives of countless other women who lack our social and economic advantages, as well as with the lives of women who may enjoy those advantages but have different social, religious, or political beliefs. Any attempt to lump the lives of very different women under a single formula—any formula—is likely to exclude more women than it includes. If the experience of men has any lessons to offer women, the first must surely be that men's interests and beliefs differ dramatically by class, race, and ethnicity, not to mention such intangibles as political or moral convictions or even intelligence and talent. And the vast majority of men who differ in these ways are, in one way or another, tied to women—to mothers, wives, partners, daughters. The same is true for women. During the past thirty years, both women and men have been living through a momentous dual revolution—the unprecedented sexual and economic revolutions of our time—that has deeply marked their expectations and their sense of their relations to others. But even as the world changes, the most meaningful stories about our lives continue to be rooted in stories we have inherited from the parents and communities that have shaped us.

Feminists might hesitate before dismissing the majority of American women as bigoted, reactionary, or stupid. NOW, the media's favorite feminist organization, claims only 300,000 members. Yet numerous other polls show that women's issues—equal pay for equal work, sexual harassment, day care, and shared responsibilities in marriage—have mass support. At the time of the 1992 election, when Clinton was strongly endorsing women's issues, the majority of women who voted claimed that health care was the issue that most mattered to them. Even in the wake of what many women perceived as the Senate's offensive grilling of Anita Hill during the Clarence Thomas confirmation hearings, only about a third of American women are willing to call themselves feminists. The proportion of college women who "definitely" consider themselves feminists is lower yet—fewer than one in five.[11] In the wake of the 1993 NOW convention, USA Today took ordinary people's attitudes toward feminism as the topic for its daily debate, asking five random people, "Has feminism become a negative label?" The respondents, one black and two white women and two men, did not offer much of a debate. Janis Hedstrom, a twenty-seven-year-old registered nurse from Minneapolis, set the tone, saying, "The feminist movement has made it a word that carries a negative connotation. And while I believe the movement has done a lot for women in helping them to become more equal to men, it has pushed an agenda that has been negative toward the family."

Thirty-seven-year-old Joe Lese likened being called a feminist to being called a chauvinist—both negative labels—but affirmed his enthusiastic support for equal rights for women. James G. Musat, who was seventy-three, was not bothered by the term unless people used it to gain unfair advantage over others. For him, equal rights must include equal responsibilities. No more than the men was Tanya Davis, a forty-seven-year-old teacher from New Mexico, "bothered" by the term feminism. She strongly favored equal pay for equal work, but did not like the movement's militancy on some issues. Victoria Haucly, an African-American, thirty-four-year-old director of marketing research for a company in Yardley, Pennsylvania, shared the others' commitment to equal rights for women, but would not herself want to be associated with the word. "It's a word that is not appropriate for the '90s and carries a negative connotation, particularly in the business world."

From these women and men, as from those with whom I have spoken, comes the really bad news for the feminist movement: The overwhelming majority of American women perceive feminism as irrelevant. In their view, feminism has no answer for the women's issues that most concern them. It is not even talking about the women's issues that most concern them. It is not writing a compelling story about women's lives. Worse, it is not writing a convincing story about our world. These are the women (and men) for whom this book is written.

NOTES

[1] Hadley Arkes, "Anti-Abortion, but Politically Smart," *The Wall Street Journal* (March 28, 1995): A26.

[2] James Wm. McClendon, Jr., *Systematic Theology*, vol. 1, *Ethics* (Nashville, TN: Abington Press, 1986), 172.

[3] Jane J. Mansbridge, *Why We Lost the ERA* (Chicago: Univ. of Chicago Press, 1986); Kristin Luker, *Abortion and the Politics of Motherhood* (Berkeley and Los Angeles: Univ. of California Press, 1984); Donald G. Mathews and Jane Sherron DeHart, *Sex, Gender, and the Politics of ERA* (New York: Oxford Univ. Press, 1990).

[4] This position emerges with special clarity in Adrienne Rich, "Cumpulsory Heterosexuality and Lesbian Existence." *Signs: Journal of Women in Culture and Society* 4 (1980); Catharine A. MacKinnon, *Feminism Unmodified: Discourses on Life and Law* (Cambridge, MA: Harvard Univ. Press, 1987); and Judith Butler, *Bodies That Matter: On the Discursive Limits of "Sex"* (New York and London: Routledge, 1993).

[5] Michael Skube, "Gender Wars Take a Ponderous Turn," *Atlanta Journal and Constitution* (July 24, 1994): N10. For the record, Michael Skube has abundant sympathy for women's issues.

[6] Kate Malloy and Maggie Jones Patterson, *Birth or Abortion: Private Struggles in a Political World* (New York: Plenum Press, 1992), 206.

[7] Naomi Wolf, *The Beauty Myth: How Images of Beauty Are Used Against Women* (New York: Morrow, 1991); Susan Faludi, *Backlash: The Undeclared War Against American Women* (New York: Crown, 1991). For a critique of feminists' and the media's misuse of statistics, see Christina Hoff Sommers, *Who Stole Feminism? How Women Have Betrayed Women* (New York: Simon and Schuster, 1994).

34   "FEMINISM IS NOT THE STORY OF MY LIFE"

[8]Betty Friedan, *The Second Stage* (New York: Summit Books, 1981); Ellen Willis, *No More Nice Girls: Countercultural Essays* (Hanover, NH: Wesleyan Univ. Press, 1992).

[9]Katie Roiphe, *The Morning After: Sex, Fear, and Feminism on Campus* (Boston: Little Brown, 1993); Naomi Wolf, *Fire With Fire: The New Female Power and How It Will Change the 21st Century* (New York: Random House, 1993).

[10]Susan Faludi, "I'm Not a Feminist But I Play One on TV," *Ms. Magazine* 5, no. 5 (1995): 30–39.

[11]Nina J. Easton, "I'm Not a Feminist But . . . ," *Los Angeles Times Magazine* (February 2, 1992).

Two

GROWING UP
FEMININE

Feminists might well be stunned to learn that Gloria Patterson's young friends think that feminism means that you must shave your legs and straighten your hair. Feminists regularly insist that they stand for freedom of choice in everything from abortion to personal style. Feminists have never promoted an image of traditional femininity, which many feminists deplore. And Brooke Mason, as a self-consciously feminine Southern woman, has some grounds for her belief that feminists do not approve of her personal style. Knowing more about feminism than Gloria's friends, Brooke believes that feminists do not approve of shaved legs or pink dresses. Brooke associates feminism with the feminist leaders of the late 1960s and early 1970s who encouraged women to burn their bras and give up high heels. In fact, leading feminists no longer lecture women about bra-burning, but even today it is sometimes hard to avoid the impression that their movement has declared war on much of what most women, especially young women, think of as typically feminine, namely style, appearance, and clothes.

Feminists have not had much patience with femininity, which they see as a trap that distracts women from the pursuit of power and independence. For what is femininity except a disguise that women adopt to appeal to men? As it happens, most women still do want to appeal to men, which may help to explain why they do not have much use for feminism. For centuries, women have shared a special interest in appearance and clothing. The femininity that feminists see as a trap, other women see as a bond to other women. And it is not difficult to understand that these women might resent feminists for trying to make them ashamed of the skills and pleasures in which they find satisfaction.

Feminism does not like differences between women and men—at least not those which disadvantage women. It has taught women to expect—and fight for—equality with men, especially in education, employment, and sports. It has encouraged women to learn self-defense and to fix their own cars. It has insisted that women should be free to participate in military combat and free not to bear children. Feminist lawyers have done their best to write these beliefs into law on the grounds that it is unfair, and should be illegal, to deny women the same advantages as men. In this spirit, feminists recently opened a new front in the fight against discrimination against women. Supported by the federal government, they have attacked the Virginia Military Institute and The Citadel, publicly funded military colleges, for their refusal to admit women.

In 1993, Shannon Faulkner applied for admission to The Citadel. Since she met the basic qualifications and had removed all references to her sex from her application and transcript, she was provisionally admitted. When The Citadel discovered her sex, it withdrew her admission. During the ensuing trial, her lawyers argued that the defense lawyers were stigmatizing and stereotyping women by suggesting that most women might not seek or benefit from the rigorous, adversarial education at The Citadel. Faulkner herself in-

What feminism has done.

sisted that she sought only to become a cadet like the others and, once admitted, would willingly comply with all expectations and regulations, no matter how strenuous.

The judge concurred with Faulkner's lawyers and ordered her immediate admission as The Citadel's only female cadet. And he ruled that The Citadel was entitled to require that her head be shaved. His decision seemed to comply with feminist demands for equality. Head-shaving has been one of the many rigors that all first-year Citadel cadets must endure. Faulkner's lawyers had grounded their case in the claims of equality, and equality with the other cadets included the shaving of her head. Or so one might think.

Head-shaving, however, was not what Faulkner's lawyers had meant by equality. During the hearing, her able and articulate lawyer rose to deliver an impassioned plea. Voice quivering with indignation, Valorie Vojdik implored Judge Houck not to subject Faulkner to such an unbearable humiliation. To shave a woman's head was to stigmatize and degrade her. To underscore the point, Vojdik tendered pictures of French women during World War II whose heads had been shaved to brand them for their collaboration with the Nazis. The about-face was mesmerizing. Equality required that Faulkner be admitted to The Citadel Corps of Cadets, not that she, as a woman, endure the shaving of her head.

For those who knew something of the rigorous life to which Faulkner was claiming admittance, head-shaving looked like the least of her problems. But not to her feminist lawyers. The very lawyers who had insisted that culture should play no role in the aspirations and opportunities of young women and men now insisted that defiance of culture would result in her degradation and humiliation. Apparently, the media believed that the public shared this sensibility, for head-shaving figured prominently in the next day's headlines. But the lawyers had not built their case upon ordinary women's feelings about the length of their hair.

It is child's play to expose the inconsistency in Faulkner's lawyers' position: If cultural differences between women and men do not count in the case of admission to The Citadel, then surely they should not count in the matter of the one-time shaving of a head. Hair grows back. More interesting than the inconsistencies, which will be evaluated by the courts, is the feminist lawyers' passionate attachment to a woman's right to have an attractive head of hair. (Significantly, they did not object to the practice of shaving the heads of the male cadets.)

Faulkner's lawyers perfectly understood that hair, like appearance in general, does matter to women. No question, appearance mattered to the lawyers, who arrived in court each day dressed as if they had just stepped off the set of *L. A. Law*. Why not? Making a good impression could not hurt—and might help—their case. There is no shame in a woman's wanting to look attractive. The shame lies in feminists' prescribing attitudes for others that they do not observe themselves. Vojdik's insistence that Faulkner not be forced to shave her head implicitly acknowledged the importance of femininity. What she did not acknowledge is that if the "natural" desire to look attractive is so important as to justify differences between women and men, then the claims to absolute equality fail.

Even in our age of male models and male cosmetics, concern for clothing and appearance mark women's experience as different from that of men. Women may not agree about specific fashions, but most agree that how you present yourself matters much more to women than to men. Even for men, appearance creates the first impression that others have of us before we so much as say a word. And women today, like their mothers and grandmothers before them, know that our clothing sends a message that permits others to place us in the swirling social scene. As recently as the 1950s our grandmothers wanted us to wear gloves in public to mark us as ladies. I have not worn white gloves in years, but I still have a box of them just in case. And what about slips? Just suppose you had an accident and fell down in the street. If you were not wearing a slip, how would the strangers who came to your assistance know that you were a lady? The days of white gloves and mandatory slips are long gone, but the importance of clothing as social marker persists. Young women who sport bright blue hair or studs in their nose or tongue are just as intent on sending a recognizable signal to others as young businesswomen in studiously correct black or navy suits.

Notoriously, women spend a lot of time worrying about how they look and, especially, what to wear. Naomi Wolf savaged these preoccupations in *The Beauty Myth*, claiming that our media-led culture conspires to keep women permanently insecure and anxious because they do not measure up to some abstract and unattainable standard of beauty. Concern with looks, she warned, literally kills women, frequently through anorexia, sometimes through breast implants. Who could doubt that it is in men's interest to keep women fixated on their looks? How better to keep them dependent and discourage them from competing with men for power and prestige?

Wolf echoes the complaints of generations of feminists who, from Mary Wollstonecraft to the present, have criticized the ways in which feminine fashion keeps women in thrall to men. Simone de Beauvoir, in her feminist classic, *The Second Sex*, especially deplored women's disadvantage in a culture in which they must always look beautiful and young, while men could grow old in the security that the character and power etched on their faces would only enhance their appeal to the opposite sex. Femininity emerges from these accounts as a mask that gullible women are forced to assume in order to pass in the world.

Women spend considerable, sometimes staggering, amounts of time and money on decorating or reshaping their bodies: nail polish, sculpted nails, hair color, perms, electrolysis, dieting programs, plastic surgery, breast implants, breast reductions—the list goes on. Many women spend their lives dieting. They try one, lose a few pounds, gain them back, and try another. All this even before we get to clothes. In extreme cases, women do jeopardize their health, and, although Wolf's statistics on deaths from anorexia have been disputed, the case of anorexia remains instructive.[1]

Like women's attempts to transform and decorate their bodies, anorexia reminds us that women, like men, develop a sense of self through their interactions with other people, especially those to whom they feel most closely connected. Women frequently display their sense of self on their own bodies. But the view of anorexia as the result of a misogynist conspiracy will not wash. Anorexia is not about being slim. It is about control—more a revolt against becoming a woman than a pathological quest of femininity. It has nothing to do with appealing to men. In fact one of the more thoughtful if controversial psychoanalytic interpretations of anorexia regards it as a young woman's desperate attempt to separate from her mother.[2]

Many women do see clothes, dieting, and self-decoration as a way to attract men, but for most women, attracting men is only part of the story. Young women develop ideas of how they want to look long before they are especially interested in attracting men. In fact, other women are much more likely to shape young women's ideas of how they want to look than are men, and many young women develop what they like to think of as their own style as much in rebellion against women (usually their mothers) as in a desire to win acceptance from other women, usually their friends.

Susan Douglas, in her book about women's relations to the media, wryly notes how her young daughter sits transfixed in front of television images of young women in sparkling, garish dresses that simultaneously capture and caricature the ideal of femininity. But to Douglas's daughter the women in those dresses embody femininity and an irresistible magic. Somehow the little girl translates those glittering images into a vision of what she would like to be. Susan Douglas understands her daughter's fascination, and, remembering the female idols of her own girlhood, she does not especially worry about the lasting harm it may cause, although her own dreams for her daughter focus on strength, independence, and accomplishment, not alluring femininity. A time may come when Douglas and her daughter, like other mothers and daughters, clash over clothes, especially if the daughter decides that clothes offer a self-definition. But the odds are good that by the time Douglas's daughter has a daughter of her own, her taste in clothes will resemble her mother's.

Not long ago, the *Geraldo* show took up the struggle between mothers and daughters over teenage clothes. The nature of the con-

flict took me back to my own adolescence when my mother ex-
pended Lord knows how much money and imagination to find me
blue jeans (what "everyone" was wearing) that did not cling to my
buttocks and thighs. At the time, my most precocious friends used
to buy the tightest jeans they could wriggle into and then bathe in
them so that the jeans would shrink and dry like a second skin. My
mother, as delicately as possible, explained to me that the flannel-
lined jeans she bought would ensure that I did not look "fat." Being
terrified of looking fat, I docilely, if unhappily, wore her purchases,
at least for a while. At thirteen, with no clothes allowance, I had
little choice. Happily, it did not take me long to acquire a couple of
pairs of jeans that conformed to the exacting standards of my peers,
and I wore them when away at school beyond the reach of her critical eye. Not until many years later did I figure out that her choice of
jeans had nothing to do with my being fat, and everything to do
with my beginning to develop a woman's figure.

At the time of our struggle, I was not conscious of wanting to look
sexy. I only wanted to look like everyone else. A few years later, when
spending the summer at a boarding school in Switzerland, another
student, an Italian girl whom I still remember as beautiful and sophisticated beyond her years, insisted upon giving me a straight skirt
because my demure full skirts struck her as hopelessly childish. I
adored that skirt, a maize and brown tweed that followed every
curve of my body and made me look older than my fifteen years.
Not long after, when my father came to take me out to dinner, I
proudly wore my new finery. I noticed something in his expression,
but paid it no mind. A few days later my mother, who had yet to see
my gorgeous skirt, wrote me that it was clearly inappropriate. This
time, benefiting from the instruction of my Italian friend, I understood the issue as what my parents saw as a provocative display of
sexuality.

The girls and mothers on the *Geraldo* show replayed my small
dramas, although this time the clothes that the girls chose for themselves shocked me and most of the audience as much as they
shocked their mothers. George, who was only fourteen and whose

name contrasted sharply with her carefully cultivated image of femininity, led the rest in daring. Accompanied by her elegant and visibly puzzled Hispanic-American mother, George appeared in a see-through black-lace body stocking under which she wore a scanty black bikini bra and panties. She allowed that her mother did not approve of her choice of clothing but insisted that it expressed her individuality. One of her friends in the audience came to her defense, insisting that George did not always dress that way—"just when we go out. I think she has the right to feel comfortable with what she's wearing."

No sooner had George's friend finished than a fiftyish-year-old African-American woman in the audience exploded, "You must be out of your mind!" Someone else added, "And don't you get a lot of wolf whistles? Do you like that?" George responded that there were plenty of wolf whistles and maybe she didn't like it, but she didn't really mind. The first woman returned to the attack. Dressing like that, she told George, was an invitation to wolf whistles and touching and worse. "When you dress like that men believe they're entitled to touch." George came back in a flash, "Oh, no, not entitled." She appeared shaken. Men and women in the audience agreed that no matter how you dress, no one is entitled to touch, but many felt she was asking for trouble. (The word "prudence" has gone out of fashion, but that is what they were talking about.) "Don't you know," an older woman asked, "that you look like a streetwalker?" Her old-fashioned language testified to the gulf that separated the generations.

None of the other young women was quite as young as George or quite as daring in her dress. All, however, were using their clothes to look older than their years. All were exposing more flesh than their mothers and the older members of the audience thought safe. And each insisted that her clothes were "me." They all seemed to believe that defining "me" led to struggles with their mother. But none was ready to take on her father, who never saw her in revealing clothes. Typically, they left the house with pants and sweaters over their "real" clothes and took them off as soon as they were safely out of sight. And when Geraldo asked nineteen-year-old Alison how her boyfriend felt about her clothes, she responded, "But he never sees me this way." Her boyfriend, it turned out, did not trust other young men to keep their hands to themselves. And the young women themselves understood, on some level, that what they called feminine or stylish was really sexually alluring.

For the young women on the Geraldo show, clothes literally define whom they are. Young women I spoke with at an exclusive private school in New York were no less concerned that their clothes be "me," but they had different ideas of what "me" should look like. They all wore blue jeans or pants to school and stressed the importance of comfort. One talked about how she shopped in boys' departments rather than girls', since "all they have are dresses with pink ruffles and pink bows and I didn't want that." Another raised the ante, cheerfully announcing that she usually borrowed her father's clothes—his sweater, shirt, belt. When she threw in the belt, I began to wonder if I were not being treated to a bit of exaggeration, since no man's belt I have ever seen would have fit around her tiny waist. But by then it was becoming clear that oversized male clothes were definitely chic.

On the surface, these girls mistrust femininity, especially the femininity they associate with pink ruffles and bows. According to their teachers, most are whizzes at math and everything else they turn their heads to. They readily admit to being ambitious and competitive about grades. The image they want to present has nothing to do with dependence, much less with sex object. Yet as they relax, hints of another side of their personalities begin to emerge. Liz admits that when she was growing up there was a lot of pressure to be feminine. Candy agrees. When she was in public school, "the girls were running around in little pink skirts. And I hated skirts."

Now that they are in high school things have changed. Candy likes "to combine: I like to play baseball, and I like to look nice." Sarah agrees. Now, she likes to wear a skirt. A few years ago, she didn't, "because the guys I was hanging out with made fun of girls in skirts. So I figured if I didn't wear a skirt they wouldn't make fun of me. And it worked. But now I love wearing skirts, I love getting dressed up. My family's all from the South, and so when I go down there I have to have the Sunday dress and all that. And I love it."

Kate spells out the sentiment of the group: "I like to dress how I want. I choose. I mean, I don't wear skirts a lot, but I wear them when I feel like wearing them. And I don't feel any different when I wear them, because I'm a woman without the skirt." But oh, she confesses, "Oh, I love shopping. I love a lot of the things that are typically girl." So does Candy, although she and her mother do not always agree on how to dress like a girl. "My mother has fits whenever I have to get dressed up for an interview, because I don't have anything in my closet. All the dresses I have are, you know, kinda wild and not really appropriate for an interview."

If this conversation, which entranced me, bears some resemblance to what one might read in *Seventeen* magazine, it may be because even these exceptionally intelligent, sophisticated young women occasionally glanced at its pages. And even if not, along the way they seem to have picked up the idiom for clothes, style, and self-representation. They would have been as appalled to be referred to as "pert" or "cute" as they were at the thought of wearing pink ruffled dresses. But by their mid-teens they had absorbed enough media culture to think of how they might look in the eyes of others. And their stated preference for blue jeans and men's clothing was, in its own way, as much a marker of their fashion-consciousness as George's attachment to her black-lace bodysuit. The two groups of girls were sharply divided by class, but each group was committed to its own culture of stylish dress. And each in its way seems to have chosen dress that contradicts the traditional ideal of feminine appearance as soft, demure, or cute for one that is tougher—more masculine or blatantly sexy.

The young women at private school had a very different sense of style than the young women on the *Geraldo* show, although they were all about the same age and lived in or around New York City. They nonetheless shared a strong sense of clothes as a kind of code —a way of defining themselves. Ironically, the young women from private school, with their independence and ambition, seemed even more concerned with how the guys they liked would view them. In contrast, as I listened to the girls on the *Geraldo* show, I began to feel that the most important audience in their quest for self-definition consisted of their female friends. No doubt they also wanted to appeal to men, but they seemed strangely naive about how they looked to men and about the signals they might be sending. And the private-school girls, who knew they wanted to pass muster with guys, mainly wanted to be accepted as interesting friends—not simply as girls.

Yet all of these girls saw clothes as a way to create a public self. And each of them believed that if she found the right "look," it would help her to be truly herself. The young women from private school compared this search for the right look with trying on costumes, by which they meant what actors wear for a theatrical part. Trying on clothes was like trying on identities. As Candy said, "If a woman is wearing a dress, it's costuming. If a woman is wearing pants and a big sweater, she's still costuming. There's nothing you can wear that's not costume—if you're a woman."

Talk to young women and you will find that the great majority have an acute and frequently whimsical sense of costume, and that they enjoy it to the hilt. The spirit of the game was captured by the young Emory undergraduate who arrived in my office to discuss what she, as a thoroughly independent young woman, thought was wrong with feminism. In a typical gesture of independence, Carla had made an appointment with me via E-mail. On the appointed day she arrived in my office in the ubiquitous undergraduate uniform of jeans, carrying a tape recorder, and with an electric head of bright fuchsia hair. After greeting me with a polite, professional handshake, she settled down to the business of the interview. And I, doing my best to respond in kind, refrained from staring at her hair. Just before leaving, she turned to me with a bright smile and said, "I suppose you have been wondering about my hair." Before I had time to gulp a polite "not at all," she continued, "It's simple. Pink for femininity, of course, but dark pink for strength and independence."

"Of course," I responded. And since then she has continued to con-sult me, via E-mail, about whether "fuschsoid" would not be the appropriate term for a strong young woman who has no patience with mainstream feminism.

Little girls begin by trying on Mama's clothes, painting their faces with lipstick, draping their bodies with the finery that engulfs them. But at very young ages, most girls begin to want costumes that fit their bodies and meet the exacting codes of their friends. And as they struggle to understand and meet prevailing standards of what looks right, they embark on what may prove to be a long process of self-definition. We all know some women who seem to have an in-stinctive gift for rightness and who always look perfect for every occasion. Normally, they are the cautious ones who never risk their self-image on a flight of fancy. Other women always risk the flight of fancy, frequently turning it into a refined art. One of my graduate students, who is fair, willowy, a bit ethereal, and gifted with an ex-quisite sense of style, frequently turns up in clinging, diaphanous, long-sleeved black dresses that sway just above her black-stockinged ankles. At her neck, she wears an antique brooch on a velvet ribbon, or perhaps a long strand of jet or pearls. On her head, shading her eyes, sits a glamorous hat, sometimes enhanced by a drooping veil. Looking for all the world like her great-grandmother as a young woman, she has turned retro-dressing into high style.

Most of us fall between the extremes, searching in fits and starts for what we hope will be our "style." And as we search, we fre-quently turn to things that remind us of other women we love, as if, through clothes, we could share a piece of their identity. Only years later did I understand that throughout my late teens and twenties, when I was trying to find my place in the world, I frequently shopped as if I were buying for other people. These "mistakes" would have looked wonderful on my best friend, my sister, my mother, a favorite professor—just not on me.

Many of us, myself included, have raged against fashion and its abuse of the female body. Feminists especially protest the ways in which women have forced themselves into shoes, skirts, bras, girdles (now resurrected as "body-toners"), and other items that may endanger their health and constrict their mobility. Women emerge from these diatribes as the helpless victims of a vast plot to undermine their independence and self-respect. And we all know how often the concern with looking "right" may gnaw at our self-confidence. It is hard to match the fury of a twelve-year-old girl ripping off a pair of pants because "they make me look fat" or throwing her hair brush against a mirror in frustration.

No doubt there are more "constructive" things for girls and women to be doing with their time than agonizing about how they look. But no amount of righteous preaching is likely to dent the pattern, although a sense of competence and self-acceptance will significantly reduce the anxiety. Women see clothes as an extension of their identities and a protection of their privacy. Clothes simultaneously expose them and encase them in armor. The concern to find clothes that "look like me" embodies both attitudes. For clothes permit women to create an image of themselves with which they are comfortable, and experienced women learn to look at themselves in clothes as if they were looking at a mannequin.

An interest in clothes binds women together, permitting them to share and even to talk about things they might usually be reluctant to mention. Nancy Wilson and I, who as busy professional women have innumerable "important" things to talk about and never enough time to scratch the surface, frequently spend one of our rare days together shopping. As we wander the aisles of store after store, we talk disjointedly but meaningfully. The clothes and our possible relation to them ("Should I try this? How would that look on you?") act as props that evoke pieces of our lives ("I need a jacket to wear with the skirt I wear for my evening classes") or people ("Do you remember your mother's polka-dot dress?") that might never come up in one of our serious talks. The special quality of our shopping conversation captures a companionship that women have always shared. Many men also care about clothes and may even enjoy shopping for them. Many even enjoy shopping for or with women—up to a point. But if there are men who shop as women do, I do not know them.

In Atlanta, where I live, Loehmann's discount clothing store attracts women of all ages, shapes, colors, and backgrounds from all over the city. At Loehmann's, men are literally relegated to the margins of the serious business: Those who are brave enough to accompany a female friend or relative sit uncomfortably on the few chairs set against a wall near the entrance. Men never get anywhere near the real center of Loehmann's, the large, crowded dressing rooms, where each woman has a peg to hang the clothes she is trying on and a bit of bench for her own things. Everyone dresses and undresses in full view of everyone else: middle-class white mothers from the suburbs with teenage daughters in tow; well-to-do young black women, toting Vuitton bags; petite Asian-American women; anxious grandmothers; working and professional women of various classes and colors.

What the dressing rooms lack in privacy, they make up for in companionship. As you look uncertainly into the mirror, pulling at the dress and craning your neck to see if it wrinkles over your hips, wondering if it makes you look too fat, the friendly voice of a stranger invariably reassures you that it looks stunning or tentatively suggests that another color would be more flattering. Across lines of race, education, income, and taste, women understand other women's anxieties about their bodies and insecurities about clothes. Some of the most accomplished and devoted Loehmann's shoppers I know are professional African-American friends who frequently have a gift for elegance that puts their white colleagues to shame. One day I conveyed my admiration to one of my African-American feminist friends. Yes, she agreed, many black women do have a rare sense of style. But then, she said sadly, "I'm not sure it's always a good thing. You know, we have always cared too much about clothes in the black community. In the end it is a kind of control."

Through years of such conversations, I have discovered that the control of which my friend complained is exercised by women over younger women. All too familiar with the dangers of an inhospitable world, generations of African-American women have learned to cultivate what Sicilian-American men are wont to call "respect." The right clothing indeed provides a kind of armor, particularly against a white world that perennially doubts your respectability and taste, but also against other women in your own community. One evening, a colleague had a group of us in stitches, describing the way her grandmother would dress for church. "Grandmama would finally get to the hat—of which she had scores. The hat had to be perfect, and she would try and retry it until it set on her head in the perfect gesture of superiority and defiance." My friend's grandmother was married to the minister, whom women found especially attractive. Her job, then, was to show by her dress and demeanor that those other women were "no 'count." "Grandmama was the minister's wife, and she knew just how to show all of them that nothing they did could touch her."

On another occasion, a college classmate, now a successful psychiatrist, and I fell into a conversation about shopping. The conversation had begun as a discussion of young women, especially her daughter, a freshman in college. As a rule, she and her daughter get on wonderfully well, but, as in any mother-daughter relation, there are moments of friction. You know, my friend confided, Gillian can be unbelievably stubborn. But, she added, "Even when things are most difficult, all I have to do is say, 'Let's go shopping.' We can always smooth things over by going shopping." No, mother and daughter did not usually agree about how Gillian wanted to look, but they could talk about clothes when they could not talk directly about other things.

It has taken years for most of the women I know well, including my sister and me, to get over dressing to please or displease our mothers. I know successful, independent women who can still be reduced to anxious girls—or even to tears—when their mothers disapprove of something they wear or, worse, suggest that maybe it does not do much for their figure. It is as if mothers unconsciously see clothes as a way of retaining control of their daughters—of keeping them girls rather than facing them as independent women. Certainly, I now believe that concern about my emerging sexuality motivated my own mother's hostility to my elegant—and revealing—straight skirt.

Who among us knows for sure what goes into all of that? Even those of us who deeply love our mothers have, at one time or another, experienced the tensions of trying to pull away—of trying to establish ourselves as independent people. For the young girls who are so determined to be "me," relations with mothers normally lie at the heart of the matter. Our mothers are the women we know best, even if we do not really know them at all. Seeing them both as extensions of ourselves and as powerful figures of authority, we search for ways to become adult women (like them) and a person in our own right (different from them).

Especially in these times, when women's roles and expectations are changing radically and rapidly, young women desperately seek to become a different kind of woman from their mothers. Today's young women enjoy opportunities from careers to sports to sexual freedom that most of their mothers never dreamed of. But no matter how successfully they prove themselves, most remain tied to their mothers and continue to pull against their authority—even when they do not entirely know what they are doing. The young women on the *Geraldo* show were proclaiming that their mothers could not control their sexuality. Moreover, by revealing their own maturing figures, they were challenging their mothers' status as sexual beings. And not unlike the female gang members in Dorchester, although without the desperation and acute alienation, these young women look to their friends to provide an alternate source of support. Their dress signifies their membership in the group.

Even though these young women have no use for conventional standards of middle-class propriety, they remain caught in a web of clothes: You are what you wear. In this respect, they are as much prisoners of the laws of their world as the women on Wall Street, who, according to Candy, one of the New York students, all wear a version of the same suit, the same correct blouse, the same neat shoes, and carefully keep the hems of their skirts one inch below their knees.

   Women today are much less dependent upon men for their livelihoods than their mothers and grandmothers have been, although a male paycheck still matters, even if most women no longer depend completely upon it. We have come a long way from the world in which the ability to attract and hold a husband was a young woman's most important career. Yet, thanks to the sexual revolution, young women are free to expose their bodies more openly than ever. The exhibitionism of George and her friends differs radically from the swirling prom dresses of the 1950s, which revealed enough to be alluring but sent a strong message of "don't touch." Those dresses labeled young women as belonging to their parents. Today's party clothes identify young women, even girls, as belonging to themselves. This is the core of the struggle between daughters who crave independence and mothers who consider their daughters too young to dispose of themselves. In this teen peer culture, young women set their own standards—in dress and most everything else.

Women have always imposed dress codes on other women, especially to keep them in line. More often than not, women isolated the bold woman who knew how to be especially alluring to men and would not play by their rules. Was this not the case of Ellen Olenska of Edith Wharton's *Age of Innocence*, who, in Martin Scorsese's film, captured the American imagination? If we may believe *Vogue*, working women still impose dress codes upon one another. The conventional suit that earned Candy's disdain remains required dress in business and the professions.[3] Former Congresswoman Marjorie Margolies-Mezvinsky of Pennsylvania told the *Vogue* reporter, "I really do think there is something in us that says it's better if our clothes are not distracting." Others worry that a fashionable or, heaven forbid, revealing dress would invite sexual harassment. Margot Parker, a director of government relations for GM, believes that women should dress according to their rank in the company: "If you're staff, I think you should look the part." And she has been known to reprimand women who did not.

Women, who well understand the fine points of dressing to fit your rank, have been known to be less than charitable toward those who fail to notice. Professional women usually fall back on their intuitive knowledge of what "looks right" without stopping to think that what is supposed to "look right" for a secretary might not be what they would want for themselves. Hierarchies of dress codes reflect differences in economic status and income. Those differences and their significance were dramatically illustrated in the film *Working Girl*. The secretary, played by Melanie Griffith, wears the clothes of her boss, played by Sigourney Weaver, and in putting on her boss's clothes assumes her executive role as well. As *Working Girl* clearly illustrates, the tasteful clothes of professional women visibly define a female elite whose work justifies the expenditure on themselves. These are women who have joined the higher echelons of what was recently a man's world. Women who work in traditional female occupations as secretaries or beauticians, women who work for minimum wages, or women who do no paid work at all can rarely justify those expenditures.

Secretaries, receptionists, and others who must, as they say, "meet the public" are obliged to spend a significant part of their earnings on their appearance simply to meet job expectations. I still wince when I recall a conversation with a manicurist friend of mine in which I referred to the stupidity of wearing artificial nails that cause decay and infection in the real nails beneath. "But, you know," she said sadly, "they have no choice. Their job requires that they have long, shiny nails." Too easily impatient with women who risk their health because they have to earn a living, I had never stopped to think. In this case, the culture does push women to a dangerous femininity. Nor do the special requirements for some secretaries and receptionists explain the countless other women who delight in manicures and artificial nails for personal reasons.

If you doubt that femininity matters to women, just pick up a woman's magazine and you will find one article after another de-

4444

voted to clothes, cosmetics, fitness, or relationships. In 1993, *Cosmopolitan* produced a special spring issue entitled "Life After College." One of five main sections was devoted to "Careers and Jobs," the remainder to "Feelings and Relationships," "Making the Adjustment," "Beauty and Fashion," and "Fun Stuff." In the section on adjustment, the opening page of an article on "The Juggling Act: Making Time for Everything" featured pictures of women doing the things for which they had to make time: exercise, bubble bath, selecting clothes, dating, and, at the end of it all, sitting at a dressing table in a lace-trimmed gown and negligee to write in a diary. The job, not pictured, was taken for granted.

These activities figure prominently in *Cosmo*'s regular offerings. During the first seven months of 1993, slightly more than half of its pages were devoted to body image, fashion, marriage and relationships, health, and leisure. Less than 5 percent of the articles discussed career and work, and only 1 percent discussed feminist issues. And *Cosmo* explicitly targets single working women. *New Woman* is not much different, even though it is designed for independent, upwardly mobile women. *Redbook*, in contrast, frequently focuses on family but still has almost as many pages on fashion, body image, sex, and health as *Cosmo* and *New Woman*. Only *Working Woman*, which devotes almost half of its pages to career and work, devotes as much space to feminism as to fashion—virtually none. *Working Woman* is, in one sense, entirely devoted to women's issues, but that makes its apparent reluctance to associate those issues with feminism all the more striking. Yet each of these magazines, in its own way, is designed to help contemporary women live rich and fulfilling lives, and each seems to assume that for its readers, the bonds of femininity frequently look like an asset rather than a liability.

These magazines, like others that flood the market, refuse to acknowledge any contradiction between femininity and women's issues. Whatever they think of feminism, which most rarely, if ever, mention, they have taken women's issues to heart. Keeping up with the times, they have followed their readers' interests, and, like those readers, they have seen femininity as a bedrock of continuity.

Why should we condemn everything associated with femininity as bad or oppressive? Those who most bitterly attack femininity assume that it has been imposed upon women by men. Yet women themselves clearly have done much to cultivate femininity and a vast number continue to value it today. It takes a breathtaking elitism, which is common among those who most vehemently denounce the presumed elitism of others, to charge that the mass of American women have let themselves be brainwashed—a charge that in effect reduces most women to "bimbos."

Elite professional women may feel especially conflicted about femininity because it stands in such sharp contrast to the masculine world they have entered. And usually, the women in that world who most clearly display femininity are secretaries and receptionists. Understandably, but not admirably, professional women recoil from the thought that their male coworkers confuse them with secretaries, and try to draw sharp lines. And because professional women may still feel uneasy about bossing or supervising other women, just as the women they boss or supervise often resent them, conflicts over status among women easily erupt.

These problems often plague relations among professional women themselves. The bonds of femininity do not offer a reliable guide for dealing with other professionals or with female employees, although they may still facilitate communication among women. From time to time, when trying to observe the rules of professionalism in dealing with other professional women whom I do not know well, I have been surprised to find that if, however accidentally, the conversation slips to clothes, parents, children, or men, the ice is suddenly broken. For men the equivalent is often professional sports, which more and more women are also becoming fans of, and women who want an easy relation with male coworkers often find that learning the language of sports eases their way. Still, to break the ice for women there is nothing like a good exchange about the difficulty of finding attractive and comfortable clothes ("I won't buy a skirt without pockets") or about what to take on a business trip ("Will one jacket do for three days if you have two skirts to go with it?"). Suddenly, we are back in the familiar conversational world in which we grew up. We have found our bearings and can more comfortably return to the business that brought us together in the first place. Like George and her friends, we recognize clothes as at once a uniform and a form of self-expression—as a way of expressing both our member-ship in a group and our individuality.

It is hard to imagine anything farther removed from George's black-lace bodysuit than what one of my successful friends mock-ingly used to call her "lady lawyer" suits. And women of different groups have styles of dress that differ from both. If we are to believe the ads and the magazines, fashion gets "freer" by the day in re-sponse to women's growing sense of their own freedom. Yet most women continue to share an interest in how they dress, even when they continue to dress in very different ways. The bond is not that we all want to wear the same things, but that we all know that what we wear—how we put ourselves together—will identify us in the eyes of others. Thus even as we choose different costumes, we share an interest in the craft of costume, for we implicitly acknowledge the truth of Candy's claim that no matter what women wear, they are costuming.

The complexities of costuming were recently brought home when I was working as an expert witness in a legal case in which many of the litigants were highly accomplished young women. When I first met two of these lawyers in a series of depositions, their clothes immediately caught my attention. One, a lovely blonde, always ap-peared in a cautious, conservative tweed suit, which she wore but-toned up to her chin. The first time I met the other, a bolder straw-berry blonde, she was wearing a low-cut, bright red dress with an oversized pearl choker and earrings to match. If the outfit did not quite match George's standards of daring, it did not miss them by much. The next time, she appeared in a long, flowing flowered print, again with a low neckline, that probably would have suited Candy's sense of what to wear for a summer party. But when they appeared in court a few days later, both were wearing impeccable black suits and white blouses. Yet even then, their individual styles showed through the uniform, and to my amazement, the cautious blonde, if anything, overmatched her bolder colleague in both elegance and femininity.

Whatever the frustration and pain, most women clearly value the distinctly female core of their identities. It offers a connection to history and to all the women who have come before. It offers a connection to other women across lines of race, ethnicity, and class. It offers a foundation for coexistence with men, who express their own anxieties and disruptions in different ways. There may be nothing especially noble in women's interest in clothes and appearance, although you might be fooled if you listen to the hype of some of the more successful designers for the new breed of upscale professional women. But for most of us it is a deeply ingrained part of who we are. When that normal interest becomes an obsession, it may, like all obsessions, undermine our independence and strength. But for most women an interest in clothes is simply the pleasant game they have played since they were children. We should be allowed to relax about it, for there is a certain sanity in treating the often maddening life around us as a costume party.

These days, more and more feminists seem to be relaxing into some of the pleasures of a modern femininity. And some designers, notably Donna Karan, are apparently designing their clothes with the new breed of upscale, feminist career woman in mind. Various feminist subcultures have developed an arresting style that frequently emphasizes black leather and exudes a heightened sense of sexuality. Many radical feminists retain a puritanical hostility to anything that suggests traditional femininity, but even their self-consciously plain clothes make a distinct "fashion" statement. And then there are the committed feminist mothers who dress their daughters in ruffles and send them to ballet lessons. In a world of costumes it is hard for any woman to avoid dressing to create an image.

NOTES

[1]Christina Hoff Somners, *Who Stole Feminism? How Women Have Betrayed Women* (New York: Simon and Schuster, 1994). The debate about deaths from anorexia are inherently misleading, since anorexia is best understood as a symptom of deep psychological disorder, frequently conflicts about independence. Typically, anorectics are more concerned with asserting control over themselves than with looking beautiful. Most do not die of anorexia, although some who suffer from anorexia die through suicide.

[2]Hilde Bruch, *The Golden Cage: The Enigma of Anorexia Nervosa* (Cambridge, MA: Harvard Univ. Press, 1978), and her *Eating Disorders: Obesity, Anorexia Nervosa, and the Person Within* (New York: Basic Books, 1973).

[3]"Fashion Taboos at Work," *Vogue* (August 1993): 219–21.

Three

SEXUAL REVOLUTION

George and the other young women from the Geraldo show seem to be experimenting with clothing as a way of experimenting with sex. But they clearly remain conflicted about their own sexuality. George fiercely defends her right to wear revealing and provocative clothing, and no less fiercely insists that no man has a right to touch. George's mother worries about the messages George's clothing is sending, in part because she knows that the rules of sexual conduct have been revolutionized since she was a girl. She does not want her daughter to court danger. Many feminists, in contrast, apparently sympathize with George's position: She does have a right to dress as she pleases, and, no matter what she wears, men do not have a right to touch. Thus even when feminists do not have much sympathy for George's preoccupation with style, they firmly support her right to a sexual freedom that can easily lead to danger. Feminism has ridden the crest of a cataclysmic sexual revolution about which feminists seem as conflicted as George herself.

If you credit leading feminists, you would have to believe that feminism is mainly about sex. Many of their conservative critics agree. Feminism has gotten most of its publicity and melodrama from the exhilarating and unsettling sexual revolution that has been sweeping across American society since the 1960s. Lurid stories of women bound and beaten by sexually predatory men have titillated a nation obsessed with sex. Some feminists have responded that for women sex means pornography, harassment, rape, acquaintance rape, and incest. Others have celebrated the liberation of women's sexuality from men's control. Some have argued that male sexuality invariably victimizes women and must be hedged in by laws and codes—by the power of the state. Others have urged women to embrace sexual freedom, even if they occasionally suffer a few knocks. But all testify to the intensity and passion with which feminists are responding to sexual issues.

Disagreements usually evaporate where abortion is concerned. For more than twenty years abortion on demand has proved the most durable feminist issue, and it has been widely viewed as the litmus test of feminism. The official feminist leaders, and many grassroots feminists as well, have been reluctant to concede that a woman who opposes abortion could legitimately call herself a feminist. Neither they nor the media want to hear that some committed feminists are pro-life and that many more support some restrictions on abortion. Feminists have consistently opposed such restrictions as the limitation of abortion to the first three or four months of a pregnancy, the imposition of a waiting period between the decision to abort and the actual abortion, and the requirement that minor girls consult a parent or guardian. So the religious and moral convictions of any number of women have been silenced by the feminist campaign to politicize sexuality and speak on behalf of all women.

This much is clear: The sexual revolution has irreversibly transformed the lives of American women, who are trying to understand what that transformation means for them. Some have embraced sexual liberation with enthusiasm, some with anxiety and doubt, some not at all. A few years ago, speaking with a group of attractive, successful college women who were busily planning independent careers, I was surprised to learn that they and their friends firmly intended to remain virgins until they married. *Virgins until marriage? You can't be serious.* They were. Chastity has been making a comeback among the young, with organized groups that include young men. This recent, and until recently unthinkable, interest in chastity confirms many women's uncertain response to a sexual liberation that too often brings them more heartache than pleasure. But even while individual women find their own way through the swirling currents of sexual liberation, images and discussions of sex continue to dominate the American scene.

When a visibly pregnant Demi Moore startled the nation by posing nude for the cover of *Vanity Fair*, most intimate sexual encounters had already been paraded before our public imagination. Adult films and pornographic magazines are nothing new, but until the last twenty years or so they have usually been shrouded in secrecy. Their recent history has been marked by open exhibitionism, as explicit sexuality has conquered fashion magazines, prime time television, and local movie theaters, to say nothing of lingerie ads in ostensibly respectable newspapers. We now live with an image of ourselves as a sexually open and adventurous people. More significant, we live in a culture that readily condemns criticism of open sexuality as evidence of religious bigotry and repression. These changes have come upon us rapidly—and they have constituted a veritable revolution.

Since the 1960s, Americans have been wrestling with the escalating implications of a sexual revolution that has replaced "traditional" stories about what it meant to be a man or a woman with a new story of limitless possibilities. Women now in late middle age came of age in a world in which "nice" girls didn't—or didn't admit that they did. Younger women came of age in a world in which nice girls, like everyone else, did—or had to have a pretty good reason why they did not. Pro-choice activists like to evoke the bad old days of back alley abortions, but few young women (or men) today have personal knowledge of a world without open abortion—one in which a young woman would die rather than admit to her parents she was pregnant. Pro-choice activists insist that women literally risked death through dangerous abortions, but at the time, "die rather than tell" meant only that we nice middle-class girls could not face our parents. This was the world of The Everly Brothers hit song "Wake Up Little Susie," in which whatever "nice" girls may have done in secret, they dared not admit to doing—a world in which an unintended pregnancy "ruined" a middle-class girl's life.[1]

At the time, most middle-class girls neither knew nor cared that many poorer girls were just as afraid of confessing a pregnancy to their parents. For historical reasons that need not concern us here, segments of the African-American community had long been more accustomed to the pregnancies of unmarried women. Some accepted them easily, but others, especially churchgoers, did not. Courtney Washington, a highly successful professor at the University of Florida, still shudders at the stories that circulated among the women of the poor black community in South Carolina where she grew up. She knows that some women had children without being married, but what she most remembers is how angry a single daughter's pregnancy could make a father. And her worst nightmare is the story of one of her own aunts—her mother's favorite sister—who did get pregnant by a man who had no intention of marrying her. Aunt Minnie hid the pregnancy as long as she could, but eventually her father, Courtney's grandfather, noticed. There were no words to describe his fury. But his actions confirmed that he could not forgive his daughter for the disgrace she brought upon the family. He shut her in her room, refused to let her sisters talk with her, and, when labor began, refused to call a doctor. After hours of painful labor, Aunt Minnie gave birth to a stillborn child and, with no medical assistance, eventually died in her own blood. Men like Aunt Minnie's father insisted upon defending the respectability of their families even at the cost of a daughter's life. Such men saw women's sexual purity as the cornerstone of morality and feared that women's "immorality" would lead to a complete moral collapse.

Gloria Patterson remembers that when she was growing up in the late 1950s and early 1960s outside of Savannah, Georgia, her father, who supplemented his meager income as a minister by working on the railroads, "would have died" if she had "fooled around" in high school. He had seven girls "and none of us had babies before we got married." Attitudes had not changed much when Aprill Ravenel was growing up in Detroit in the 1980s. Aprill unintentionally became pregnant, and she did not "tell a soul, not my sisters, no one." When her parents found out, her mother "wanted to kick me out of the house." To Aprill's surprise, her father was loving and support- ive, but his response was unusual for fathers in their respectable, churchgoing community. She thinks that most of her friends' dads "would have hit the roof." One of her friends left home when she discovered she was pregnant because she knew that she could not tell her father. "He would have killed her, you know."

Living at home during their teens, Aprill and her friend, like Glo- ria and her sisters, lived intimately with their parents' values. So did most white working-class women of all ethnic backgrounds. The more affluent young women who went away to college had more freedom to pursue independent lives and were more likely to iden- tify with an emerging women's movement that defended women's sexual freedom as their individual right. But throughout the sixties and beyond, many working and lower-middle-class white and black families viewed a daughter's pregnancy outside of marriage as a hu- miliation. For them, the free expression of female sexuality, espe- cially for unmarried daughters, represented social and cultural chaos.

Today, the link between women's sexual purity and morality has snapped. The revolution in attitudes occurred almost overnight, and the rapidity of the change makes it all the more important to try to understand it. Sexuality does lie at the core of each of our sense of self. Sexuality does join women and men across the divide of biolog- ical difference. Sexuality does produce babies. Most societies, even the sexually permissive, have taken a grave view of sexuality. Not many societies have believed they could afford to be permissive about the sexuality of young women. Not for nothing does sexuality claim an important place in most religions and moral codes, for sexuality, perhaps more than any other human activity, links danger and promise: the danger of violence, rape, and abuse to the promise of love, union, and new life. Even those with jaded modern sensibilities should be able to understand that most societies have reasonably seen sexuality as a moral issue.

Those who embrace the sexual revolution reject the idea that sexuality has anything to do with morality, and during the 1960s and 1970s their views triumphed. The sexual revolution freed women from centuries of imposed "virtue." It especially freed them from the double standard that had deprived "respectable" women of the freedoms enjoyed by men. Almost overnight, women and girls rejected the notion that they could never have sex outside of marriage and still be "nice." For those of us who entered college in the late 1950s, the loss of virginity was a momentous event. Would the man still respect us? Would any man respect us? Many of us would not even tell our closest women friends that we were "sleeping with" our boyfriend. Yet by the time we had graduated, younger undergraduates were announcing that they and their friends regarded virginity as a burden to be shed as soon as possible. They enthusiastically linked the struggle for sexual liberation to the struggle for women's rights. After all, had not women's sexuality too often been used as the main justification for "protecting" women from everything from challenging work to walking the streets alone? Thus, sexual "morality" simply enforced the inequality between women and men. Women would never be equal to men until they could enjoy the same sexual freedom as men. What these apostles of liberation were unwilling to imagine was that sex itself might make women unequal to men.

By the 1960s, modern contraception, especially the diaphragm, was opening the possibility that young women might enjoy sexual freedom without cost. But the risk of pregnancy, while reduced, remained. And frequently a sense of guilt or shame still haunted women who engaged in premarital or extramarital sex. By the 1990s, the ghosts of sexual guilt had all but disappeared, and most women of all social groups were free to have premarital or even extramarital sex. They might now choose to abort a baby or to bear and raise it alone. Substantial pockets of traditional values remained, but the culture at large had embraced women's sexual freedom with a vengeance. Beneath that surface, however, women continue to disagree about whether their new freedom is good or bad. What some women have embraced as liberation, others have experienced as dangerous abandonment. And, as the women who fear abandonment are quick to point out—and as the polls confirm—men have tended to be much more enthusiastic about women's sexual liberation than many women themselves.

Since the sixties, both feminists and conservatives have debated sexual liberation as if it had a life of its own. Feminists defend sexual liberation as a good in its own right, while traditionalist conservatives attack it as a free-floating moral failure. Both groups talk as if sexual freedom means the same thing for women of different classes, races, and ethnic groups—as if all women are vulnerable to the same kinds of abuse and as if all could afford the same sexual risks.

Sexual revolution came upon us so rapidly that few, if any, had a clear picture of where it was leading and, especially, its implications for a consensus on moral values. In hindsight, its most important consequence was a growing conviction that consensus is impossible—that moral standards are a personal, not a community, matter. But at the time, nothing could have been less clear. Many Americans who welcomed the first stages of the sexual revolution never expected it to affect moral values at all. Others saw it as the beginning of moral collapse. From the start, controversy was brewing, and it has escalated. The different sides seem to be speaking different languages, and perhaps more important, the sexual revolution has forced everyone to reconsider what morality means.

Traditionally, religion had grounded morality. But in 1968 a Gallup poll showed that half of all Americans, especially the younger and more educated, believed that religious values were eroding, although most did not view the decline in religion, which was also occurring in other industrialized nations, as especially dangerous.[2] In contrast, they did worry deeply about a perceived decline in honesty. Morality, broadly understood, was a different matter. More than three quarters of Americans saw a decline in morality, women more so than men. Above all, people's views of morality reflected their income and education: The less of each they had, the more likely they were to worry about moral decline. In this climate, three quarters of the more urban, educated, and affluent favored making information on birth control available to anyone who wanted it, which suggests that the elite no longer saw birth control as a moral issue. Working-class women saw this "open-mindedness" as a luxury they could not afford.[3]

In complaining about moral decline and in accepting or rejecting birth control, Americans were responding in the light of their own values, traditions, and circumstances. It probably never occurred to the privileged folks who favored the broad distribution of birth control that their views might be contributing to a decline in morals among those young women with limited economic resources for whom marriage promised economic security. And we may doubt that they cared. The elite assumed that since "those people" do not respect middle-class morality anyway, we might as well make sure that they do not go on having more and more babies. Even today, when the open expression of elitism meets harsh denunciation, Planned Parenthood still reminds potential contributors about how much the pregnancies of poor unmarried women cost taxpayers, suggesting that the wide availability of birth control and abortion will reduce the bill. And conservatives use the same economic arguments to support the abolition of Aid to Families with Dependent Children (AFDC), although they usually want out-of-wedlock births to be reduced by abstinence rather than abortion.

During the late 1960s and early 1970s, the sense of cultural up-
heaval escalated as students engaged in protests against the Vietnam
War and demonstrated at the Democratic Convention in Chicago.
In working-class communities, families of Italian, Irish, Jewish, and
Eastern European backgrounds were quick to perceive the calls to
liberation not only as symptoms of declining morality but as a direct
threat to their families, especially their daughters. Most African-
Americans, like Gloria Patterson's father, also saw sexual liberation
as a promise of poverty and social despair. Sexual revolution threat-
ened their fragile hopes to pull families together so that children
could get educations and look forward to doing better than their
parents had done. Contraception might also encourage young girls
to "fool around." For poor black people, contraception carried a
double risk: It was less understood by their kids and less readily
available. So long as fooling around was likely, sooner or later, to
result in a pregnancy, they preferred their daughters to live with the
fear of its consequences.

By 1970, concern about consequences was leading many to rethink the desirability of making free birth control available on demand, and the number of those who did dropped sharply from three
years previously. Predictably, elite white men continued to support
the wide distribution of birth control, if only because it facilitated
their ability to play without risk, but polls showed that people with
no college education, including black and white men, had doubts.
From the perspective of Gloria Patterson's father and Aprill
Ravenel's mother, free birth control spelled trouble for their daughters. In this context, the Pill emerged as the very symbol of sexual
revolution. Many less affluent Americans seem to have blamed the
Pill for a dramatic increase in premarital sex, although initially it
mainly affected the lives of younger, more affluent, and better educated people, especially college students. By 1970, a Gallup poll
found that three in four college students, women as well as men, did
not consider it important that the person they marry be a virgin.
College men were still more likely than college women to have sex

before marriage, but more college women than ever before were doing so. And the wealthier a college woman's parents, the more likely
she was to feel that her own virginity did not affect her chances for
marriage.[4]

These elite college women would also be the first to benefit from
the new professional and occupational opportunities that were opening up for women. They belonged to the cutting edge of the baby
boomers and were the first generation of women to graduate with
new expectations for their lives. Where earlier generations of college
women had frequently worked before marriage or until they had
children, more and more of the new generation were beginning to
plan to pursue careers throughout their lives even if they married
and had children. For them, the new possibilities of sexual freedom
were there for the taking. Even if they planned to defer marriage
while they completed professional training, they neither expected to
defer sex nor wanted an inconvenient pregnancy to interfere with
their plans. They were the elite of a generation that would bring a
new set of attitudes and expectations to American culture.

Lucy Goldfarb was still a virgin when she arrived at Wellesley
College in the late 1960s. She had attended an exclusive girls' school
in New York, and had had little contact with boys except at heavily
chaperoned dances. At Wellesley, however, she rapidly became
caught up in a social whirl and, together with a group of friends,
started dating young men from Harvard. Suddenly, she was playing
in a new league, and when after a couple of months of steady dating
her boyfriend started pushing her to "go all the way," she had trouble thinking of reasons not to. The first couple of times, she resisted.
But without much conviction. Don Feldman, too, came from a
wealthy New York Jewish family; he was attractive, he was fun, and
she adored him. So, why not? He had a friend who was happy to give
them access to his apartment in Cambridge, and soon Lucy and her
boyfriend were having sex on a regular basis. At first, she used a
diaphragm, but over Christmas vacation she persuaded her mother's
gynecologist to give her a prescription for the Pill. Over that first
summer, she and Don broke up, and Lucy stopped taking the Pill

because she did not want to feel like a party girl who was ready to have sex with anyone she dated once or twice. By the next spring, she was seeing Bill Saxon, another Harvard man, and they started having sex before she thought about going back on the Pill. In June, she missed her period. By July, she feared she was pregnant. Mustering her courage, she talked to her mother, who was concerned but not shocked. And her mother arranged a quiet abortion at a private clinic. In the fall, Lucy returned to Wellesley, promising herself that she would be more careful the next time.

Lucy's experience did not lead her to turn her back on sexual freedom, which she and her college friends easily accepted as a way of life. College students in general led the way in embracing the sexual revolution, but they were not the only young Americans to do so. Baby boomers of every class, race, and ethnicity shared the new attitudes that were transforming American culture. The new mood could be seen in their attitudes toward family size, which changed dramatically between 1967 and 1973. That the young baby boomers wanted more sex did not mean that they wanted more children. By 1973, only about one fifth liked the idea of a family with four or more children, fewer than at any point since the Great Depression of the 1930s.[5]

The most dramatic change occurred in the attitudes of young women. Within a few years, they rejected large families as the main justification for their lives, and they were acting on their convictions. Not only did they want fewer children; in the early 1970s, whether rich or poor, they were having fewer than at any time in the nation's history. Obviously, there were many reasons for this sudden decline, including concerns for zero population growth and the rising cost of raising children, especially of educating them, but the sexual revolution played a major role. Effective contraception and more liberal abortion laws permitted women of the baby boom generation more control over their fertility than their mothers and grandmothers had had, and increasing numbers enthusiastically used that power to pursue new values and opportunities.[6]

In the early 1970s, those who rejected these new attitudes tended to view increased sexual freedom for women as a direct cause of moral decline, especially the majority of adults who still believed that premarital sex was "wrong." And many of the nearly 80 percent of Americans who thought that morals were getting worse blamed the new sexual permissiveness. Parents especially worried about the new sexual freedom among young people, and a large majority of adults, who saw sexual freedom as a general moral problem, favored stricter state and local laws on obscene literature and stricter standards for magazines available at newsstands.

Not everyone agreed about the moral dangers of sexual liberation. People in their twenties were less likely to worry about its morality than those over thirty, and some people opposed premarital sex for practical rather than moral reasons. Unlike those who held marriage sacred, they primarily worried that premarital sex would lead to illegitimate children, damaged reputations, or psychological difficulties. Even the minority who refused to condemn premarital sex disagreed about its moral implications. Some believed that traditional moral codes had become irrelevant. Others believed that sexual codes should be left to individuals. And some believed that premarital sex was a practical test of compatibility for marriage.

From the start, those who approved of premarital sex tended to be politically liberal and those who opposed it conservative.[7] But the association between political and sexual attitudes remained, as it would for the next two decades, something less than hard and fast. Thus, African-American parents who worry about premarital sexuality often support liberal politicians, primarily for economic reasons. And elite white parents who have a fairly relaxed attitude toward their daughters' sexual behavior support conservative politicians, again for economic reasons. Here, as in so many other areas, the interlocking of economic and sexual change has had confusing effects. The only clear result of the sexual revolution was that more and more people were coming to see sexual morality as a purely personal issue.

The sexual revolution touched people differently according to income and education—their ability to prosper in a rapidly changing society. The differences emerged with special clarity from the continuing discussions about birth control, which eventually spilled into the debate over abortion. More accessible and effective contraception encouraged freer sexual attitudes, but it did not solve the problem of premarital pregnancy and may even have made it worse. In fact, it remains unclear whether the number of premarital pregnancies rose or fell during the 1960s; certainly, it did not fall drastically, as most assumed it would. During the 1960s the young women in their late teens and twenties who first benefited from improved, accessible contraception and freer sexual attitudes had been shaped by the older respectability of the 1950s. Even when they started having sex, they were not always sure that they should. Thus, however improbable it may seem today, many wrestled with their own conflicted emotions, and some felt less responsible—and less guilty—if their boyfriend swept them off their feet in a moment of passion than if they themselves had planned to have sex. And what could be better evidence of planning than to come prepared with a diaphragm? So they came without. Or they "forgot" to take their pill.

Such conflicted feelings influenced Lucy Goldfarb's decision to stop taking the Pill after she broke up with Don Feldman. One of Lucy's Wellesley classmates, Pauline Stern, who came from a less affluent and more conservative family, also started to have sex with her boyfriend during her first year at college. Her boyfriend, Jonathan Barnes, was a scholarship student at Amherst, and he and Pauline could afford to see each other only a few times a semester. But they rapidly decided that they wanted to get married, which eased her mind about their sexual relations. Even so, she felt conflicted enough that she did not always use contraception, and during her junior year she became pregnant. There was no possibility of telling either set of their deeply religious parents, and they could not afford to marry until Jonathan had finished college and found a job. So they saved their money, he borrowed some from a friend, and they went to Mexico for her to have an abortion. The experience deeply depressed them, and for several years thereafter, she would burst into tears whenever she thought about what they had done. Other young women "forgot" to use contraception because they wanted the young man to marry them. Some were just irresponsible. Whatever the reasons, young women who had not been raised to take responsibility for their own sexual lives frequently got "in trouble." And one solution was to try to get an abortion.

Although obtaining an abortion, as Pauline and Jonathan discovered, might prove difficult, expensive, and even dangerous, roughly as many women had abortions before *Roe* v. *Wade* as after it.[8] The sexual revolution brought discussion about abortion into the open, and the polls showed that people's feelings were conflicted. Most Americans did not see abortion as a simple yes or no issue, believing that its legality should depend upon the circumstances. Overwhelmingly and unhesitatingly they favored abortion when the health of the mother was endangered. But only about half favored abortion when the child might be born deformed. More telling, fewer than one in five viewed economic considerations as relevant.[9] These responses suggest that in thinking about abortion, Americans above all thought about the life or potential life of the fetus rather than of the mother's convenience. Even presumably hardheaded men refused to accept finances as an adequate justification for abortion, although men with college educations and younger, more affluent women were more likely to do so.[10] Thus some of those who were most in favor of abortion as a solution to financial problems were probably young people who planned to have successful careers and knew that marriage and a child would interrupt training and limit their future standard of living.

The public discussion of abortion has flowed directly from the growing acceptance of young women's premarital sexual activity and was accordingly shaped by the concerns of the more vocal elite women who most benefited from it. The attitudes of the less affluent remained more conflicted and conservative. Once again, class proved more important than gender in shaping people's views, although men were always more likely than women to favor abortion, since it relieved them of responsibility for their sexual activities.[11] By

1970, support for legalization of abortion during the first three months of a pregnancy was growing rapidly.[12]

As with abortion, so with divorce, and for similar reasons. Throughout the late 1960s, more than half of all Americans believed that divorce should be more difficult to obtain. Of all the sexual and moral issues, divorce has most readily united women. Because so many women depended upon men for support, divorce was clearly a women's issue, but young upscale women were beginning to change their minds. With divorce, as with abortion, the baby boomer elite—the younger, wealthier, college-educated people, who lived in large cities—were the most liberal.[13] But on divorce, unlike abortion, their views did not easily triumph.[14] By the 1960s, Americans already knew a good deal, perhaps too much, about divorce, which was steadily increasing, and their distaste for it may well have been linked to a lingering attachment to a more traditional Ozzie and Harriet image of American culture. They may even have instinctively seen a link between morality and the stability of families that they did not see between morality and the sexual behavior of young women.

For whatever reasons, Americans remained deeply divided about the implications of the sexual revolution. Even now, the best one can safely say is that the youngest, most affluent, and best educated people—the elite—were the most likely to welcome new sexual mores and the social changes, notably legal abortion and easier divorce, to which they seemed logically to lead. Elite women and men did not always agree about the issues, because in the case of sex, marriage, and pregnancy, they had different interests. But increasingly, the interests of elite women were diverging from those of poorer women, and the interests of children were beginning to drop from view.

Roe v. Wade, the symbolic turning point of January 1973, cast a long shadow over the debates of subsequent decades. The legalization of abortion marked the beginning of a protracted war. Most feminists saw Roe v. Wade as nothing less than women's own Declaration of Independence. They now claimed abortion as a woman's natural as well as constitutional right, as important as the right to freedom of speech and as necessary to every woman's right to life, liberty, and the pursuit of happiness. For opponents, *Roe* v. *Wade* ran roughshod over the conflicting right of the fetus to life and was nothing less than the legalization of baby-killing.

While passions on both sides burned ever more fiercely, the great majority of Americans persisted in the more cautious belief that abortion should be available but only under certain circumstances, by which they normally meant during the first trimester. Yet the voices of the majority, which supports abortion conditionally, have been drowned by the louder, more insistent voices of those who demand total access or prohibition. Pro-life and pro-choice militants have carried their war from the courts and the legislatures into the streets and to the doors of abortion clinics. Each side has framed the issue as a matter of fundamental and inalienable right: the right to life of the fetus against the individual right of the woman to her own body. Neither side can accept even the most modest compromise, for those who defend fundamental truths and absolute rights must regard compromise as a cowardly betrayal of principle.

Then as now, for those who defend the fetus's right to life, abortion kills babies. Then as now, for those who defend the woman's right to choose, denial of abortion kills women—either physically through back-alley abortions or spiritually through the curtailment of their autonomy. The struggle thus reduces to a decision in favor of the life of the unborn child or the life of the pregnant woman. Which side are you on?

The battle lines have been clear, but the issues frequently have not. Those on the pro-choice side have focused on the story of women for whom denial of abortion has allegedly meant virtual enslavement to the domination of men and their own bodies. For them, abortion becomes the key to women's "liberation" and, especially, women's "equality" with men. As they emphasize the story of women's long struggle for individual freedom, they minimize the story of the babies. Those on the pro-choice side focus on the babies, for whom abortion allegedly means endorsement of the selfishness of women who refuse to accept responsibility for the most vulnerable members of American society. For them, abortion mocks any respect for the rights of others—and even complicity in murder. And as they emphasize the story of the babies, they minimize the story of women.

To the extent that the pro-choice forces acknowledge the claims of babies, they insist, with astonishing presumption and no less astonishing absurdity, that no self-respecting baby would want to be born deformed or poor, and some might not even want to be born in the sex that its mother did not choose. To the extent that the pro-life forces acknowledge the claims of women, they insist that no self-respecting woman would want a personal and sexual freedom that would relieve men of the responsibility to support her and their children. But too often, their concern for life seems to begin and end with life in the womb, since they show little enthusiasm for the support and education of the many babies who are born poor and, frequently, fatherless.

Even as the rhetoric escalates, these passionate debates still bear the imprint of their origins in the early years of the sexual revolution. Could women ever hope for equality and independence if they do not enjoy the same sexual freedom as men? Could women ever enjoy the same sexual freedom as men if they remain tied to women's unique capacity to bear and nurture life? Increasingly, the two sides have differed over whether to view women's sexuality as an encumbrance or a potential asset: Are women basically similar to men and in direct competition with them or are they essentially different and in need of male cooperation? Although the lines that divide women among themselves have never been as clear as social scientists would like to think, they have tended to divide upscale, career women from less affluent and less well educated women of all ethnicities.

In a survey published in April 1973, the *Gallup Opinion Index* announced that a sexual revolution was underway and called attention to "dramatic" changes in American attitudes toward sex and nudity. Now, almost half of the American public saw both pictures of nudes in magazines and premarital sex as acceptable, whereas only four years earlier a large majority had seen the pictures as offensive and the sex as "wrong." More important, almost half had come to doubt that premarital sex was a moral issue. In their view, young women who engaged in it were making a personal choice, not violating a community standard. And a solid majority of young people in their late teens and twenties saw no connection between premarital sex and morality at all.[15] There is nothing surprising either in the enthusiasm of the young or in the reservations of older married people. More surprising is the rapidity with which women, especially the young and single, were coming to accept premarital sex for themselves. For although women remained somewhat more cautious than men, the gap between the sexes was steadily decreasing, doubtless because in the new world of young singles they were leading lives increasingly similar to those of men.

The young, elite baby boomers who carried these new attitudes were living very different lives than were poorer and less well educated Americans, especially nonwhites. And nonwhites, notably poor African-Americans in cities and rural areas, were much less likely than whites to condone premarital sex, however many practiced it. Their conservatism reflected their fears about the social breakdown of their communities. Economic hardship and lack of education do not automatically lead people to take a casual attitude toward premarital sex. Indeed, they are just as likely to have the opposite effect. Long before white Americans awoke to the problems of single motherhood, welfare, and family disintegration, black Americans were reading the handwriting on the wall and doing their best to forestall the disaster.

Although groups differed in their attitudes toward premarital sex, they tended to agree about its close ties to the availability of abortion, which most viewed as primarily a single woman's issue. The availability of abortion also affected married women, but single women were most visibly at risk. And those who were coming to view a young woman's premarital sexual activity as a personal matter were coming to regard her decision to have an abortion as no less personal. The same people were likely to believe that professional birth control information, services, and counseling should be available to unmarried sexually active teenagers. By the same token, people who did not approve of premarital sex or abortion were unlikely to approve of making birth control available to unmarried sexually active teenagers—especially their own daughters.[16]

Gabriella Ortiz, a colleague of Maria Ramirez in the GED class at Lehman College, worries constantly about how she, as a divorced mother, can be sure what is the best way to raise her two teenage daughters. Living close to New York's dangerous streets, Gabriella has encouraged her teenage daughters to take responsibility for themselves. "When my daughters reached eighteen I gave them both cards to the medical clinic and told them they didn't have to tell me anything. Nobody has to tell me anything." Many of Gabriella's friends and family criticize her decision, but she wants her daughters to know that they have a mother who does not "want to go prying into their lives." And her colleagues in the GED class all agree that things—sex and drugs—have become so open that you have to make hard choices. In the end, they believe you're damned if you do tell them about the world, and you're damned if you don't. There is no middle ground for mothers' advice to daughters, although some mothers, especially religious believers, may urge their daughters to remain virgins, and many oppose abortion.

Like the majority of Americans since *Roe* v. *Wade*, Gabriella and her friends especially worry about the specific circumstances under which abortion is justified.[17] As early as 1975, most Americans were prepared to live with abortion, but only with restrictions. The more advanced the pregnancy, the less Americans supported abortion. Most thought abortion should be legal at any time during the first trimester, at least under certain circumstances; but less than half were comfortable with abortion on demand during the second trimester, and more than half would make all abortions illegal during the last trimester. Then and since, feminists have argued that abortion is a woman's issue, and, at least in the obvious sense, it is. But there was no evidence that men were seeking to dominate women by imposing unwanted pregnancies on them. For although men and women agreed about abortion during the first trimester, women, not men, were more likely to favor total prohibition in the later months. And a close look at Americans' attitudes toward abortion leaves no doubt that it is also a man's issue.[18] Indeed, the closer one looks, the more abortion looks like a moral issue rather than like a woman's issue, at least as most Americans define women's issues.

The point is underscored by Americans' attitudes toward the Equal Rights Amendment to the Constitution, which was under consideration during the 1970s. By 1976, only a quarter of the population opposed the ERA, which simply stated that "Equality of rights under the law shall not be denied or abridged by the United States or by any State on account of sex." Although the amendment was never ratified, the general support for it suggests that most people agreed that women should have the same opportunities as men in work and politics. Yet many more people opposed abortion than opposed the ERA, which suggests that they did not view access to abortion as identical to equality in work and politics.[19] Even women themselves divided almost equally over an outright ban on abortion, although once again nonwhite women were more opposed to abortion than white women, and women with the lowest incomes and the least education were more opposed than wealthier and better educated white women.[20]

To complicate matters further, women's attitudes toward abortion do not necessarily predict whether they are likely to have abortions. By 1987, it was clear that in practice abortion was indeed a young single woman's issue, for 70 percent of all abortions were performed on women between nineteen and twenty-nine years of age, and 80 percent were performed on women who were not married. Thus, as one scholar has noted, most abortions take place "for precisely the reasons most Americans disapprove: financial or psychological reasons or convenience."[21] Furthermore, although black women are more likely than white women to disapprove of abortion on moral and religious grounds, they are somewhat more likely to have one.[22]

Apparently, the dramatic proliferation of single motherhood within African-American communities during the 1980s had an impact, and, by 1986, African-Americans were, for the first time, more likely than not to support *Roe* v. *Wade*.[23]

○ In retrospect, it appears that, for most Americans, the main point of the sexual revolution was that single women should be able to engage in premarital sex as they chose. But by the time that point had been generally accepted, sexual liberation had acquired a life of its own. Throughout the late 1970s and 1980s, as public nudity, sexual display, and sexual violence paraded their way through the media, there seemed no end to the successive assaults on sexual taboos. Yet, during those same years, attitudes toward abortion changed little. The constancy of these views about abortion in the midst of escalating sexual freedom suggests that most people refused to see abortion only as a matter of sexual freedom.

From the mid-seventies until now, only about 20 percent of Americans have consistently supported abortion with no restrictions, and only about 20 percent have consistently supported no abortion at all. These have remained minority positions. Meanwhile, most Americans continue to believe that abortion should be legal but subject to a variety of restrictions, especially the stage of the pregnancy. In the late 1970s, most people firmly opposed second and third trimester abortions, except to save the life of the mother, and only about 15 percent believed that economic considerations justified abortion. Hence a contradiction: Most Americans have opposed personal convenience as a rationale for abortion, even while they have increasingly believed that the decision to have an abortion is a matter of personal conscience.[24]

Ironically most Americans, especially the least affluent, for whom an unplanned pregnancy would impose the greatest economic burden, have especially opposed abortion for economic reasons.[25] Poverty alone did not lead people to favor easy access to abortion, even though throughout the 1980s and 1990s the number of poor single mothers has been increasing dramatically. Typically, the wealthier, better educated elite remained much more liberal about abortion and sexual freedom than the less fortunate. But then, many members of the elite no longer believed that sexual behavior was a matter of moral concern, and they viewed abortion as the guarantee that women (and men) could enjoy sexual freedom without consequences. Many other Americans, who linked abortion to children, found *Roe* v. *Wade* troubling. It was not that they necessarily thought the decision wrong or less "right" than the obvious alternatives. They could live with it, but they did not like it.

Throughout history, societies have regarded the birth of children as a sign of renewal and a cause for celebration. Most have also tacitly accepted various forms of population control, including abortion and even infanticide. But they have not celebrated them. It is one thing to live with abortion or infanticide, another to establish them as legal rights, and yet another to try to assimilate them as "natural rights." Natural rights necessarily derive from the notion of a natural law that no legal system should violate. In principle, then, natural law upholds the dignity of the human being. In the modern world, natural rights have been taken to include the inalienable right to life, liberty, and the pursuit of happiness. Secular theories of natural law like the Darwinian theory of evolution, however, have emphasized the unrelenting struggle for survival within nature, thus undercutting the ideal of a fundamental dignity and worth of the human person.

It is difficult to extract a moral obligation from the view of the world as an unending struggle for the survival of the fittest. Abortion and infanticide may indeed obey a natural law of survival of the fittest, especially if survival demands that the mother wants the child and must be able to care for it. But the claim that abortion is a natural right derives from no discernible moral obligation. At most, one might argue that the human dignity of the mother requires that her right to life, liberty, and the pursuit of happiness not be limited by the claims of the child. This position, however, simply invokes natural right to individual convenience or the defense of one social policy against another. Indeed, it is difficult to imagine a compelling argument for natural law that is not grounded in the Word of God, for without an appeal to God as an absolute standard for human dignity, the defense of natural right simply embodies the preferences of individuals or groups. Most cultures have assumed that laws express and shape the relations among human beings. Since so many cultures have viewed the relation between mother and child as close to sacred, they have been reluctant to enact laws that sanction what they consider baby-killing.

Roe v. Wade may therefore be seen as reflecting the failures of American society more than its promises. For Roe v. Wade tells of women who experienced pregnancy and childbearing as unacceptable emotional and economic burdens and thus threatens the ideal of women's "natural" devotion to the preservation and protection of life. Nor was everyone reassured by the knowledge that some women supported Roe v. Wade precisely because they wanted freedom from traditional maternal responsibilities. But beneath the real, and frequently painful, struggles about women's roles lies the more disturbing problem of Americans' attitudes toward human life. For even the majority of Americans who are prepared to live with abortion "under certain circumstances" remain uneasy about the public affirmation of one person's right to take the life of another at will, and they remain uneasy about the notion that an as yet only partially formed person should be considered no person at all.

The concern with abortion as the taking of life does not primarily divide Americans along religious lines. A decade after Roe v. Wade, all the major religious groups divided evenly between supporters and opponents, as they still do.[26] But then and since, attitudes toward the relation between abortion and life have divided Americans by income, education, and, frequently, race or ethnicity. For, during the years since Roe v. Wade, the expectations of women of different classes have been diverging. And since most Americans see abortion as primarily a woman's issue, they are likely to see the debate as primarily about young women's prospects—as a struggle over the appropriate story of a young woman's life. Thus, the debate about abortion has consistently intertwined with Americans' attempt to come to terms with the implications of the sexual revolution for women.

NOTES

[1]Rickie Solinger, *Wake Up Little Susie: Single Pregnancy and Race Before Roe v. Wade* (New York and London: Routledge, 1992).

[2]*Gallup*, 39, September 1968. And here, those most likely to lament the decline in honesty were most likely to be working people. Gender did not influence people's attitudes in this regard. Affluent and well-educated women and men found less cause to worry about the decline in honesty than women and men with less income and education.

[3]*Gallup*, 39, September 1968.

[4]*Gallup*, 60, June 1970. Within just a few years, the percentage of college students who said they had engaged in premarital sex jumped twelve points from 51 percent to 63 percent.

[5]In 1967, four in ten Americans, and slightly more women (45 percent of women) than men, still thought that the ideal family would have four or more children.

[6]*Gallup*, 92, February 1973.

[7]*Gallup*, 85, July 1972.

[8]Kate Maloy and Maggie Jones Patterson, *Birth or Abortion: Private Struggles in a Political World* (New York: Plenum, 1992).

[9]Only 18 percent favored legal abortion for women whose reasons were simply economic.

[10]*Gallup*, 8, January 1966.

[11]*Gallup*, 50, August 1969.

[12]*Gallup*, 63, September 1970. As late as 1969, three years before *Roe v. Wade*, less than half the population favored legalization of abortion during the first three months of a pregnancy. Only a year later roughly half of all Americans, especially the younger, better educated, and more affluent, did.

[13]*Gallup*, 9, February 1966.

[14]*Gallup*, 63, September 1970. As late as 1970, almost two thirds of American

women and more than half of American men still wanted divorce to be more difficult to obtain.

[15]*Gallup*, 94, April 1973. Only four years before almost three quarters had found pictures of nudes offensive. Two years later, even fewer students condemned premarital sex (19 percent) and more than three quarters accepted it. *Gallup*, 124, September 1975.

[16]*Gallup*, 87, September 1972.

[17]At the time of *Roe* v. *Wade*, 46 percent of Americans favored it, 45 percent opposed, and 9 percent were unsure. *Gallup*, 92, February 1973. For the persistence of these attitudes, see Roger Rosenblatt, *Life Itself: Abortion in the American Mind* (New York: Random House, 1992) and Barbara Hinkson Craig and David M. O'Brien, *Abortion and American Politics* (Chatham, NJ: Chatham House, 1993).

[18]With abortion, as with other sexual issues, the differences among groups by income, education, and race or ethnicity vastly outweigh the differences between women and men. Young white people, especially those from the Northeast and California and those in the upscale groups (upper income and education and in the professions and white-collar occupations) invariably showed the strongest support for liberal positions. By sex: legal under any circumstances, men 20 percent, women 22 percent; under certain circumstances, men 54 percent, women 53 percent; illegal, men 22 percent, women 23 percent. By race: legal under any circumstances, white 21 percent, nonwhite 20 percent; under certain circumstances, white 56 percent, nonwhite, 40 percent; illegal, white 21 percent, nonwhite 32 percent. *Gallup*, 121, July 1975.

[19]Except in the case of danger to the life of the mother. *Gallup*, 128, March 1976.

[20]By 57 percent to 46 percent. *Gallup*, 128, March 1976.

[21]Victoria A. Sackett, "Between Pro-Life and Pro-Choice," *Public Opinion* (April/May 1985): 55.

[22]Craig and O'Brien, *Abortion in American Politics*, 256.

[23]*Gallup*, 244–45, January–February 1986.

[24]*Gallup*, 166, May 1979.

[25]At least until the mid-eighties, nonwhites consistently favored more limitations than whites, and a quarter to a third wanted abortion illegal under all circumstances. Hispanic men and women remained the most consistently opposed.

[26]*Gallup*, 229, October 1984. See also Craig and O'Brien, *Abortion and American Politics*.

Four

LIVING WITH
SEXUAL
LIBERATION

✗ abortion

uring the early 1960s, when Lucy Goldfarb and Pauline
Stern were starting out at Wellesley, Lucy's friend Maggie Farrell arrived at Smith College, reeling from the
last-minute advice of her wealthy Catholic mother. Until then, Mrs.
Farrell had not much bothered to instruct Maggie about the dangers
of men and sex. Living at home and attending an exclusive girls'
school, Maggie had not needed much advice, or so Mrs. Farrell assumed. Curfews in the Farrell household were strict, and Maggie
never challenged them by more than a few minutes. By the time
Mrs. Farrell got around to telling Maggie that young men might ask
her to do things that no "nice" girl would do, Maggie had collected
a fund of information from her friends, but she was not about to tell
her mother that she needed no instruction.

As it happened, neither Maggie's knowledge nor Mrs. Farrell's advice were relevant to the world in which Maggie found herself. Toward the end of her first year, Maggie met Tony McDonald, senior at Yale, son of another wealthy Catholic family from New York. They dated during the summer and, by the next fall, when Tony went to the Harvard Business School, they had become seriously involved. By Christmas, they were sleeping together; by Easter, Tony had given Maggie a stunning diamond engagement ring. Their parents, who knew nothing about their sleeping together, could not have been happier. This was exactly what they wanted for their children. Everyone agreed that Maggie would finish college. Mrs. Farrell and Mrs. McDonald were already planning the lavish wedding. And then Maggie discovered she was pregnant. Abortion was out of the question, although Maggie had heard from Lucy about Pauline's trip to Mexico to have one. Maggie and Tony had a small, private wedding, and she left college. Maggie's friends were delighted, her mother was confused. In a few years, the world had changed beyond recognition. Maggie was doing exactly what her mother had always wanted her to do, but not in the way she had imagined.

Ten years later, Tracey Thomas, who grew up in a middle-class Catholic family in Dayton, Ohio, started college at the University of Ohio. Although less affluent than Maggie Farrell, Tracey had been, if anything, more carefully supervised during her teens, when she attended a Catholic girls' high school. The excitement and turmoil of the university during the early seventies threw her into an exhilarating but totally unfamiliar world. None of her friends expected to remain virgins, and many had already had sexual relations with boys they were dating. Some of them had had sexual relations with women. During her first semester, Tracey, a beauty with black hair to her waist and light blue eyes, dated at least twelve different men, all of whom pressed her to have sex with them. She resisted. Then, during the second semester, one of her radical young professors invited her to coffee. Soon, they were seeing each other regularly, and when he invited her to his apartment for dinner she accepted with pleasure. By the end of the evening, she was slightly heady with wine and Professor Marchand's attentions, and she easily yielded to his pressure to go to bed.

For the next few months, Tracey spent most of her evenings at Jim Marchand's apartment, seduced as much by his feisty radicalism as his physical presence. In fact, she did not much enjoy the sex, but she came to depend heavily on him for a support and approval that she did not get from the men of her own age. Nothing had prepared Tracey for the confusing life of a large university, much less for an affair. She was torn between a guilty sense that she was defying the religion and standards of her upbringing and fascination with the unsettling world into which she had moved. Jim arranged an appointment for her with a local gynecologist, who fit her for a diaphragm. Tracey refused the Pill, because that would make the affair seem a way of life, but she told herself and Jim that she was scared of gaining weight. Sometimes she "forgot" to use the diaphragm. Some days, she did not believe she could get pregnant. Other days, she told herself that if she did, Jim would have to marry her. When she did get pregnant he told her that marriage was out of the question. By then, *Roe* v. *Wade* had made abortion legal, and he paid for her abortion at a local clinic.

The abortion left Tracey feeling more dependent upon Jim than ever, which made him more determined to pull away. Looking back, she can understand that her constant tears and clinging were more than he could handle, although she also sees that he was a weak man who fed on the admiration of younger women. At the time, she simply felt guilty and abandoned. She could not tell her parents, she could not go to confession, she could not concentrate on her work. Even the spring flowers seemed to mock her. Finally, the semester ended, and Tracey, who could not face a summer under her mother's loving concern, took a job at a work camp in Montana. The fresh air and physical labor helped to restore her health but not her self-confidence. And, when she returned to the university in the fall, she quickly fell into a series of brief affairs. Over Christmas, she missed her period, and by January she knew she was pregnant again.

Not knowing for sure who was the father, she arranged her own abortion. Her junior year, she had a stormy relationship with a lesbian friend. Her senior year, she focused on her work because she had decided to apply to graduate school.

Tracey could not believe her luck in being admitted to New York University with a full fellowship, and she promised herself that from now on she would devote herself to her work. But two months into her first semester, a senior professor in her department asked her to come to his office to discuss her paper topic for his seminar. Since Professor Schwartz was married and twenty years older than she, Tracey did not think twice about being alone with him. And, during her first visit to his office, he was all business. His interest in her work helped to ease the insecurity and anxiety she had felt since moving to New York, and she asked if she might return in a couple of weeks to show him a draft of the paper. When the time came, he moved her chair next to his, and, while leafing through her paper, brushed her hand with his. And, when she tearfully confessed her fears that her work was not good enough, he reassured her with a hug. Within weeks, they had started an affair, and three months later she was again pregnant. That winter, Tracey had her third abortion. By the time she had finished graduate school, she had had five, and she was beginning to fear that she could never have a child. Tracey's story ended happily. Her second year as a professor at a small college in Oregon, she met a young professor in physics, and, after dating for several months, they married. A year later, she was again pregnant, and this time she gave birth to a healthy daughter. Josie's birth, a happy marriage, and three years of therapy all helped Tracey to take hold of her life. She has made some peace with what she calls her "crazy" behavior. She is once more going to church because she and her husband want Josie to have a sense of "moral values."

As Tracey's story suggests, living with sexual liberation has proved more confusing than many of us initially expected, primarily because of conflicts about the claims of morality. By the 1980s, most Americans no longer saw sex as a moral issue in the way our grandparents did. Moral concerns did not disappear, but in a period of exceptionally rapid change agreement on a public standard seemed elusive, if not impossible. So, people turned to private standards: I act according to my conscience (if any), and you act according to yours. By no means did this live-and-let-live attitude come easily. Many still believed that private behavior had public consequences, and others believed that morality was inherently public and that its privatization would leave us with no morality at all.

Abortion has dramatized this controversy. For unconditional opponents, abortion is murder, and private conscience cannot be invoked to justify murder. For unconditional supporters, abortion on demand guarantees a woman's freedom. Meanwhile, most Americans continue to believe that women should be able to choose abortion but not under all circumstances. Regulations have changed, attitudes have not. This stalemate, which has persisted since the early 1980s, reflects a widespread attempt to come to terms with rapidly changing attitudes toward sex, morality, and the relations among them.

Acceptance of abortion under some conditions might have provided grounds for a compromise, but it did not. For it implicitly raises the moral questions that few have wanted to talk about—the specifics of the conditions and then the reasons for them. And for the majority of Americans the question of conditions remains a moral one: At what point does the termination of a pregnancy become the murder of a baby? Logically, one's position on conditions need have little or nothing to do with one's attitude toward women's sexual freedom. But pro-choice and pro-life advocates have been unwilling to accept that logic. In their view, women's sexual freedom cannot be separated from women's capacity to bear children: If we free sex from the shackles of morality, we must necessarily free reproduction from them as well.

On a humane and practical level, most Americans willingly acknowledged that easily available, publicly funded abortion would deter society from punishing women whose new sexual opportunities led them into a mistake. To those who welcomed greater sexual freedom for women, and even those simply prepared to live with it, abortion seemed an unpleasant necessity. This spirit of realism has led to the acceptance of abortion even among those who are unhappy with it. They prefer to view abortion in relation to sex rather than life—as only the termination of an unplanned pregnancy that threatens to disrupt a woman's life. They are not necessarily insensitive to the moral questions, but they do not apply them to the act that leads to the pregnancy, for, in their view, women's sexual freedom should not be treated as a moral issue. That the fate of the fetus might have more pressing claims on public morality than anyone's sexual freedom understandably troubles many. They therefore worry about conditions. For they instinctively acknowledge that the underlying moral issues are precisely what Americans cannot agree on—and perhaps not even discuss.

Those enmeshed in the rapid expansion of what Stephen Carter has called the "culture of disbelief" thus prefer to regard the legalization of abortion as a practical rather than a moral question.[1] Americans increasingly view religious faith, like morality, as an entirely private matter. This spirit has made it easier for people who doubt the morality of abortion to accept it as a matter of public policy, as many Catholics do.[2] Even many passionate supporters of abortion will admit that it is not desirable. Privately, many pro-choice women have told me that they could never bring themselves to have an abortion, even when the pregnancy was not merely unplanned but seriously inconvenient. And one after another has told me that she thinks abortion wrong but would not impose her views on others.

One evening, during a dinner with two male colleagues, the conversation turned to abortion. Both of these highly successful men attend church and observe an exacting moral code in their personal lives; both have traditional families, in which they are the primary breadwinners; both are generally conservative in politics. Yet, primarily for personal reasons, they hold opposing positions on abortion. The younger of the two, now in his forties, still remembers every detail of the day he was called away from work because his wife had unexpectedly been found to be suffering complications from an ectopic pregnancy. Confronted with an emergency, he and his wife had a few minutes in which to decide whether to abort the fetus. At the time, they had very little money and wanted to postpone having children until he had completed his training. But, in those few minutes, they decided to have the child. Today, every time he thinks of abortion, he thinks of Julie, the daughter he adores. Knowing that if he and his wife had decided on an abortion, Julie would not be here, he realizes that he could never support abortion. The discussion of abortion led his older colleague to think of his own daughter, Sue, whom he and his wife adopted when they thought they could not have children of their own. No more than his friend does he like the idea of abortion, but he reluctantly supports legalization, in part because he does not want Sue to have to pay too high a price for a "mistake."

Both men have resolved their personal conflicts about abortion by defining it as a matter of individual conscience, which leaves it to individuals to decide which circumstances justify abortion and which do not. After conducting extensive interviews about attitudes toward abortion and consulting polls, the sociologist James Davison Hunter and his colleagues found that people's private views differed from their public positions, primarily because they were unwilling to impose their views upon others. One woman captured the attitudes of many: "I would say my views are true for me, but I can't put that on someone else. I just can't force my truths on other people." And another admitted that she might be "wimping out," but she could not bring herself to tell another woman that the fetus she was carrying was a person, "because she's the one that ultimately makes that decision." She obviously did not consider the "opinion" of the unborn child, who cannot be consulted and whom we easily ignore. Many other respondents acknowledged inconsistency in their views, but fell back on "that's just how I feel."[3] Some admitted—privately—that concerns about overpopulation by "poor" and "minority" children influenced their views.

Thus even as people acknowledge abortion as a moral or ethical issue, they tend to make it relative and personal. What matters most is "how I feel about it." How a society—any society—can survive without at least a minimal moral standard remains obscure. And how even a minimal moral standard can be established if "how I feel" prevails remains totally incomprehensible. What seems to worry most people is the unfairness of judging others. If you do not know how life "feels" to someone else, how can you possibly tell them what to do? Even many Americans with traditional moral and religious views refuse to regard their beliefs as publicly binding. So out of deference to the personal experience of others, most Americans have come to support *Roe* v. *Wade*, even if they do not know precisely what it says and even if they, like Governor Mario Cuomo in his widely reported speech at Notre Dame, do not believe in abortion themselves. This reluctance to impose one's views has further confused the relation between sexual and reproductive morality and discouraged many from acknowledging that reproduction has claims upon public morality that personal sexual behavior may not.

What James Davison Hunter and his colleagues in *Before the Shooting Starts* missed—or prudentially avoided—is how closely this flight from a public moral standard has been linked to the sexual revolution and the emergence of feminism.[4] Feminists, insisting on the need to liberate women from morality, have frequently suggested that the morality was imposed by men. In fact, women were just as likely as men to enforce standards of female sexual morality, if only to protect themselves from danger. But feminism has convinced a surprising number of Americans that "fairness" to women requires permitting them virtually the same sexual freedom as men, although they obviously face immeasurably greater risks. Uncertainty about what that freedom should mean has undermined their willingness to defend any single public moral standard. As a result, we have lost sight of the main issues: What should be the link between morality and sexuality? between morality and reproduction? between personal and public morality?

Both sides of the abortion debate have strong views on the relation between sexual liberation and morality. Pro-choicers claim that they are fighting for women's freedom against those who want to imprison women in domesticity. Pro-lifers claim that they are fighting for the needs of children and women. Both agree that the debate is indeed about women's sexuality and reproductive capacities. But they differ in their vision of the relation between sexuality and reproduction in women's lives. The pro-choicers seek to cut the link between sex and reproduction; the pro-lifers seek to sustain and even strengthen it.

Opponents view abortion as the linchpin of a sexual liberation they mistrust and fear. Few, if any, want to limit women's general freedom, but they do believe that sexual freedom does women more harm than good, mainly by freeing men to seduce and abandon women with impunity. Above all, opponents of abortion focus on babies, and their poignant commercials graphically equate the abortion of a three-month-old fetus with the destruction of a potentially happy, healthy child. But their willful confusion of abortion with infanticide does not further the discussion.

Neither group of militants discusses life, broadly understood. The pro-life militants stonewall discussion by insisting that, from the moment of conception, the fetus embodies a life endowed with its own inalienable rights. The pro-choice militants deny that fetal life should limit a woman's right to abort, which explains their insistence that a woman's right to an "effective abortion" may require killing a baby that survives abortion. Yet most Americans' opinions about *Roe* v. *Wade* depend precisely upon a judgment of when life begins. Those who believe that life begins at conception oppose *Roe* v. *Wade*; those who believe that life begins at birth favor it. Most women and men reject both views and continue to worry and to differ among themselves about when meaningful life begins and, therefore, about the circumstances under which abortion would be appropriate.[5]

Roe v. *Wade* does not provide much help. For, although it distinguishes among the three trimesters of a pregnancy, it does not say anything about the life of the fetus, nor does it absolutely prohibit abortion at any point during a pregnancy.[6] Given the nature of the debates, there is a certain irony that *Roe* v. *Wade* mentions neither the life of the fetus nor the rights of the woman. It is nonetheless clear that the decision directly affects our attitudes toward motherhood. American culture long placed a high, not to say sacred, value on the relation between mother and child. It especially assumed that mothers willingly devote themselves to the children whose lives and characters they help to shape. Feminist scholars quickly point out that this vision of motherhood has not told the whole story of real-life mothers who might not always have been able to stay home and care for their children full-time, and who sometimes might not even have wanted to. But most Americans still find comfort in the idea that mothers have a special inclination to care for the young and the vulnerable. And even today feminists frequently argue that motherhood endows women with a special moral sensibility.[7]

The tendency to bind motherhood to morality embodies the knowledge, shared by most cultures, that responsibility for the young is taxing despite its also being an extraordinary source of joy. It is a commonplace that infants experience an unusually long stage of dependence, during which adults must be inspired, persuaded, or coerced to care for them. Since most people want children both for the delight they afford and to perpetuate themselves or their families, the positive incentives to care for them remain strong. But since all cultures instinctively know that positive incentives alone will not suffice, they normally portray the relations between parents, especially mothers, and children as a moral obligation. And American culture traditionally tried to convince women that motherhood embodied a noble calling.

The debate over abortion has raised the disquieting possibility that women might choose not to be mothers after all. At the very least, the pro-choice position suggests that some women see a conflict between being a "person" and being a mother. A few decades ago new opportunities opened for women, but social policies to support their ability to combine work with motherhood did not keep pace. Hence, a significant number of young women first began to delay motherhood and then to forego it entirely. Megan Beatty, an ambitious young woman from a very modest background who had won a scholarship to Princeton and was planning to go on to graduate school, confided to me that she was becoming anxious about her husband's desire for children. Now that he had finished his training as an engineer and had secured a fine position, he was ready to start a family. "But what about me," she plaintively asked. "I still have to finish graduate school, and then I want to work. You know, I am not even sure that I want children."

Megan openly admits to being ambitious. "I have to prove that I can be successful." She also admits to a desire to enjoy the material comforts she had not known as a child or when she had to work to supplement her scholarship at college. At twenty-three, with the world opening before her, she really means that she does not want children if they are going to limit her professional life. Megan likes to think of herself as a feminist, and she has uncritically absorbed some upscale feminist assumptions. So far, nothing has encouraged her to consider that there might be very special rewards in bearing and rearing a child. Dawn Rivers, who, as a forty-year-old African-American, has worked her way up to director of personnel in a growing engineering firm, has no interest in feminism, but no more than Megan does she want motherhood to interfere with her career. Recently, Dawn sent her nine-year-old daughter, Serena, back to live with her former husband because "I simply can't cope with her needs, and she will be fine with her dad."

Many Americans still do not like the idea that women might not want to be mothers, but not because they favor large families. Most do not want women to have more children, and many want poor young women to have fewer or only as many as they can support.[8] But most also want women to want to have children and want mothers selflessly to love babies. Most, in other words, still see motherhood as a comforting sign of moral commitment. Yet, the precise relation between morality and reproduction troubles them. If women wish to be free of one pregnancy, does that mean they want permanently to be free from motherhood? At times, feminist rhetoric almost sounds as if that were precisely what women want: For women to be truly liberated, they must be liberated from babies.

Opponents of abortion—the more orthodox in all faiths—have been quick to pick up on the implication, blaming feminists for refusing to be women. But they usually complain about the collapse of sexual morality while they skirt the issue of who will care for the children. Liberals are quick to trivialize or reject any insistence upon the special moral responsibilities of mothers as cheap sentimentalism. But while their opponents of the religious right have taken extreme ground, they have never been alone in their desire to put some limits on the progress of sexual liberation. And as concern about the plight of children rises nationally, and as the difficulties of combining motherhood with high-powered careers persist, a growing number of women are beginning to wonder about what their priorities should be.

The attempts to make sense of the sexual revolution began in the 1980s and have continued into the 1990s as the baby boomers, the first generation to benefit from the new sexual freedom, are sorting out which parts of it they accept and which they would like to end or even reverse.[9] The vast majority think that the Pill has had a positive impact, and half accept legal abortion. But conflicts persist. Slightly more than half have come to believe that the increased acceptance of premarital sex has been bad for society, and only 30 percent think more sexual freedom in the future a good idea. Premarital sex remains, as it had been at the start, the most widely accepted feature of the sexual revolution. As in 1985, more than half of the baby boomers do not consider it wrong. When one recalls that as recently as 1969 only one in five (20 percent) Americans accepted premarital sex, the change seems remarkable.[10] Yet even the majority that refuses to condemn premarital sex frets over its exact meaning and ramifications.

Women have consistently been more cautious than men, but almost half do not consider premarital sex immoral, whereas twenty years previously, two thirds had. A majority also wants abortion to be legal. These attitudes reflect a recognition that women might well have to live all or some part of their lives as single individuals. Yet most women clearly continue to cherish dreams of a more lasting connection. Two thirds believe that a woman should share the decision to have an abortion with the man, and only one third believes that marriages would be improved if couples live together for a while before getting married. These attitudes reflect a commitment to cooperation between women and men and especially a commitment to marriage, which more than four in five believe is important to the future of our society.[11] And although most men, especially young men, are more sexually permissive than most women, they share women's commitment to the importance of marriage.[12]

The most striking consequence of the sexual revolution has been the virtual disappearance of the double standard. Although men and women have different views on a variety of sexual issues, the vast majority agree that they should be bound by the same sexual standards after marriage as well as before, and more than 90 percent condemns extramarital affairs for both women and men.[13] This growing acceptance of sexual parity between women and men does not mean that people do not want limits on sexual freedom: It means that they want limits to apply equally to women and men.

Similarly, the wide acceptance of premarital sex does not mean that most people accept sexual promiscuity. Both women and men continue to prefer stable relationships before marriage and to value sexual fidelity within marriage. The threat of AIDS has surely strengthened this new caution, which some are bizarrely calling a new puritanism. But there are also signs that companionate marriages are becoming more common, not least because both men and women see marriage as the foundation of personal and economic security.[14] Although divorce rates have reached an all-time high, many of those who get divorced rapidly remarry. Thus, while a majority of Americans have welcomed an easing of traditional sexual morality, they apparently do not want sexual liberation to destroy marriage. By the mid-1980s, only one in three men and fewer than one in five women favored an increase in sexual liberation. The majority of people who did not favor an increase did not regret the sexual revolution or want to see it reversed, but they were worried about how to live with it and, especially, where and how to draw lines.[15] What, they were asking, follows from acceptance of premarital sex: X-rated movies nightly on TV and at neighborhood theaters? sexual activity for twelve year-olds? "open" marriages?

As people have tried to make sense of the crosscurrents, they have increasingly worried that sexual liberation is undermining families. By 1982, more than nine in ten Americans wanted to see a greater emphasis on traditional family ties, although it is not clear that they agreed about what "family" meant.[16] Disagreements about the meaning of family have, if anything, become more heated during the 1990s as single-motherhood has proliferated and the campaign for recognition of domestic partnerships has intensified, and they have fueled Americans' concerns about the relation between strong families and sexual freedom.

Americans, who believe in marriage for love rather than as a social arrangement, have never been especially tolerant of marital infidelity. We practice extramarital sex as much as any other people, but we are still more likely than others to expect affairs to end in divorce and remarriage. Today, the word "adultery" has virtually disappeared from our vocabulary. The brief vogue for open marriages during the 1970s fizzled out, perhaps in part because many people discovered that married life without sexual fidelity was charged with anxiety, resentment, and a sense of betrayal. But virtually no one condemned open marriage because it violated a moral standard. So sexual fidelity became essentially a matter of personal well-being rather than of moral obligation, or even an obligation to others.

Feminists, not surprisingly, tend to be more tolerant of women's infidelities than of men's. If we are to credit the media, the feminist elite has no difficulty with Patricia Ireland's open pursuit of an extramarital affair, although its approval may have something to do with her having the affair with a woman. But the feminist belief that women needed freedom from traditional sexual restrictions helps to explain the disappearance of the notion of fidelity. In *The Erotic Silence of the American Wife*, Dalma Heyn defends adultery as "a revolutionary way for women to rise above the conventional."[17] Extramarital affairs, Heyn argues, give women a new sense of power and a freedom from dependence upon their husbands. "Freed from the model of silence and goodness—an image that in no way enriched or enlarged them—through the consummate act of transgression they once would have labeled 'selfish' and 'bad,' they now felt 'released.' "[18] Thus does infidelity become a weapon of women's liberation.

Notwithstanding the warm reception that Heyn's book received among feminists, not to mention Larry King, sexual infidelity still troubles many women deeply. Tess London, a successful lawyer, knew that many of the men in her firm engaged in extramarital affairs and that one of her partners was having an affair with her closest friend. Accustomed to the sophistication of professional circles in New York, it never occurred to her to judge their conduct. And then she discovered that her husband of ten years had been having an affair with one of her young associates, whom he met at a party Tess gave for the firm. She was devastated. Suddenly her tolerance for infidelity evaporated. Ultimately, she decided not to divorce him, primarily because of their two sons, but she could hardly bear the sense of betrayal and uncertainty. And for years thereafter, she was afraid to trust him—or anyone else. Women of all classes share her aversion to disloyalty, and many behave as if marital loyalty is indeed a moral issue.

One of the main reasons Gloria Patterson left her first husband was his playing around. Years later, after she had remarried, she discovered that several of the men in her lower-middle-class community had ideas about playing around with her. Especially after her husband had his first heart attack, she found that Brother so-and-so, a member of their church no less, would propose to help her by taking her out for a drink and a drive. It did not take long for her to figure out where the neighborly solicitude was leading. "No way I would have done that," she told me. "Can you believe it? And they

call themselves his friends—his brothers!" Gloria, a devout Methodist, took her marriage vows seriously. But she was not naive about
the standards of the world, and, as she saw the old rules crumbling,
she devised her own code. "Bill," she said of her present husband,
"is my best friend. He was a friend to me when I needed him worst,
and now he's having hard times, I'm going to be a friend to him."
Gloria knows women who cheat on their husbands, and more men
who cheat on their wives, but she persists in her belief that cheating
is cheating, not to say betrayal. Christian that she is, she knows it to
be immoral, although she also knows that others would not use the
word.

Gloria is not alone in her belief that sexual relations are a matter
of morality. She invokes the Bible, but others are hard pressed to
explain their similar conviction. Listening to her, I was struck that
although she has no desire to judge what other people do, she continues to worry about what they do to others. That her single nieces
were engaging in premarital sex bothered her not at all. That married men were pushing her to be unfaithful to her husband and were
themselves being unfaithful to their wives bothered her considerably. She finds it difficult to draw hard lines, but she knows that
individual sexual behavior implicates others. And if it implicates
others, then, in her view, it has moral implications and consequences.

The widespread acceptance of premarital sex that had conquered
American opinion by the mid-1980s raised these issues with a vengeance. It is one thing to assimilate premarital sex into conventional
stories about young men's and, especially, young women's lives. It is
another to say that since premarital sex is okay promiscuity is also
okay. But what, under the new conditions, constitutes promiscuity?
One man, two men, three men, ten, more than ten—in sequence or
simultaneously? Presumably, these concerns explain the willingness
to accept premarital sex but simultaneously to oppose an increase in
sexual freedom.

The confusion about how to define promiscuity in an age of sexual liberation spills over into debates about the public expression and discussion of sexuality. Concern about the proliferation of sexually explicit materials rose throughout the 1970s and especially the 1980s. Beginning in the late 1970s, some feminists launched an attack on pornography, claiming that the sexual degradation of women encouraged rape. The evidence for this connection is, at best, ambiguous, but they have continued to insist that pornography should be banned or seriously restricted because it is, literally, a form of violence against women. And their slogan, "Pornography is the theory, rape is the practice," intuitively appeals to many.[19]

Other feminists oppose censorship because they favor freedom of expression, including all forms of sexuality. The debate divides those who see pornography as a dangerous weapon from those who see it as simply words and images. Neither side has any interest in sexual morality or obscenity. Radical feminists define the issue exclusively as one of power—men's power over women. According to the feminist theorist Catharine MacKinnon, questions of morality—of decency and obscenity—are irrelevant, since obscenity laws define morals "from the male point of view" in order to perpetuate male dominance.[20]

Even those who remain uncomfortable with both positions cavil at child pornography. Throughout the 1980s, more than 90 percent of Americans, men as well as women, wanted a total ban on the sale or rental of videos showing sexual acts that involved children, while most opposed an outright ban on the portrayal of sexual violence in magazines, movies, and video cassettes, especially in their own communities.[21] But beyond this instinctive response, people recognize that pornography, like abortion, raises questions of public policy, and they remain divided about how best to handle them. Again the divorce of sex from morality has prevented the formulation of a clear position. If the grossest pornography cannot be condemned as immoral or obscene, on what grounds can it be prohibited?

Sex education in public schools has raised similar problems. The rapid increase in teenage pregnancies and especially the spread of AIDS has brought sex education to national attention, and more than three quarters of Americans now favor some form of sex education in the schools.[22] And as the numbers of teen pregnancies have skyrocketed, growing numbers of people also want to provide contraception to the young, even the very young. Suddenly, the stakes have become frighteningly high. Suddenly, sex can kill. And those at risk to be killed or to kill others include young teenagers. Some groups still oppose sex education on the grounds that it encourages children to do things that they should not be doing and that it usurps the role of the family. Most Americans recognize, however reluctantly, that some basic information on birth control and sexually transmitted diseases might help to prevent the worst calamities, but even they disagree about the appropriate content. Whose morality should prevail? Is it possible to prepare kids for safe sex without encouraging them to indulge and at ever younger ages?

Linda Maldonado, who grew up in poverty in New York City and is now a health-care worker, sees the problems firsthand. Experience has taught her that protection literally means survival, although she is more concerned with the risk of HIV/AIDS than the risk of pregnancy. A tearful young girl who had just tested positive for the virus told her that she had met the guy who infected her while she was on vacation. They had met and just hit it off. But when, after a delightful week, he saw her off on the plane, he handed her a package to open after takeoff. In it, she found a small black coffin and a note. He had the virus. The experience prompted Linda to call the daughter of her very conservative sister to warn her that if she was going "to fool around" she must use protection. She told her, "I don't care how bad it gets, I don't care how heated it gets, if you gotta go to the store, you gotta stop. If you gotta put it on yourself, you put it on yourself."

Things were different when Linda was growing up. Then it was not "if you're going to fool around," it was "you don't fool around, period." Now Linda works in a hospital and sees a lot of female AIDS patients, all of whom claim that it happened the first time.

"They hear it, they hear the danger, they hear the warning, but for some reason it's like it's not going to happen to me." Linda believes that these young girls "hear about AIDS and they don't connect." The failure or unwillingness to connect affects many middle-class girls as well. Too many young women, no matter how sexually active, still believe that "it could never happen to me."

To women who have to raise daughters—and sons—close to the streets, an always dangerous world has become a nightmare. Teen pregnancy, AIDS, drugs, and pornography intertwine to threaten everything they believe in and, especially, everything they want for their children. They do not view the collapse of traditional values as liberation. Some, like Polly Hobson and Amanda Thomas, have responded by attempting to protect their daughters by never letting them go out alone. Polly worries that she is being overprotective and that, given the first opportunity, her daughter may rebel. But she does not know what else to do. Gabriella Ortiz, who gave her daughters cards to the medical clinic, has attempted to prepare them to deal with the world on their own. Both Gabriella and Polly respect the other's choice. Neither is sure that she has the right answer; both believe that this dangerous new world makes it impossible for anyone to be certain about any answers.

They and countless women like them face special problems that most middle-class women have rarely known, although each day more are encountering them. Today, women of every class and race share the problems of dealing with a new sexual freedom that has forced them to take care of themselves. Even reasonably well-to-do, young college-educated women, who are in the strongest position to enjoy their freedom and autonomy, have learned that each time they go to bed with a man they go to bed with the assorted women who have preceded them. Significantly, by the early 1990s, the college graduates who do so much to shape public opinion have had more direct experience of AIDS than the rest of the population. Almost a third knows someone with AIDS, and one in three single people now fears that he or she might contract it.

Among young single professionals, the AIDS test has apparently become a kind of continuing ritual that must be regularly reenacted but never makes you feel completely safe. This time you are okay, but what about the next? A young woman who is successfully pursuing a career in environmental administration tells me that funding for AIDS research has become one of her top political priorities because she and her friends worry constantly that anyone they have sex with could infect them. The realities make a mockery of stories of mutual trust between sexual partners. How can you ever be sure? Yet, for most women, nothing has destroyed the older stories of love and marriage. Danger coexists with hopes and dreams, and young women try to find ways to combine their sexual independence with their hope for a lasting relationship.

Growing acceptance of premarital sex and sexual parity has especially benefited the wealthiest, best-educated members of the population. Before the sexual revolution, a poor woman might well have engaged in premarital sex with the expectation that the man would eventually marry her. Today, such women face altogether more threatening problems. For them premarital sex and sexual equality are likely to result in abandonment with one or more children, which in turn reinforces economic deprivation. Then and now, for them the most ominous manifestations of sexual freedom walk the streets and prey upon women and children.

The continuing debates about abortion during the late 1980s reflected these confused feelings, but they took a new turn when the Supreme Court began to hand down decisions that restricted access to abortion. First the Court prohibited the use of federal funds, notably Medicare, for abortions (*Webster* v. *Reproductive Services*, 1989); then it prohibited family planning clinics that received federal funds from providing patients with information about abortion (*Rust* v. *Sullivan*, 1991). Both of these decisions struck directly at poor women who lacked the money to pay for an abortion and frequently lacked information about its availability. President Clinton reversed *Rust* v. *Sullivan* by executive order immediately upon taking office in January 1993. But the denial of Medicare funding for abortion continued to strike especially hard at the growing numbers of very young poor women who were becoming pregnant, having their babies, and falling into a debilitating cycle of poverty and dependency.

Each of the new restrictions has provoked heated debates without significantly changing most people's attitudes. The wealthiest and best-educated members of the population remain most committed to *Roe* v. *Wade*.[23] Some worry about the welfare bill, although others, especially women, want poor women to have the same opportunities that wealthier women enjoy, notably careers and a problematic "independence."[24] But while some poor women assuredly did dream of those things, many more continued to dream of stable marriages and fulfillment through children. And while the battle of words continues to rage, policy is beginning to inch toward pragmatic economic ground, and, in preparation for the 1996 presidential election, even many pro-life Republican politicians are softening their position.[25]

Planned Parenthood v. *Casey* (1992) simultaneously reaffirmed a woman's right to abortion and imposed new restrictions. The decision satisfied few. Abortion-rights activists insisted that it abolished "a woman's fundamental right to choose"; right-to-life activists pronounced it a "victory for pro-abortion forces." What the Court had done in fact, was to insist that *Roe* v. *Wade* had become a permanent part of the law of the land, although it also held that a woman who sought an abortion would have to wait twenty-four hours between requesting and having an abortion and that minors would have to secure the consent of one parent, an appropriate guardian, or a judge.[26] Thus a majority of the Supreme Court justices recognized that pregnancy burdens a woman and places her liberty "at stake in a sense unique to the human condition and so unique to the law." They also insisted that since her decision to terminate a pregnancy affects others, abortion is never entirely a private act.[27] Pregnancy and abortion stand alone in human experience, challenging us to fit them into a world with which they are incompatible.

In attempting to fit pregnancy into the world we know, the justices focused on pragmatic considerations. Neither sex nor morality ranked as their main concern. Their real concern lay in protecting women's freedom to engage in activities with which pregnancy is often incompatible—specifically the labor force. For women to participate equally in the economic and social life of the nation, the justices reasoned, they must in some measure be freed from their "unique" reproductive capacities—by which they apparently meant that to be "equal," women as workers must have the opportunity to become as sexually autonomous as men. This blatant transformation of sexuality, reproduction, and morals into economic commodities came from the "conservative" Chief Justice Rehnquist.

The justices effectively announced that, in the absence of strong government support for women's unique reproductive capacities and for the children they produce, women's ability to bear children too easily leads to economic inequality and, in some instances, economic deprivation. To prohibit women from protecting themselves and their children from such deprivation would, indeed, be punitive. Worse, it would undercut the assumption that women, like men, bear complete economic responsibility for their own lives. Significantly, although the justices held that minor girls must obtain an adult's consent, they did not require that a married woman obtain her partner's consent. Thus they implicitly labeled reproduction as solely the responsibility of women.

Planned Parenthood v. *Casey* reflected the realities of a world in which 82 percent of abortions were performed on single women, 70 percent on women between eighteen and twenty-nine, and 57 percent on nonwhite women. These figures confirm that the majority of women who seek abortions must be concerned about their ability to support themselves and the children they already have. They are women who cannot wholly or even partially count upon the support of a man.[28] Girls may be having sex at very early ages, even as young as twelve, but they are not getting abortions in significant numbers. It is by no means clear that the imposition of a strict sexual morality on teenage girls would significantly change the number of abortions, although it might limit the number of unplanned pregnancies. The debate over abortion primarily reflects people's anxieties about the new freedoms and responsibilities of adult women. And it has as much to do with economics as with sex.

As a sixteen-year-old, Judy Swift was shattered by her parents' divorce. Since her father made an excellent income as head of his own construction firm and contributed generously to her and her mother's support, money was not an issue. But the emotional blow was severe, and Judy responded to it by becoming very withdrawn. Two years later, when she went off to Swarthmore College, she met a young man and, almost immediately, they began to have sex. Judy's mother had arranged to have her fitted for a diaphragm, but Judy stopped using it after she and Larry, her boyfriend, broke up. From time to time, Judy and Larry would still see each other, and occasionally they even ended the evening in bed. Two months after one of these evenings, she discovered she was pregnant.

After the first shock and fear of what her mother would say, Judy recognized, to her surprise, that she desperately wanted to keep the baby. She and her mother had not been close for several years, especially since Judy tended to blame her mother for the divorce. Finally, however, she went home to talk to her mother, whose main goal was to see Judy become a successful lawyer. Mrs. Swift never said a word about Judy's sexual activity, although she sadly asked her why she had not been more careful. But, deeply committed to Judy's professional success, she did urge her to have an abortion. When Judy refused, her mother pushed harder. Didn't Judy understand what a child would do to her prospects for a career? Judy held her ground. And, suddenly, Mrs. Swift gave her a hug and said, "All right. If that's what you want, we'll do it together."

Planned Parenthood v. *Casey* may have disappointed both pro-choice and pro-life activists, but it scrupulously reflects the sensibilities of taxpayers and business. An adult woman's sexual life is no one's business but her own, but her reproductive life concerns those who might have to foot the bill. If she can afford to support children, as Judy Swift could with her mother's help, then she may have as many as she pleases. If she cannot afford to support them, then she should be free to have none. The decision reflects the feminist commitment to women's liberation and autonomy and, no less clearly, the conservative determination not to subsidize other people's children. The decision thus chillingly presents the relation between morality and childbearing as a cold question of economics. The justices accepted women's traditional responsibility for children but gave it a new twist. For by holding women solely responsible for children, they all but told women that to be fully autonomous they must forgo children—unless they earn enough to pay someone else to care for the child or have a husband who can support both mother and child.

Change has come upon us so swiftly that public policies and attitudes have not been able to keep pace. At the heart of the confusion lies the relation between economic realities and moral values. Since women must now be able to support themselves, it seems reasonable to expect that they will need the same education and training as men. And if so, young women may also be expected to need something like the personal freedom, including sexual freedom, that young men have typically enjoyed. So far, so good. In theory, there is no reason that young women could not engage in premarital sex without guilt or censure and still regard motherhood as a moral responsibility. In practice, however, as the Court recognized in *Planned Parenthood* v. *Casey*, women frequently wish or need to work outside the home throughout their adult lives. And working women confront a working world that has been adapted to the lives of men, who are not expected to be burdened with primary responsibility for children.

These are the conditions under which the debate about the morality of reproduction could not occur. For under these conditions, how can any humane person hold women to a moral responsibility they cannot meet except at the price of their own economic well-being or even survival? Many Americans are not prepared to insist that a poor woman is morally bound to have a child she cannot possibly support. And, sadly, too many of those who say she is morally obligated to have it are not willing to fund the services that would permit her to support it with dignity and some chance of a decent future. Thus, it is easy for many to assume that everyone, including poor women themselves, would be better off without the economic burden of poor women's children. But however compelling the practical economic argument may be, it avoids the central issue. Until we agree that at some point during a pregnancy the abortion of a fetus becomes the murder of a baby, we will continue to run the risk of measuring the sanctity of life by the yardstick of dollars and cents. If the mother can afford the baby or if society is prepared to support it and her, the fetus is a life. If she cannot afford it and we will not support it and her, it is an inconvenience. Yet feminists, in their determination to defend women's freedom, have fallen into the trap, leaving the uncomfortable impression that their real purpose has been not so much to free women from men as to free them from babies.

NOTES

[1] Stephen L. Carter, *The Culture of Disbelief: How American Law and Politics Trivialize Religious Devotion* (New York: Basic Books, 1993).

[2] Barbara Hinkson Craig and David M. O'Brien, *Abortion and American Politics* (Chatham, NJ: Chatham House, 1993), 254–56.

[3] James Davison Hunter, *Before the Shooting Starts* (New York: Free Press, 1994), 139. The problem of people's conflicted moral and personal feelings have also been discussed by Roger Rosenblatt, *Life Itself: Abortion in the American Mind* (New York: Random House, 1992) and Ronald Dworkin, *Life's Dominion: An Argument about Abortion, Euthanasia, and Individual Freedom* (New York: Knopf, 1993).

[4] For an insightful discussion of the relations among the sexual revolution, women's sexual liberation, and morality, see Richard Posner, *Sex and Reason* (Chicago: Univ. of Chicago Press, 1992).

[5] *Gallup*, 190, July 1981.

[6] Above all, the decision focuses upon who has the right to decide when an abortion is appropriate. Thus, it holds that during the first trimester the decision should lie with "the pregnant woman's attending physician." During the second and third trimesters, in contrast, authority falls to the State. During the

second trimester, the State may regulate abortion to promote maternal health, and, during the third, it may even prohibit abortion except when medical judgment views abortion as necessary "to preserve the life or health of the mother." *Roe* v. *Wade*, 410 U.S. 113 (1973). For a thorough discussion of the decision, see Barbara Milbauer with Bert N. Obrentz, *The Law Giveth: Legal Aspects of the Abortion Controversy* (New York: McGraw Hill, 1983).

[7]The most thoughtful discussion of the qualities and practices that motherhood evokes in women, notably a kind of attentive care, may be found in Sara Ruddick, *Maternal Thinking: Toward a Politics of Peace* (Boston: Beacon Press, 1989).

[8]*Gallup*, 176, March 1980. In the mid-eighties, the proportion of Americans who favored families with four or more children, declining since 1945, dropped sharply. True, some who oppose abortion, especially people with only grade school education, still prefer large families.

[9]Those who are 27–45 in 1991.

[10]*Gallup*, 313, October 1991.

[11]*1990 Virginia Slims*, 41.

[12]Almost one half (46 percent) of all men ages 18–45 claimed that during the previous year they had enjoyed one or more forms of pornography: erotic magazines, X-rated movies, adult bookstores, nude stage shows. *Gallup* 313 (October 1991).

[13]*Gallup* 313, October 1991; *1990 Virginia Slims*, 41.

[14]Robert T. Michael, John H. Gagnon, Edward O. Laumann, and Gina Kolata, *Sex in America: A Definitive Survey* (Boston: Little Brown, 1994).

[15]*Gallup*, 197, February 1982.

[16]Ibid.

[17]Dalma Heyn, *The Erotic Silence of the American Wife* (New York: Signet, 1993), 11.

[18]Heyn, *Erotic Silence*, 315.

[19]I have discussed the contradictions and complexities of this issue in *Feminism Without Illusions: A Critique of Individualism* (Chapel Hill, NC: Univ. of North Carolina Press, 1991).

[20]Catharine A. MacKinnon, *Toward a Feminist Theory of the State* (Cambridge, MA: Harvard Univ. Press, 1989), 197.

[21]Almost three quarters wanted a ban on the sale or rental of videocassettes that displayed sexual violence in their communities; a ban on theaters that ran movies depicting sexual violence; and a ban on magazines that showed sexual violence. In the single year between 1985 and 1986, the opposition to violent sex materials jumped sharply by 10 points, *Gallup*, 251, August 1986.

[22]Young, college-educated, affluent women and black men are the strongest supporters, while black women are the least. Black women were the only group in which fewer than three quarters approved. *Harris*, 871028, July 1987.

[23]*Gallup*, September 1991.

[24]*Gallup*, 309, June 1991.

[25]Gerald F. Seib and John Harwood, "Abortion Issue Takes on a Growing Importance in the Welfare Debate and Republican Politics," *The Wall Street Journal* (March 23, 1995): A16; and Hadley Arkes, "Anti-Abortion, But Politically Smart," *The Wall Street Journal* (March 28, 1995): A26.

[26]Justice Scalia forcefully and plausibly denies that the Court has the constitutional authority to legislate on abortion at all—that the issue concerns social policy, not abstract right, and that in a democratic society all such decisions should be made by the elected representatives of the people.

[27]According to the justices, an abortion also affects those who perform the abortion, the woman's family, "and society which must confront the knowledge that these procedures exist."

[28]Craig and O'Brien, *Abortion and American Politics*, 251. *U.S.A. Today*, April 21, 1992, 11A, reported that 55 percent were performed on women between the ages of twenty and thirty, which suggests that eighteen- and nineteen-year-old women are especially likely to have abortions.

Five

ECONOMIC
REVOLUTION

L ucy Goldfarb, Pauline Stern, Maggie Farrell, Tracey Thomas,
and Judy Swift differ in background and generation, but
they all faced an unplanned pregnancy. As young middle-
class women, they expected to have careers that would permit them
to support themselves if necessary. And although the unplanned
pregnancy affected each of them somewhat differently, it did not
destroy, or even radically alter, the lives they were planning. Judy
Swift had to leave Swarthmore, but, with her mother's support, she
finished college on schedule at Hunter in New York and went on to
law school at Fordham. All of the others progressed steadily in their
careers, although Pauline Stern chose to remain at home for a few
years after her daughter was born. For all of them, the sexual revolution that had both freed and complicated their lives seemed a natural partner of the economic revolution that was helping them to

enter and succeed in careers that had been closed to most of their mothers.

Career women have conquered the American imagination. These days, even Barbie of Barbie doll fame can be dressed for any career that strikes her owner's fancy. In almost any television show you turn to, the main women characters have jobs. Paid employment has brought many women a new independence that most of their mothers and grandmothers could not have imagined. Jobs permit single women to support themselves, sometimes in considerable comfort. Jobs give married women greater power within their marriages. Most feminists see paid employment as the bedrock of women's new freedom, and they have devoted much of their attention to campaigning for better pay and working conditions for women. Feminism has successfully and constructively encouraged middle-class women to view paid employment as vital to their lives before and after they marry, if they marry at all.

Since the 1940s, movies like *His Girl Friday*, in which Rosalind Russell played a dynamic, ambitious newswoman, have glamorized the image of the working girl. Feisty, determined, taking no sass from any man, Russell rubbed shoulders with the boys in the newsroom while writing her way up the ladder of her profession. Russell marries and keeps her career, but—as Betty Friedan complained—by the 1950s working heroines were giving up careers for marriages. Even Friedan probably did not guess, when she published her book in 1963, that women's proclivity to trade pad and pencil for apron and baby was about to be drowned in the wave of economic changes that were sweeping over the country. American women owe Friedan an incalculable debt for *The Feminine Mystique*, and the feminism it did so much to mobilize stirred tens of thousands of middle-class young women to rethink their lives. But with or without the rethinking, our lives are now in the throes of irreversible change.

Modern feminism emerged as a direct response to the economic revolution that has transformed our world. In *The Feminine Mystique*, Friedan emphasized the importance of meaningful work to women's lives and the frustration of the upscale, elite, affluent young women who had received excellent college educations that they were putting to no direct use. Why should women who had been as well educated as aspiring male lawyers, doctors, and stockbrokers choose to stay at home to bake meat loaf and change diapers? Domesticity was not a satisfactory story of an intelligent woman's life.

✳ Contrary to both supporters and opponents, feminism did not create the new working woman. She is the product of an economic revolution that has drawn the United States into a global economy and transformed economic opportunities and relations. Women have not merely entered the labor force in unprecedented numbers. They have entered a labor force that is changing dramatically, and their entry is changing it further. The technological revolution has not just facilitated the way we do business: it has changed the way we do it, where we do it, and who does it. Male skills that had been passed from father to son have become outmoded, and the jobs they prepared men to hold have disappeared. Gone are the days in which a skilled steel or auto worker could earn enough to own a house and support a wife and children. Big businesses have merged and become global, while small and medium businesses wrestle with new challenges. The complex features of this economic revolution have intimately affected the lives of women, promoting some to unprecedented prosperity, condemning others to debilitating poverty, and leaving most to juggle their lives as women and as workers as best they can.

Martha Miller, whose husband Michael is an airline pilot, teaches in a private high school in Baltimore while working on a Ph.D. in English at the University of Maryland. Martha sees her life as a kind of jigsaw puzzle in which she is always trying to make the pieces fit. Mainly, however, she worries about Benjamin, Michael's fourteen-year-old son from his first marriage who is living with them. More than once, she has thought that if only she could teach half days everything would be possible. Then, she says, "I could still keep track of this teenager and run the house and do a decent job teaching. But it isn't an option." Martha has never had a child of her own, but friends tell her that you worry less about infants than about teenagers. She cannot judge which is more difficult, but she knows that Benjamin "is a very challenging young man," and she worries constantly. "There's so much to worry about. You know, if he's late, or if he's not home when I come home from school." Martha suspects she exaggerates what Benjamin might be doing, but her concerns are real. And other working parents of teenage children share them. Today, more than three quarters of all children between fourteen and seventeen have working mothers, whose teenagers come home after school to empty houses and cars.[1] Martha and Mike live in a nice, upscale neighborhood, "but drugs are everywhere and you can't hide them and you can't hide from the alcohol and all the sexual problems . . ."

When Martha was young, her own mother had worked, but she was only able to do so because Martha's grandmother, her mother's mother, lived in the same town, "and I would come home from school and go to her house or else she would be at our house until my mother came home and my mother would take her home." Finally, when Martha was in ninth grade, her grandmother moved in with them. "So my mother didn't have to worry about the teenage daughter who was always raising hell. Grandma was there." Martha, who had more than a few conflicts with her own mother, adored her grandmother and would do anything for her. "If my mother came home and she was tired, my grandmother was always willing to step in and cook. And that gave my mother the ability to do a lot of things." Martha does not have that kind of help at home, and she occasionally gets angry when she needs to go out in the evening and Michael is late, since both of them dislike leaving Benjamin alone at night. "And I get real angry, especially since he isn't even my child." But then, she adds, "What can you do? You can't just say 'hit the road' because a man won't wash the dishes or something."

For Martha, as for so many women, paid work, which women had previously done now and then, has become a way of life. But women have not mindlessly been slipping out of an old life and into a new one. They have consciously been trying to combine both. And so we now have the myth of the superwoman who does it all and with ease. Unfortunately, the life of a superwoman is easier to dream than to live. Real women find that their lives as mothers clash with their lives as workers. Economic mobility and job schedules make no concessions to nursing, diapers, or colic. Nursing, diapers, and colic make no concessions to production schedules or board meetings. All of which, any working mother could tell us, if only she were being asked. For there are no superwomen, and something has to give. Hence the grim threat of the economic revolution: As workers, women need to be liberated from children; as mothers, they need to be liberated from work. Whatever the consequences of the economic revolution, women's lives lie at the center.

A few cold facts tell a dramatic story. In 1992, women were working in greater numbers than ever before in our nation's history. Of the 100 million women in the United States, more than half (58 million) were working or looking for work.[2] But work means different things to different women. One fourth work only part-time, many because of responsibilities to children. Family responsibilities help to explain why single women are more likely to work than married women. Yet divorced women, who frequently have children to support, are more likely to work than women who have never been married, many of whom are still in graduate or professional schools.[3] Among poorer women, school or teenage pregnancies may also make it difficult to work full-time, or even to work at all. And teenage women who are not in school do not normally have enough education for a good job. Overall, the best jobs have gone to women at the upper end of the economic spectrum, who, not surprisingly, have benefited the most from the economic revolution. As early as 1983, women held 40 percent of the lucrative jobs in the professions and management. By 1992 they held almost half of them (47 percent).[4]

Before the 1960s women who worked outside the home tended to move in and out of the labor force, depending upon whether they were married or had children at home. Young women of all classes and races frequently worked between school and marriage; single women might work throughout their lives; older women might work as their children grew older or after the children had left home. But few women remained in the labor force throughout their adult lives, and perhaps even fewer saw their job or career as a permanent feature of their life.[5]

As a result, it was easy to assume that women did not "really" work the way men did, or to assume that women's earnings were merely supplements to the basic male wage that supported the family. This was the working-class world of Archie and Edith Bunker in which "girls were girls, and men were men." It was also the world of the towns and, increasingly, the suburbs, which most Americans thought of as home. Today that world has disappeared for men as well as women. The global economy has left most men unable to support a family without a second wage earner. A thirty-year-old construction worker from Tennessee, who might have been expected to share Archie's attitudes, said simply: "My wife works part-time; you have to nowadays. Of course, it would be nice if a person could go out and work and support your family at home, but you can't do that nowadays."[6]

Significantly, the most dramatic, indeed revolutionary economic changes exploded during the late 1960s and early 1970s, precisely the years during which the feminist movement took shape.[7] Almost overnight, wage labor became as important in women's lives as it had always been in men's. The no-fault divorce laws, beginning in 1970, might have warned those who cared to pay attention: Women could no longer look to marriage as a reliable source of financial support. But long before the changes were understood, people had begun to live their lives in response to them.

When Myra, the heroine of Marilyn French's best-selling novel, *The Woman's Room*, discovers that the doctor husband whom she had supported through medical school has been cheating on her, she is devastated. With two young children and no profession, how can she manage, especially since the divorce leaves her with virtually no resources? Myra manages by returning to graduate school and becoming a feminist. Innumerable other women in her position have not had the options or have not wanted them. They have struggled along as secretaries, medical assistants, waitresses, whatever. Where experience made Myra a feminist, it has made other women long for the security of remarriage. But like Myra, they have learned the hard way that marriage is no longer a reliable career. And even those who remarry frequently find that their family's security requires that they continue to work—which growing numbers of married women throughout the country are now doing.

From Friedan on, feminists have grasped the importance of work and economic independence to women's lives. Equality of economic opportunity and earnings have consistently figured as a major rallying point. Yet during the 1970s, when feminists first angrily and accurately proclaimed that a woman earned a mere fifty-nine cents for every dollar earned by a man, the idea that women should earn as much as men was novel. Most people still assumed that women's primary goals and responsibilities were domestic and that a wife's earnings would be secondary to those of her husband. And since most women still worked in "female" occupations, equal pay for equal work was not the main issue. For young professional women, however, earning less than men for the same work came as a rude shock. The early feminist anger about unequal salaries spoke directly to the young professional woman's life.

Feminists have been reluctant to acknowledge that the aspiring professionals for whom they primarily spoke were atypical. Rather, they took professional women as their model and assumed that women's working lives should resemble those of men. And pollsters confirm that the attitudes of single women toward work do very much resemble those of men. If anything, women are even more concerned than men with finding work that offers chances for promotion, skill development, and higher pay.[8] Yet many who do not expect women's working lives to mirror those of men firmly believe that women should receive equal pay for equal work, and many, if not all, are beginning to agree that women should be doing the same work as men if they choose. These attitudes testify to the rapid change in women's economic position during the past thirty years.

It is one thing to recognize change and another to understand it. We all know that some women are doing much worse, but do not always understand why. Feminists are quick to blame discrimination. But the poorest women in the United States are more likely to be poor because of the disintegration of families than because of discrimination in the labor market. And the blanket charge of discrimination masks another truth, namely, that some women are doing well. Professional and managerial women are doing much better— almost as well as the men of their group. And what we almost never hear is that in a mere thirty years the improvement in entry-level women's economic position relative to that of men has been without precedent in human history. Thus, whether a young woman starts in a prestigious law firm or at McDonald's, she is likely to earn the same as her male peers.

The hard truth is that women are disadvantaged in the workforce not so much because of the behavior and biases of employers as because they have children. Many employers are biased and behave badly, but more and more recognize that it is no longer in their interest to do so. As a result, the women who are most economically vulnerable are as likely to be vulnerable relative to other women as relative to men. Feminism has not acknowledged the truth that during the past thirty years some women's lives have improved dramatically while other women's have worsened. Feminists are reluctant to focus upon the widening gap among women in part because they have a vested interest in emphasizing the disadvantages that women share and, perhaps, in part because some of the women who are doing best are doing well because they belong to two-career marriages. Others commentators frequently pay little attention to the widening gap among women because they are primarily interested in the difference in income among families rather than the differences among women as individual wage-earners.[9]

Since 1960 women's participation in the labor force has reshaped their relations to their families and to the world of work. Whether undertaken from choice or necessity, paid work has drastically reduced women's economic dependence upon men, providing many with the resources to function as independent individuals. Most women continue to value marriage and family life, but they are less likely to define themselves exclusively in relation to families. And families are exercising decreasing influence over their lives.[10] But women's growing economic independence from families has not automatically lessened their commitment to family life. Indeed, the competing pulls of work and family define many women's lives.

Feminists have frequently expressed sympathy for women who are caught in those conflicting pulls, but mainly to insist that women need more help from husbands or more and cheaper day care in order to break free of burdensome family responsibilities. And although feminists regularly insist that they respect any choice a woman makes about her life, it is difficult to find much feminist support for women who decide that their commitment to family must, at least for a while, take precedence over their commitment to work. As a result, many women who do decide to treat family responsibilities as their primary "job" believe that feminists have contempt for their choice. And, not surprisingly, more than a few return the contempt, holding feminists responsible for the weakening of families.

It may come as a surprise, but more often than not, women like their work. A fifty-six-year-old grandmother from Pittsburgh, who is now running a college post office by day and a bed-and-breakfast by night, claims, "I was always doing something to bring a little extra income into the house, because it made me feel like I was doing more than filling salt and pepper shakers." Across the continent in Los Angeles, a fifty-four-year-old African-American woman, who takes medical billing work into her home and sells real estate on the side, concurs. "There are certain things you want out of life, and you have to work to get them." She values her work: "I enjoy it; it's not a burden. I've been a single parent for many years, so I have always had a second job; now my son is full-time in graduate school. I made a choice to do something I enjoy to have the money to have the standard I enjoy, and by working for those things I also gratify the other side."[11]

Even the postal supervisor from Pittsburgh, who says her work has ruined her health, will not give it up. "I'm on a cement floor for seven and a half hours a day. It's ruined my feet, my legs, my back." But, she insists, "I really enjoy the job; it's a challenge. To get everything coordinated and do it accurately is a real chore, but you get a lot of satisfaction out of it. And you know when you get it done, you did it."[12]

At forty, Marcy Matthews believes that growing up the youngest girl in a Catholic family of six children shaped her determination to work. Marcy's father died when she was young, and she grew up "very poor. Grew up knowing that we would never, ever, ever go to college—that we had to get into programs where we would learn a trade, learn a skill, so we could get out and support ourselves." Her mother was raised the same way and expected her daughters to be able to support themselves. But as soon as Marcy started to work, she went back to school. "It was just real important to me to have a college degree just—just to prove that I could." She did not complete the degree until twenty years after she had graduated from high school, and by then she had established herself as a very successful sales and marketing executive for an engineering firm.

Marcy loves her work and the economic independence it brings. She also loves her second husband, who is proud of her achievements and from whom she gets "nothing but support." She admires him and relies heavily on his advice, especially his political skill and his "horse sense" about people. She has never had a child, but even if she had, she could not imagine herself not working. "That's definitely from the environment in which I was raised. I would never allow myself to be totally dependent on one person's income, because of the struggle my mom had and her having to go back into the workforce." Doing what she loves to do "is an awesome feeling. Every Sunday night you can't wait, can't wait to get to work, and that's how this job is." Marcy's exuberant delight in her work may not be typical, but even women who can easily wait to get to work and sometimes would prefer not to go at all understand her satisfaction in being an effective working person.

Married or single, old or young, women of all races, ethnic groups, and classes are coming to see work as an important part of who they are. Work previously undertaken out of economic necessity has become central to identity. Work helps married women to think of themselves as full partners rather than dependents. Economic necessity weighs most heavily on the growing numbers of single women, especially single mothers. But even when pushed to the limit they, too, frequently appreciate the sense of competence and independence that work brings. Yes, many single women would give a lot to have someone to share the burdens, but many would no longer choose simply to stay home and be supported.

Anslie Davis, a mid-level sales and marketing executive for a growing company, is bemused by how seriously she takes her work. She enjoys her own femininity, yet sees herself as "very dominating." She is often frustrated that her corporation does not give her more opportunity to make decisions, but she does love the work. "I live work, it never ends, it never does end for me." Her friends at work challenge her: "Challenge my way of thinking, or improve me, help me as an individual." For Anslie, work has helped her to grow beyond the partying of her undergraduate days and to respect herself.

Anslie comes from the solid, white middle class, but her views of work do not differ sharply from those of women from other classes. Patricia Sanders values her job as a secretary for the edge of economic independence it offers her. As her husband frequently reminds her, they could afford to have her stop working for a year or two so that she could finish her teaching degree rapidly. She appreciates his generosity but declines. She loves her husband and knows they could afford it, but she still prefers to earn her own salary. Anna, a young black single mother on Aid to Families with Dependent Children, says: "I feel so much better about myself when I'm working because I'm also doing something for myself, and all the time I'm trying to better myself."[13]

My women graduate students and other young professionals share these women's feelings about self-improvement and independence. Cecilia MacDonald, a devout Catholic and a "pro-life feminist," believes deeply in women's responsibilities to children and families. Yet she is avidly pursuing her career. What sense does it make, she asked me, to receive this lengthy and demanding education and not use it? Melanie Johnson puts it even more forcefully. Ambitious from a young age, she has worked hard to have a career and is not about to stop. Both of these young women, like most of their friends, hope to marry and have children, but they do not want to sacrifice their hard-won professional identities and accomplishments. Dawn Grayson, who grew up in a lower-middle-class African-American family in the mountains of western Virginia, shares their feelings. The first in her family even to try for a BA, she went to a small women's college with no idea of what she might hope to become. But her ambition progressed with her education, and by her senior year she was planning to pursue a doctorate and then a career in teaching.

Women are taking genuine pleasure in their work, even when it is far from glamorous. They like to be working to get out of the house, to interact with other adults, to earn money they can call their own. Even when the money they call their own is necessary to the survival of their families, earning it gives them a larger say in family decisions. The security of a full-time job gives women a kind of insurance against a husband's death, disability, or desertion. It makes women indispensable to their families and simultaneously helps them feel themselves discrete individuals. A woman who can support herself has some hope of leaving an abusive marriage. A woman who cannot support herself almost always feels she cannot leave. And even the dullest, most routine work may give a woman a sense of competence, which translates into a sense of individuality.

For years, women got the same sense of accomplishment from presiding over a household and raising children. Even today, there is no reason that being a housewife cannot serve that function, and for countless women it does. Yet, sadly, in what has been a "man's world," housewives have often been denied the respect they deserve. More sadly yet, the growing tendency for women to work, even while their children are very young, has led many women to treat women who choose to remain at home with barely veiled condescension or worse. Countless women who have made that choice have told me, sometimes with sorrow, sometimes with bitterness, that their former friends from work no longer have time for them. What they do not understand is that some of those friends may secretly envy the opportunity to stay home, but cannot afford it. Be that as it may, increasing numbers of women have come to believe that they must pursue some kind of nondomestic career if they expect to be taken seriously. These attitudes are especially prevalent among upscale women for whom work means status, even though increasing numbers of young professional mothers are deciding to stay home or cut back on their work while their children are young. But sadly, the option to stay home is rarely available for the many ordinary working women who want to.

Many women, who believe they face impossible choices, still prefer not to work. A Louis Harris poll of the late 1980s found at every level of education, age, and income men are more enthusiastic about work than women, and a 1991 Gallup poll showed men are more likely than women to depend upon work for a sense of purpose and identity. And contrary to stereotype, it is especially striking that black and Hispanic men, who are more likely to be unemployed than white men, claim to care even more about working.[14] Thus, as we think about women's problems, we need to remember that, as important as work is to growing numbers of women, it may be even more important to those men who have the greatest difficulty in finding jobs.

We should also remember that women's new commitment to work has not led them to value marriage and family less, even if it has led many to value them differently. Most women see work as a complement to the more traditional domestic story of their lives, not as a replacement for it. But work has forced young married women and mothers to modify both stories. That women work is one thing, that mothers work another. The most dramatic consequence of the economic revolution that began in the late 1960s has been the growing tendency of mothers with young children to work. Almost overnight, after 1960 significant numbers were remaining in the labor force while they raised their children. Thus, the economic revolution has not merely transformed the lives of women but transformed the lives of children, more and more of whom have been spending much of their time with nannies, baby-sitters, or in day care.

Today, at least three quarters of all American women between ages twenty-five and forty-four are working full-time or part-time for wages, and they are precisely the women who are most likely to have children. Since 1950, the number of working mothers has almost doubled. Even in 1975 most mothers of children under six did not work, whether they were married or single. By 1992, more than half of the women with children under three were in the labor force, and more than two thirds of those with children under eighteen.[15]

Most of us know that mothers work, but most of us do not normally stop to think about the larger significance of the numbers. Today, mothers of young children are not only working, they are the women who are most likely to be working, especially if they are black.[16] The story of working women is primarily the story of working mothers. More and more women must fit children around their work, or fit work around their children. And the fit has rarely been easy. Working mothers rely heavily upon day care, and many worry about whether it is adequate or even how they can afford it. Children increasingly know that they cannot count on their mothers' always being there. Many children cannot play quietly at home with a friend because there is no one there to supervise them. An administrator at a private school in New York told me that the school has steadily been pushed to extend its hours because some children are dropped off before breakfast and not picked up until ten at night. As Megan Beatty said to me, "Michael and I have always known we wanted to have a family, but now, when I think about my own career, the right time for having kids gets pushed further and further back. First it was twenty-five, then it was thirty, now who knows?" The truth is that for a young woman who wants to succeed in a profession, no time seems right. Yet my friend, like so many others, still wants children—or at least one child.

Women who want professional careers believe they face special problems, primarily because they compete directly with men who ostensibly are free to devote all their time first to professional training and then to their work. Understandably, these women feel that if they take time off to have one or more children they will fall too far behind the competition to be able to catch up. More often than not they are right, although some of them, like Zoe Baird, a vice president at Aetna Life Insurance and an ill-fated nominee for attorney general, solve the worst of the practical difficulties by hiring nannies. Most women cannot afford nannies.

Single mothers have the hardest time. With minor exceptions, they either work or go on welfare. It is harder for single women to work than for married women, harder for poor women than for affluent, and harder for women with children than those without. Most single mothers, many of whom are young, unskilled, and poor, have young children at home. They cannot afford full-time home day care, much less nannies, yet must rely upon some form of day care. Day care centers normally will not take sick children, so each time a child is sick, the mother must miss work or leave the child alone. Poor women sometimes feel they must lock their children in the apartment, or, perhaps worse, leave them to unsupervised play in the street. Married women face similar problems, but they at least have some possibility of taking turns with their husbands in staying home with the child. Single or married, the vast majority of working women live with two "shifts"—one on the job and one at home. And although more and more men, working-class as well as middle-class, are beginning to shoulder domestic responsibilities, the burden still falls primarily on women.

The problems of working mothers lie at the center of women's relation to work, but no one is giving them the attention they deserve. Feminists who enthusiastically defend women's right to work tend to argue that enough day care or cooperation from fathers can solve the problems. Conservatives tend to argue that women with young children simply should not work since children need and deserve one parent's full attention. Both of these attitudes ignore the hard realities of the world in which women find themselves. Working mothers are not exceptions among women: They are the norm, and they are here to stay. Mothers and women who may soon be mothers are the most numerous and important group of women in the labor force, and most must work at least part-time, whether they want to or not.

Janelle Morrison works as an administrative assistant in the African-American studies department at one of the campuses of the University of California. Having started as a part-time secretary, she rapidly advanced until now she virtually runs the department's programs. Janelle could not be happier with her job, which she insists she loves, but its demands can be crushing. Above all, the schedule is unpredictable since the lectures and meetings she is responsible for organizing may easily run over, or a visitor may need to be driven to the airport, or students may just drop in with a problem. When the annual budget or course listings are due, the working day may stretch until six or seven at night. When things run smoothly, Janelle's three-year-old son and twelve-year-old daughter do fine. Little Mark normally loves his day care, and Solange has a full schedule of after-school activities. If one of them, especially Mark, gets sick, everything collapses, and Janelle has to stay home. But, in some ways, the hardest times come when Mark has recovered enough to return to day care but does not really want to, or when Solange wants her to come to a soccer game or dance recital in the afternoon. It kills Janelle to disappoint them; it kills her to give less than 100 percent at her job; and, frequently, the stress makes her feel as if her head will burst. Her husband, Bennett, spends as much time with the children as he can, but he works as a salesman for a big publishing company and is frequently on the road.

Women's earnings have become essential to a family's standard of living, as Janelle's are to hers. Single mothers provide their family's main source of support, although in some cases fathers or welfare payments also contribute. Married women's earnings account for a growing—and, among the less affluent—necessary share of their family's income, even when women do not earn as much as their husbands. But women's freedom to go out to work costs families. Rachel Landsman's position as assistant provost at a small liberal arts college near Chicago requires that she dress tastefully, which is never cheap, and her long hours require her to have extensive child care for her two young daughters. Because her job often requires her to attend breakfasts, receptions, dinners, or even school concerts and sports events, she decided to hire a full-time nanny after the birth of her second daughter, Trish. She, her husband, and the girls have all been delighted with the arrangement, and Lillian has practically become a member of the family. But, for years, Lillian's salary was almost as large as Rachel's, which meant that Rachel was working for the pleasure and freedom of being able to work. Eventually, Rachel began to earn substantial raises, so that each year a larger proportion of her salary was available for other expenses. But, while the girls were young, she earned barely enough to pay for Lillian and her own clothes.

In the early 1970s many young professional mothers claimed that they spent virtually their entire salary on a nanny or other forms of domestic help. Their earnings increased family incomes, but if you take their expenditures into account, the net increase over the incomes of families in which wives did not work was minimal—a mere 5 percent.[17] Thus most of the money married women earned was spent on permitting them to work. Indeed, many married women wanted to work, at least in part because they preferred to buy services for the household rather than perform the services themselves.

Having the money to spend on domestic labor means that women do not have to do it themselves. Working wives can justify the expenditure on cleaning help; they can afford to send out laundry rather than do it themselves; they can pay for baby-sitters, meals at restaurants, or quality prepared foods. Like Hillary Rodham Clinton, they do not have to make cookies. But their new freedom from much ordinary domestic labor establishes a cruel hierarchy between them and women who do not work outside the home. Their ability to buy services defines the roles of women who do their own domestic labor as servants' roles. And their ability to spend money on themselves for travel, restaurants, clothes, hairdressers, and manicurists etches the distinction in a sharp visual image. You do not need an elegant suit and a chic haircut to go to the playground, and if you are spending your time at the playground you probably cannot afford them.

Since the 1970s, the difference in income between families with and without a wage-earning wife has steadily increased.[18] By 1991, on average, families in which the wife worked for wages earned $48,000 per year, whereas families in which she did not earned $30,000—a difference of $18,000 per year or more than 60 percent, and a difference between modest comfort and scrimping. But even families without a wage-earning wife were doing almost twice as well as the families of single mothers, for which the average income was less than $17,000.[19] As women's wages are catching up to those of men, the gap between married women who have jobs and those who do not is steadily widening, and the gap between two-parent and female-headed families is widening even faster. In short, women are not benefiting equally from new opportunities in the workplace. Many are not benefiting at all.

The big winners from women's new employment opportunities have been upscale young women who are pursuing careers in business and the professions—the women for whom the official feminist lobby, despite pretensions, actually speaks. By 1994, women were receiving almost half of the doctorates awarded to U.S. citizens, more than double the percentage they had received in 1973. They were also receiving more than one third of the master's degrees in business administration, a nineteen-fold increase since 1972. The story for law schools and medical schools is comparable.[20] In recent years women's level of education and experience has been increasing at a faster rate than that of men. The gap between women and men is narrowing at an astounding rate, and as it narrows, the gap in earnings narrows as well.

From the start, pay equity—equal pay for equal work—has ranked as a major feminist issue and, of all feminist issues, has spoken the most directly to ordinary women—and men. "Fifty-nine cents on the dollar" swiftly captured the popular imagination. And from 1960 to 1980, it captured the reality of women's experience.[21] Today, it does not. By 1991, the fifty-nine cents had become seventy cents for women in general—an amazing improvement for a brief period. Equal pay for equal work is no longer the main problem and probably will soon be no problem at all. The real problem is how little difference the closing of that gap makes in the lives of many women, whose earnings have become more important to their own support and the support of their families.

When feminists first called attention to the inequality of men's and women's earnings, they seemed to assume that if women made as much as men they would be economically self-sufficient, if not comfortable. But equal pay for equal work always meant precisely that: For women to earn the same as men, they must hold the same jobs and must hold them for the same amount of time. As we all now know, this is not a scenario that easily includes motherhood. Beyond the difficulties of juggling employment and motherhood lies the reality of our economy. Just because a woman who works at McDonald's earns as much as a male coworker with the same amount of experience does not mean that she earns enough to support herself and one or two children.

The debates over AFDC have brought public attention to the difficulties that swamp a single mother with one or two children, not to mention those who have more than two. In forty-five states, all-day day care for two children now costs more than welfare mothers receive for all of their living expenses, and women who work at or near the minimum wage do not earn much more. When Gloria Patterson left her first husband, Bobby, she had a decent part-time job at Macy's. Thanks to that job, she and Bobby could afford a two-bedroom apartment and some minimal comforts, including part-time day care for her toddler, Johnny. But without Bobby's wages, her job at Macy's could not even cover the rent. Gloria had completed high school but had not attended college. She had more basic skills, and especially more self-confidence, experience, and presence, than many welfare mothers, but even she did not have adequate training for a job that would have paid for both rent and full-time day care. Gloria briefly tried to make ends meet by working in a school cafeteria, where she earned as much as the men she worked with, but she rapidly discovered she could not. So, rather than fall into debt, she moved back to her parents' house in low-country Georgia, where her mother and sisters could help her with Johnny, and she could work part-time while taking some courses in nutrition at the local community college.

Gloria's situation differed from that of welfare mothers who have no family to turn to, but, without her family's assistance and her own second marriage, it did not differ much. Her situation also differed from that of women with only a little more education, but with the skills to work as a secretary, the supervisor of a school cafeteria, a nurse, or even a truck driver or law enforcement officer. And it differed radically from that of upscale career women, who earn enough as lawyers, doctors, university professors, corporate managers, or television executives to support children on their own earnings. We cannot possibly understand what has been happening to women's earnings if we group all women together. "Fifty-nine cents on the dollar" reflected the average experience of all women in the labor force no matter what their age or education or how much of their lives they had worked. Typically, older women had always earned less than the men of their age, especially if they left the labor force or worked part-time when their children were young. They rarely had the opportunities to enter lucrative careers and professions that young women enjoy today. Poor women still do not have the appropriate education. So the average improvement in women's earnings disguises the radically different circumstances of different groups.

While some groups of women saw little or no improvement in their earnings, others leapfrogged into the highest brackets. The real story concerns which women won and which women lost or barely held steady in the new employment lottery. In general, younger women have been the big winners, and today young full-time women workers are earning 90 percent or more of what their male colleagues earn.[22] Of this group, the women with the most education have done the best of all. Tellingly, the more education a woman has, the more likely she is to seek employment—and, apparently, to find it. As of 1992, women held almost half of all managerial and professional positions.[23] Education, enhanced by affirmative action, thus helped women to move into the white collar and managerial sectors that were previously dominated by men.[24] But women who have entered nontraditional occupations that do not require as much education have also done remarkably well, although they have frequently faced serious challenges in getting their coworkers to accept them.[25]

Women who become mechanics and skilled repair workers, like women who become welders, engineers, law enforcement officers, or firefighters still enter a man's world. The plus is that they are taking up occupations that offer reasonably high wages. The minus is that many of their male coworkers offer them a less than cordial welcome. Geraldine Walker, a ship scaler and the only black woman supervisor at her shipyard, likes working in the yards, even though she believes her work contributed to her divorce. "I'm a lot stronger now than when I started in the yards. I don't doubt now that I can take care of myself. Financially, emotionally, I'm more confident."[26] So, to earn their wages they not only have to do their jobs, they frequently have to contend with subtle and not-so-subtle forms of harassment. It should come as no surprise that many of the men with whom they work do not think that they belong there. Marge

Kirk, who works as a concrete truck driver, remembers putting up with a lot of sexual innuendoes, especially from the dispatcher who was her supervisor. "It takes a lot of energy just to stand your ground—balancing male egos with your right to survive." But she "wanted to be a good truck driver," and "somehow I survived." Other women have done the same as mechanics, skilled repair workers, security guards, police, or firefighters, and the wages of women in these occupations have been steadily rising. But working in "male" occupations does not alone explain the general improvement in women's earnings; secretaries, who are mainly women, have enjoyed the biggest increase of all.[27]

The numbers challenge feminism's picture of the Reagan and Bush years as a period of backlash against women. The 1980s did very well by many women. They did not do well by others. The many women in service occupations such as food preparation or day care and in typically "female" occupations such as manicurist or beautician did badly, and they may soon do worse, especially those with children to support. But men from similar backgrounds, with similar educations, are doing no better. If anything, women are more likely than men to pursue the education that our modern economy demands. According to the Census Bureau, the number of women who enter the labor force with a college degree is rising one and one-half times as rapidly as the number of men. The continuing decline of occupational segregation is producing more and more direct competition between women and men for jobs and wages. This direct competition is new, and it is pushing down men's wages. During the years of the so-called backlash, women's average income grew by almost 30 percent, while the average income of men actually declined slightly.[28]

No, women in general are still not doing as well as men in general. Yes, some men do resent the gains that women have made and do their best to prevent them from making more. It should not be difficult to understand that direct competition between women and men for employment and wages could result in men's resentment of women—and even a backlash. But no backlash has prevented significant numbers of upscale white women from prospering. More important, even while most women still do less well than men in absolute terms, women's economic position continues to improve while men's is beginning to decline. The gap is steadily closing.

So why, in the face of improvement, do feminists continue to stress discrimination? One may only assume that, understandably, they resent not having advanced as rapidly or as far as they had hoped. Each of us sees the world through the lens of her own life. Naomi Wolf, who acknowledges that women have made terrific gains in many areas, continues to protest, probably with good reason, their disadvantage in the media—her own world.[29] Women who have butted their heads against the notorious corporate "glass ceiling" feel the same about theirs. Knowing themselves to be as talented and accomplished (often more so) than the men with whom they work, they find it tempting to blame their troubles upon men who are determined to keep them down. In this frame of mind, they are unlikely to be impressed by reminders of the extraordinary improvement in the situation of women like themselves.

We should not lightly dismiss men's persisting determination to continue to control the workplace. Most successful women in business or the professions will at least privately complain of a male network that they simply cannot crack. The workings of these networks are subtle, private, and elusive, consisting in conversations over a drink or a game of golf at which women just happen not to be present. Sexual harassment, even in its mildest form of passing remarks, remains a problem. As women have entered the labor force in ever greater numbers, their perception of discrimination has increased. And college women perceive more discrimination than women with less education.[30] Meanwhile, the women and men who have the least chance to become executives—nonwhites or those with only a grade school education—are the most likely to believe that a woman has as good a chance as a man to become one.[31] Doubtless, some men do resent female competition, but others benefit directly from the improvement in women's earnings through their wives, daughters, and partners. And increasing numbers of working-class as well as middle-class men are making a successful effort to come to terms with their women coworkers.

In fairness to the feminist elite, it is clear that as of the 1990s women still have not made significant inroads on the top executive positions. In 1991, when women accounted for almost half the labor force and, depending upon the estimate, 25 to 40 percent of all managers, they held less, by some counts much less, than 10 percent of the top executive positions. Variations in job classifications make statistical precision difficult, but during the past ten years, women have been making dramatic gains in upper management. Some companies have let it be known that women only need apply for some of their top jobs.[32] Even so, the only women who are faring better than the men of their own group are black women professionals, who, as of 1994, outnumbered black male professionals by nearly two to one in the 38,000 companies that report to the Equal Employment Opportunity Commission.[33]

In 1992, *Business Week* surveyed four hundred female managers, only to find that they divided equally among those who believed that corporate America was doing "somewhat better" in hiring and promoting women and those who believed that the rate of progress was slowing. The main difficulty in assessing any of these numbers or even the responses to them is that the numbers themselves are so small. If a company that has one woman in a senior executive position adds a second, it will have increased the percentage of women by 100 percent. If its one woman retires or leaves and is replaced with a man, it will be left with no senior women executives at all. These are indeed circumstances designed to provoke bitterness and outrage, and they are circumstances upon which feminists have readily focused. After all, does not the low number of women at the top of the corporate ladder confirm the prevalence of blatant sexism? Doubtless it does. The rage and frustration of the women caught in it should surprise no one. But the corporate world that still treats women shabbily is beginning to treat many men even worse. For between 1982 and 1992, when men lost a net 93,000 management jobs, women gained a net 520,000 management jobs.

Under these conditions, men are easily tempted to see a sexism in reverse. What, in fact, they are seeing is a ruthlessness that knows neither sex nor race in its concern for the bottom line of its ledgers and need to appease one or another political lobby. Sometimes women are simply taking over men's jobs; sometimes the men's jobs are eliminated entirely, and the women are hired for new jobs at lower pay.

In principle, Americans have long favored paying women the same as men for the same work.[34] As early as 1976, two thirds also approved of working wives, with the strongest support coming from the upscale and the young.[35] And in 1982, when women were entering the labor force in growing numbers the vast majority, especially those with the most education, believed that women should enjoy the same job opportunities as men.[36] Today, virtually everyone agrees that women and men who do the same work should receive the same pay.[37] But support for working women in principle does not necessarily mean support in practice. And even people with the best of intentions often find it difficult to act on their beliefs. Continuing inequalities persist and should not be brushed aside. The essential point nonetheless remains: The gap between men and women in wages and salaries is on the verge of extinction. The one exception is the most important case of all, namely mothers. But their needs do not rank at the top of anyone's agenda.

No one can pretend that women and men started out on an equal —or level—playing field. Thirty years ago men monopolized the best positions and the highest incomes throughout our economy. Today, women are claiming a steadily increasing share of both positions and incomes, but women as a group have still not attained equality with men as a group. Nor, as many women are quick to point out, have specific women always attained parity with specific men where parity seems appropriate. But the average of all women and the cases of specific women both obscure what may well be more important: The economic revolution that has drawn women into the labor force has transformed our economy, widening the gap between social classes and races but narrowing the gap between women and men within classes and races.

Feminism has ridden the crest of an economic wave that is pushing a disquieting number of Americans into a poverty from which they have little hope of escape. The same economic wave has been assaulting the security and self-confidence of many middle-class families, largely through the declining value of wages and the loss of male jobs.[38] Between 1973 and 1992, the average wages for the bottom 60 percent of male workers fell by 20 percent, and among young full-time male workers (ages eighteen to twenty-four) the percentage earning less than $12,195 a year jumped from 18 to 40—that is, it more than doubled. For comparable young women, the percentage went from 29 to 48. These stark figures draw a bleak picture for everyone: First, young women have consistently earned less than young men; second, the gap between the earnings of young women and those of young men has narrowed; and third, the numbers of both young men and young women who have poor prospects for earning a decent living has skyrocketed. Meanwhile, the richest Americans have increased their numbers and grown richer.

In this new and threatening economic world, two incomes are not just better than one: For most Americans, they are necessary. It is a world in which many, if not most, women must work, struggling to raise their children as best they can. It is a world in which the woman worker is a mother and often is poor because she is a mother. Feminism has been inclined to focus on professional and managerial women and to blame men for the disadvantages that women still suffer. But the young upscale women on whom official feminism focuses are doing remarkably well, and in the measure that they still have not attained full equality with men it is normally because of their responsibilities to children. Yet the economic revolution that has brought this group of women to an unprecedented independence and prosperity has condemned others to insecurity and even poverty.

What, in such a world, does equality mean? So long as women bear children, they will not be identical to men—and hence not equal to them. The measures of mathematical equality have little to do with the fabric of human lives. They have everything to do with the size of paychecks, whether equal or not. The differences between paychecks have more to do with the differences between social classes—and increasingly the education that, more than anything else today, determines class membership—than with the differences between the sexes. Within classes, differences between women and men persist, although they are steadily lessening. And, in the end, the best explanation for them remains women's ability to bear children—the inequality that no amount of social policy can erase. Social policy can ease the consequences of that inequality. But it is unlikely to accomplish even that much until we replace the feminist quest for an illusory equality with compassionate attention to the lives most women actually live.

NOTES

[1]Ellen Graham, "Working Parents' Torment: Teens After School," *The Wall Street Journal* (May 9, 1995): B1.

[2]Women now account for almost half (45 percent) of the entire labor force, and the percentage is steadily increasing; two thirds of all part-time workers are women.

[3]Three quarters of all divorced women and two thirds of all single (never married) women are working.

[4]U.S. Department of Labor, Women's Bureau, "Facts on Working Women," 93–92 (June 1993).

[5]African-American women were much more likely than women of other ethnic groups to remain in the labor force throughout their adult lives, including when their children were young.

[6]*Gallup*, 312, September 1991, 6.

[7]Steven D. McLaughlin, Barbara D. Miller, John O. G. Billy, Denise M. Zimmerle, Linda D. Winges, Terry R. Johnson, *The Changing Lives of American Women* (Chapel Hill, NC: Univ. of North Carolina Press, 1988).

[8]63 percent compared with 53 percent of all workers. *Gallup*, 312, September 1991.

[9]Richard J. Herrnstein and Charles A. Murray, *The Bell Curve: Intelligence*

and Class Structure in American Life (New York: Free Press, 1994); see also Charles Murray, *Losing Ground: American Social Policy 1950–1980*. 2nd ed. (New York: Basic Books, 1994).

[10]McLaughlin et al., *Changing Lives*.

[11]Quoted in *Gallup*, 312, September 1991, 5–6.

[12]*Gallup*, 312, September 1991, 5.

[13]Valerie Polakow, *Lives on the Edge: Single Mothers and Their Children in the Other America* (Chicago: Univ. of Chicago Press, 1993).

[14]*Harris*, 861011, February 18, 1987. 68 percent of men and 56 percent of women, *Gallup*, 312, September 1991.

[15]Paula Ries and Anne J. Stone, eds., *The American Woman 1992–93: A Status Report* (New York: W. W. Norton, 1992), 321; U.S. Department of Labor, Women's Bureau, "Facts on Working Women," 93–92 (June 1993).

[16]Ries and Stone, eds., *The American Woman 1992–93*, 319; Bureau of Labor Statistics, *Handbook of Labor Statistics,* Bulletin 2340 (August 1989), 27.

[17]See E. P. Lazear and R. T. Michael, "Family Size and Distribution of Real Per Capita Income," *American Economic Review* (1980) 70: 91–107. In 1972–73, when married women were entering the labor force in large numbers, two-person households in which the wife worked had an income 35 percent higher than those in which the wife did not work, although if you take into account taxes and other expenses associated with the wife's working (clothes, meals out, etc.) the net advantage reduced to 5 percent. By the late 1980s, working wives were contributing 23 to 28 percent of household income, although the actual percentage diminishes when you take expenditures into account.

[18]Cynthia Taeuber, ed. and comp., *Statistical Handbook of Women in America* (Phoenix, AZ: Oryx Press, 1991). In 1970, the mean income of couples without working wives was $6,800 less than those in which wives worked for wages; in 1984, families in which the wife did not work earned, on average, $12,600 less than those in which she did; and by 1987, they earned $14,000 less.

[19]U.S. Department of Labor, Women's Bureau, "Facts on Working Women."

[20]Alison Bernstein and Jacklyn Cock, "A Troubling Picture of Gender Equity," *The Chronicle of Higher Education* (June 15, 1994): B1. In 1990, women received 34 percent of medical degrees (up from 5.5 percent in 1960), 30.9 percent of degrees in dentistry (up from .8 percent in 1960), 42.2 percent of the degrees in law (up from 2.5 percent in 1960). Bureau of the Census, *Statistical Abstract of the United States 1993* (Washington, 1993), 185.

[21]From 1960 to 1980, full-time women workers on average earned roughly 60 percent of the hourly wages of men.

[22]Ries and Stone, eds., *The American Woman 1992–93*, 357. U.S. Department

of Labor, Women's Bureau, "Facts on Working Women"; 9, U.S. Bureau of Labor Statistics, *Handbook of Labor Statistics,* 1989.

[23]The figure is 47 percent, up from 40 percent in 1983. U.S. Department of Labor, Women's Bureau, "Facts on Working Women."

[24]In 1960, about 60 percent of all female workers were in occupations that were at least 80 percent female; by 1980, only 46 percent of female workers were.

[25]"1993 Salary Survey," *Working Woman* (January 1993), 43.

[26]Jean Reith Schroedel, *Alone in a Crowd: Women in the Trades Tell Their Stories* (Philadelphia: Temple Univ. Press, 1985), 117.

[27]Schroedel, *Alone in a Crowd,* 157; "1993 Salary Survey," *Working Woman* (January 1993), 43. On average, those who joined the police or became security guards or firefighters enjoyed a 20 percent increase in wages between 1983 and 1991. For mechanics and skilled repair workers, the increase was not quite as large, but the wages were consistently higher than for police, guards, or firefighters.

[28]Between 1980 and 1993, women's median income rose by 28.7 percent and men's declined by 1.3 percent. "1993 Salary Survey," *Working Woman* (January 1993), 40.

[29]Naomi Wolf, *Fire With Fire: The New Female Power and How It Will Change the 21st Century* (New York: Random House, 1993).

[30]*Gallup,* 202, July 1982. Half of the men polled consistently maintained that indeed women did not have equal opportunities. Women have always been more doubtful than men about the reality of equity, and during the past twenty years or so their doubts have markedly increased. Thus, in 1975, half of the women Gallup polled believed they had equal opportunities, but by 1982 only about 40 percent did. By 1982, women were also more likely to attribute the lack of opportunity to bias and discrimination in the job market. *Gallup,* 128, March 1976.

[31]*Gallup,* 202, July 1982.

[32]Anna Troy Segal with Wendy Zellner, "Corporate Women," *Business Week* (June 8, 1992): 74, put the percentage of women managers at 27 for 1981 and 41 for 1991. Rochelle Sharpe, "The Waiting Game," *The Wall Street Journal* (March 29, 1994), claims that in 1992, among the nation's two hundred largest companies women held only one quarter of the jobs that the EEOC classifies as "officials and managers." And Joann S. Lublin, "Firms Designate Some Openings for Women Only," *The Wall Street Journal* (February 7, 1994), says that in 1992, women held 8 percent of the top twenty jobs at 208 of the Fortune 500 companies.

[33]Dorothy J. Gaiter, "Black Women's Gains in Corporate America Outstrip Black Men's," *The Wall Street Journal* (March 8, 1994): 1.

[34]A poll in June 1954 showed that, by a majority of almost 90 percent, they approved of pay equity in general, with slightly more favoring equal pay for professionals and slightly fewer favoring equal pay for factory workers. To put these attitudes in context, it should be noted that fewer than two thirds of the British regarded equal pay for women and men as desirable. In the American survey women were strongest supporters of pay equity, but men favored it by more than a four to one ratio. Among regions, Southerners showed strongest approval. Little difference was observed by economic class or city vs. country. *Gallup*, 89, November 1972.

[35]68 percent–70 percent of women, 65 percent of men. *Gallup*, 128, March 1976.

[36]82 percent of men, 89 percent of women, 86 percent of whites, 84 percent of nonwhites say yes. So do 93 percent of college and 84 percent of high school, but only 73 percent of grade school. *Gallup*, 202, July 1982.

[37]99 percent of men and 98 percent of women. Gallup poll, August 23–25, 1993.

[38]Katherine S. Newman, *Falling From Grace: The Experience of Downward Mobility in the American Middle Class* (New York: Free Press, 1988); Jack Beatty, "Who Speaks for the Middle Class?" *The Atlantic Monthly* (May 1994): 65–79.

Six

WE ARE ALSO
OUR MOTHERS'
DAUGHTERS

N*icole Stewart left the affluent suburb of Shaker Heights,* Ohio, for Bennington College in the fall of 1959. By then, she had seen enough of the pain of relations between women and men to last her a lifetime. For as long as Nicole could remember, her mother, who had once shown real talent as a painter, had been drinking heavily. But the year Nicole entered high school, the drinking suddenly got worse. Nicole never fully understood the reasons. But she did know that her exotically beautiful mother, who had always seemed to live more in her own thoughts than in the real world, stopped paying attention to her appearance, almost stopped talking to Nicole and her thirteen-year-old younger sister, and frequently turned up with bruises on her face and arms. Nicole did not suspect her father of causing the bruises, for he was spending most nights away from home. He expressed his anger through silence, withdrawal, and visible disgust, which made Nicole's mother frantic. Only several years later, after Nicole had left for college and her mother was dying of sclerosis of the liver, did she begin to understand that her mother must have been having violent affairs with some of the men she met in the seedy bars where she sometimes spent afternoons and evenings.

Early on, Nicole acquired an uneasy feeling that her mother wanted or needed more love and attention than she was getting from her reserved husband. Nicole never blamed her father, whom she adored, but she, too, sometimes thought that he was not entirely there for either her mother or herself. Her mother was imaginative and passionate, her father was not. During high school, Nicole had compensated for the lack of attention by spending most of her time with a wild crowd. She never had a special boyfriend, but she did enjoy late nights, wild dancing, and fast cars. College removed her from daily contact with her parents' problems, but did not ease her craving for excitement—or for affection. The first year at Bennington, she met a young man from Williams College who showered her with attention and affection, and for a while his adoration gave her a warm sense of security. But by the spring of that year, she was becoming restless without quite understanding why. At the end of the semester, she told David, her boyfriend, that she needed some time to herself, and she went off to Cambridge with the intention of attending summer school at Harvard.

In Cambridge, Nicole moved into an apartment with two high-school women friends who were attending Radcliffe and had also decided to attend summer school. Nicole was stunned by how the year had changed Kathy and Sharon, who had left Shaker Heights in conventional kilts and Shetland sweaters. Kathy had cut off her rich auburn hair, which was now little longer than a boy's, and Sharon had let her black curls grow long and wild. On Nicole's first night, they invited her to go with them to a party at some friends' apartment in Central Square. By the time they arrived, the noisy crowd was packed into three smoke-filled rooms, and Nicole immediately recognized some of the smoke as marijuana. In one room, people were dancing to Buddy Holly, while in another one of the guests was playing folk songs on a guitar. In the third room, people were sprawled on the floor and a couple of bare mattresses, drinking corn liquor and smoking marijuana. At about three in the morning, when Kathy and Sharon had long since disappeared, Nicole left the party with Ron Bowles, whom she had met earlier in the evening. When they got back to her apartment, Ron, who was some combination of drunk and high, told her he would spend the night.

Nicole, who had had a good deal to drink herself, did not resist. To her surprise, the evening had eased her anxieties and almost made her feel comfortable. That night, Ron and Nicole began an affair that would last, off and on, for six years. Their relations were never smooth, or even happy, but Nicole could not break away. She soon discovered that Ron's drinking and drug use were serious problems. He never finished college or held a job, but each semester he attended a few classes at Tufts University. Occasionally, when the class caught his attention, he performed brilliantly. Most of the time, he failed or squeaked by with a D. The problem was not intelligence: Ron had an exceptionally good mind. Rather, he could not commit himself to any serious effort. And, as Nicole rapidly discovered, things were no different in his relations with women. More often than not, he would fail to turn up when promised or would turn up high or drunk. He claimed to love Nicole, but she knew he had other women on the side. Sometimes he withdrew into depression, sometimes he lashed out with cutting criticisms of Nicole's clinging and dependence.

By the end of the summer, even Nicole's radical friends were worried about her. She had arranged to transfer from Bennington to Boston University to be close to Ron. Ron, meanwhile, had started to live with a woman graduate student at Harvard. It was as if he meant to taunt Nicole, whom he still claimed to love. His weakness and unreliability only bound Nicole more tightly to him. When her friends asked her how she could continue to see a man who was openly flaunting an affair with another woman, she replied, "You just don't understand. You can't tell me what to do." During Nicole's junior year, her mother died, and her father immediately re-married. That summer, she went to Europe to learn French and to try to break free of Ron. She had only been there a month when she discovered she was pregnant. She came back. Ron, who was more heavily into drugs than ever, refused to marry her, although he still claimed to love her. Nicole's father arranged for an abortion at a private clinic in Cleveland. She spent the fall semester of her senior year with him and his new wife. In the spring she returned to Cam-bridge because she could not stand to be away from Ron, and they fell into the old patterns.

Nicole could not break with Ron because she was addicted to his special form of emotional abuse—a combination of love and aban-donment. Finally, when the woman graduate student with whom he had been living off and on put her foot down, he broke with her. Nicole was devastated. She felt the way she had felt as a girl when her mother withdrew into alcohol. But the depression forced her to see a therapist, and she began to understand why she was driven to love someone who had so little to give. As a child and then as a confused adolescent, she had come to associate love with two par-ents who, for different reasons, were never "there" for her. Two years later, she started medical school with the intention of becoming a therapist for troubled adolescents. Shortly after she finished her resi-dency, she married a successful lawyer, whom she had met during her first summer in Cambridge and remained friends with since.

Women have always known that sex and love can be dangerous. If sex is a joining of bodies and love a joining of souls, both are a joining of differences in which both partners seek to lose as well as gain themselves. This is a dangerous game. Women (and men) may easily get hurt. But throughout time, women, as readily as men, have risked the hurt in their quest for the joy and satisfaction promised by the union of difference. And throughout time, mothers have passed these stories on to daughters and done their best to prepare them.

The sexual and economic revolutions have cut women loose from such traditional roles and expectations. Even girls barely in their teens are now free to engage in sexual relations as they please without much, if any, guidance from parents, teachers, or other adults. But women's new freedom has neither made sex and love any less dangerous nor diminished their appeal. If anything, by stripping away the conventions that were intended to offer women at least minimal protection, sexual freedom has made sex and love more dangerous than ever. For without conventions that encourage men to respect women's sexual vulnerability, women are "free" to confront men as equals—free to take pleasure where they find it and to be hurt and abandoned if something goes wrong—which it frequently does.

◉ Our mothers and grandmothers understood women's sexual vulnerability, especially as manifested in their ability to bear children and in their special responsibility to care for them. Women do suffer discrete vulnerabilities that may expose them to physical, emotional, and economic abuse by men. The literature and lore of all cultures abounds with women who have been used and abused, deserted, or simply taken advantage of. It also abounds with women who have found passion, meaning, and fulfillment in their relations with men and their love for children. Commonly, women's vulnerability has been the stuff of romance and tragedy, rarely of political programs. Women have understood both the dangers and the promise of sex and love as the stuff of everyday life—as an integral part of what it means to be a woman, and many still cherish a dream of love even if they recognize that reality differs from the "happily-ever-after" stories. Feminists tend to disapprove of love stories, arguing that most cultures, especially our own, have invoked love and devotion to coerce women into roles that perpetuate their subordination.

Feminists have been lobbying to transform female vulnerability into a political agenda. With reason, they insist that no woman should accept exploitation and abuse, much less accept them as norms, and feminist campaigns have effectively drawn public attention to rape, battering, and sexual harassment. Indeed, with much greater success than many feminists acknowledge, they have aroused public opinion against such indignities. To take a relatively benign example, men, who only a few years ago would have thought nothing of hugging an unreceptive female coworker, now think twice about it.

Some feminists, not satisfied with these gains, have turned a worthy campaign for equity, justice, and common decency into an assault on all manifestations of masculinity. Believe it or not, there are feminist theorists, genuinely intelligent and with well-earned high academic credentials, who denounce an erection as "an act of aggression." The terribly punitive temper of our times forbids us from laughing, but we might be permitted to object that the denunciation can only numb our consciousness of genuine male aggression— of which there is more than enough to concern us. For a denunciation of erections is tailor-made to convince sensible women, especially those with a sense of humor, that male aggression can't be all bad. The radicals' penchant for upping the ante into a sex war puts at risk the real gains that have been made. This is not primarily a question of male "backlash." Pushed to the wall, men may well begin to fight back, but, more important and dangerous, many women are beginning to see the struggle against men as actually an attack on their own femininity and sense of what it means to be a woman. Increasingly, the "backlash" against feminism is coming from women who are appalled by the claims and efforts presumptuously made on their behalf.

It is hard to read feminist indictments of male brutality without concluding that men are naturally brutal. But if so, should we not conclude that men and women are naturally different? Most feminists reject that obvious conclusion, fearing that any recognition of sexual differences might justify policies that exclude women from desirable opportunities. So, they do not want to hear of natural or biological differences. Their position is puzzling since many also write of women's different sense of morality or women's different "ways of knowing." But even those who suggest that women are morally superior or have a special compassion for the vulnerable deny that such differences mean that women might have different talents and ambitions than men—that they might not really want to do all of the things that men do.[1]

We are left with an absurdity: Men are portrayed as sexually predatory, and women are encouraged to see themselves as equal to and no different from men. To date, no one has explained satisfactorily how men may be sexual brutes and women their victims—how men may be vicious predators and women embodiments of mercy and compassion—when there is no essential difference between them. But I am happy to leave that problem to postmodern feminist theorists. Meanwhile, most women sensibly proceed on the assumption that women and men do differ, at least with respect to their experience of sexuality and their sense of personal relations. Most women, in other words, seem perfectly comfortable with the idea that a woman might perform brilliantly as a pilot or a lawyer or a law enforcement officer and still be happy to think of herself as a woman.

Since childhood, officer Dora McKinney of the Dade County Police Department in Florida had become accustomed to being complimented on her delicate blond prettiness. In a pinch, she had even used people's delight in her feminine charm to wiggle her way out of a difficult situation. Neither her father nor her teachers could ever stay angry with her for long, and, as she got older, the boys who crowded around her would put up with almost anything. Dora understood the value of her looks and took pride in looking her best. But a fierce independence accompanied her self-conscious femininity. After finishing high school at the top of her class, she went on to nursing school even though most of her friends were getting married. After graduation, she pleased her family by marrying Patrick, one of her high school boyfriends, but she insisted upon taking a job as a nurse. The marriage proved stormy, primarily because of Patrick's jealous, moody temperament. The birth of their two children, Julie and Tommy, eased things for a while. Dora adored her children and, for a few years, was happy to stay home with them. But when Tommy, the younger, started kindergarten, she started to talk about going back to work.

Eventually, Dora found the perfect part-time job at a local clinic, but her happiness in her work only intensified Patrick's jealousy and black moods. After two more impossible years, Dora moved out and filed for divorce. She had to work full-time to support herself and the children, but her mother helped with child care, and her life rapidly settled into a comfortable routine. As beautiful as ever, Dora attracted men without lifting a finger. But this time, she decided she wanted something else. As a child, she had dreamed of becoming a police officer like her father, but during the 1970s it had not seemed possible. In the early 1980s, Dora began to believe she might realize her dream. She enrolled in night classes and soon found that she was doing wonderfully well. With assistance from her parents, she completed the training in three years and joined the police force. Two years later, she was studying for her sergeant's exam.

Dora's silvery blond curls, purple eyes, and carefully manicured fingernails contrasted sharply with her severe uniform. Indeed, when I met her, she looked a bit like Goldie Hawn in *Private Benjamin*. And, on the police force, her looks brought her more trouble than advantages. During her first couple of years, she warred constantly with sexual harassment from her fellow officers, who enjoyed nothing more than treating her like a "girl." Dora gave as good as she got. Her acid words and contemptuous looks normally reduced the offenders to pouting little boys, and when words and looks were not enough, she would rap knuckles or elbows with her stick. "It's a colossal pain," she told me, "but I love my job, and I'll be damned if those yokels are going to spoil it for me. Their problem," she added, "is that they don't know how to take orders from a woman—especially not if she's pretty." For Dora, pretty and good cop were perfectly compatible, and she is determined to be both. But then, Larry, the man she has been seeing for the past year, agrees.

Dora has as little patience with bullying men as any feminist, whether the men are domineering husbands or hassling coworkers. Yet her insistence that men behave themselves and respect her does not conflict with her enjoyment of her own femininity. Feminists who denounce male brutality claim to speak for all women, yet we all know that women divide decisively in their economic prospects and interests, not to mention their social experience. In many ways women have more in common with the men of their class, race, or social group than they have in common with women of different classes and races. Increasingly, feminists acknowledge these differences, but they resist the corollary that many women may feel closer to some men than they do to all women. So the question arises: Just what do women have in common? When income, education, ethnicity, race, and other specifics of a woman's life and identity are stripped away, what can possibly justify the feminist claim to speak of and for "women"? Precious little, you may answer. For all that remains is a woman's being the daughter of a woman and the ability of her own body to bear a child. But that precious little is indeed precious, and it brings us back to some basic differences between women and men. In that core lies not only women's greatest vulnerability, but our sense of personal identity, which resolutely resists politicization.

Throughout history, women's bodies have simultaneously been the source of our greatest vulnerability and our greatest strength and joy. As the title of the pathbreaking women's health guide, *Our Bodies, Ourselves*, suggests, women's bodies have helped to shape women's identities. Men may be raped and in prison frequently are, but rape remains preeminently a woman's story. Conservatives accept all too lightly the notion that men have always been the primary sexual predators and women those primarily preyed upon. The conservative analysis of men's propensity for sexual aggression has much in common with the more radical feminists' rabid condemnation of it. Conservatives yield nothing to feminists in their hostility to rape and abuse, but they conclude that we would solve most of the problems by strengthening families under the leadership and protection of men. Radical feminists, in contrast, insist that most violence and abuse occurs within families and that it is high time to treat all men as the potential rapists they are. The problem for most women is that neither the conservative nor the radical feminist position adequately captures the everyday reality of their own lives.

No one doubts that women are sexually vulnerable, but most women do not see victimization or unrelenting struggles against male brutality as the main story of their lives. In the measure that feminists seize upon male brutality as an excuse for everything wrong in their lives, they degrade rather than empower women. Feminist stories of victimization are no more convincing than conservative stories of women's need to rely on the protection of men. Most women know that they have fashioned their own lives from a mixture of pleasure and danger—of good and bad—that has little to do with such abstractions. And the bolder spirits cannot be faulted for finding some pleasure in the danger, at least within limits. Women rely upon common sense and direct experience. That is what used to be called folk wisdom, and notwithstanding the rapid changes of today, more women live by it than public discussions even hint at.

Today, as in the past, women transmit folk wisdom through stories, through the endless flow of conversation that eases and makes sense of our lives and binds us to those with whom we share it. Our talk about men, even when harshly critical, often merges with talk of love and romance. It blends with the dreams embodied in the romances we read and the films and soap operas we watch. Romances, films, and soaps obviously spin fantasies that have little to do with everyday life. Women turn to them precisely for escape. But for most of us, the lines blur, and it is an easy step from losing oneself in a romance or reading a magazine for advice to trading stories with other women. The shared experiences of these conversations acknowledge and domesticate the dangers of sexual encounters with men, weaving a web of lore that binds women to one another.

We rely heavily on stories to make sense of our lives. As the somewhat awkward six- and seven-year-old daughter of middle-class, intellectual parents, I would wheel my treasured new bicycle around the front yard of our house, pretending to be a "normal" girl named Nancy who rode her bike to school. We lived far enough out in the country that I had to ride the schoolbus. My mother, long before healthy food had become fashionable, insisted on feeding me whole wheat bread. Possessed of exquisite taste, she dressed me in simple, elegant clothes—vaguely reminiscent of those occasionally pictured in *Vogue*—when everyone else was wearing plaid taffeta and Mary Janes. "Normal," about which I instinctively felt I understood very little, promised a safe, predictable way to ease my growing up. At about the same time, I delighted in making long braids (from left-over rags from the rugs my grandmother used to make) and pinning them to my head to pretend that I was like Laura Ingalls Wilder, whose *Little House* books I loved. Other girls had different heroines, some radically different, but I am willing to bet that all of us had one or more to help us weave the seemingly random events of our lives into patterns.

The most significant aspect of those stories may well have been that in hearing or reading about other girls and women, we assimilated bits of them into our own experience, we anchored them in our own lives. Susan Douglas, writing of women's relation to the mass media, insists that you can always tell a genuine woman member of the baby-boomer generation because she will know by heart every single word of The Shirelles' hit song "Will You Love Me Tomorrow?"[2] Like the traditional Scottish ballads that women once sang at work, the Shirelles' music told of women's experiences of love and loss, of the dangers and uncertainties, as well as the delights, of courtship. In singing those songs, as in telling stories, women took possession of their experience, even when it was painful or ended badly. As Douglas insists, the excitement of the Shirelles came from their being a girl group that sang girls' music for girls. She sees the Shirelles as something new in the world of mass media, but in telling women's stories for other women they were not new at all. And the women who delighted in them were not new in relishing women's stories of women's experience.

Women never outgrow the need for stories about women's lives, even if, as we get older, the stories change. And although recent generations have been establishing new patterns and expectations, many of the stories that we cherish and that most deeply touch us have much in common with stories that women throughout time have relied upon to make sense of their lives. The stories always contain a measure of fantasy, a bit of how we would like our lives to be. Sometimes, especially when real life gets especially painful, fantasy gets the upper hand. Even then, it can provide a kind of safety valve or an escape that permits us to bear the pain more easily. Or it can simply provide a bit of color or hope in a drab life. But among all the variations, certain kinds of stories tend to become so general that they shape very different kinds of dreams for the lives of very different kinds of women. Among them, love, marriage, and motherhood have always enjoyed a privileged place.

Marriage and motherhood retain a powerful hold on very different kinds of women's imaginations. We have modified the story here and there, but nothing has replaced it. "Nice" girls may now have sex before marriage without penalty, but most continue to hope that sooner or later they will marry. The number of single mothers has grown dramatically, but more often than not the women in question have wanted to become mothers and hoped for marriage as well. The great rise in the rate of divorce has barely affected the story of marriage at all. Second, third, or more marriages follow early mistakes, but marriage endures. Many women have expanded that story to include their own careers, but a large number of successful career women acknowledge that they, too, see themselves as wives and mothers.

Today these oldest of women's stories have become a battleground across which two warring ideological camps hurl charges and countercharges. One side punitively asserts that good girls don't have sex. The other side adamantly counters that good girls are entitled to do as they please. One side argues that mothers should stay at home and take care of the children who need them. The other retorts that mothers, like everyone else, have a self-evident right to develop and enjoy the fruits of their own talents. One side assumes that every fetus has a God-given right to be born. The other assumes that a woman has an absolute right to her own body. Thus, conservatives preach duty, sacrifice, traditional values, and womanly virtue, while feminists preach autonomy, self-determination, and independence. Conservatives condemn feminists as selfish, irresponsible, and man-hating. Feminists condemn conservatives as repressive and women-hating. It is hard to imagine what conservatives make of the many feminists who are devoted wives and mothers. It is no less hard to imagine what feminists make of self-reliant and professionally accomplished conservative women, some of whom even call themselves feminists and fight for women's rights as hard as left-wing feminists do.

Meanwhile, many—I believe most—American women try to make sense of their lives, in full knowledge that neither polarized story will fit the rich and messy complexities of the lives we actually live. We want pieces of each story: a successful career and a happy marriage; equal pay for equal work and conditions that allow us to care for our children; freedom from sexual harassment and discrimination and a measure of sexual freedom. Sensible women, knowing they cannot "have it all," do not want to be trapped in one story or the other. Feminism is not essentially a story about our lives, but neither is full-time domesticity, which many conservatives push even when they know it is not possible for most women, even those who are most committed to their families.

This war of "values" ignores the circumstances of women's everyday lives and fondest hopes. The hopes vary tremendously from one woman to the next according to race, ethnicity, income, education, age, and individual preferences. They vary according to personality (the unique combination of genetic inheritance and early experience that shapes our expectations and ambitions) and according to luck (the sum of the accidents and contingencies that life has given us). But when all the variations are taken into account—and they are much more numerous than the few mentioned—women's stories still seem to cluster in recognizable patterns.

What remains striking is how much women of different

backgrounds and ages have in common. It is rare for one woman to talk to another for more than a few minutes without stumbling on something that leads to a heartfelt: "I know just how you feel." Frequently, the common ground appears in response to a passing reference to some man in the other woman's life. "Oh, men! Tell me about it." And a smile of understanding will greet the other woman's frustration with a household chore that has been left undone or poorly done, or some clothes that have been forgotten at the cleaners, or a message that has not been delivered. Young women share impatience with men who want sexual relations too fast; with men who do not know how to be just friends or who want to be only friends; with men who never seem to show up on time.

African-American mothers worry constantly about their husbands, boyfriends, and sons—"those black boys," as they are wont to call them—who so easily get into trouble. Veronica Taylor, who is now in her fifties, left her husband years ago and now works in a wealthy section of Atlanta as a full-time housekeeper to support herself and her teenage son. She nearly fainted when she heard he had been arrested for murder. Later, she explained to the woman friends from her church, who had rallied to support her, "One of his buddies pulled a gun during a quarrel, and my boy turned it back on the buddy just to protect himself." One of those friends, Selina Brown, understood perfectly. Selina works as a manicurist and has been happily married for years to "a good, steady man," but she worries that something similar could happen to her son. After Selina's son, Lester, graduated high school, he had a terrible time finding a job. She insists that he is a good boy, but the part-time jobs he could find did not pay much and left him with too much free time on his hands. So, he spends most of his time working out in a gym downtown. Selina is delighted that he is burning off energy, "but you know the kind of guys who hang out at that place . . ."

One day Gloria Patterson, who was working in the lunchroom of an Atlanta school, got word that her sister's boy had been killed up in Jersey. At first she thought the shooting was random, "but they told me he had fallen in with some dudes who did drugs, so what could you expect?" She had always feared that something like that would happen, and several years previously she had sent her own son, Johnny, off to the army right after high school. Johnny had a great record in the service, but after he got out he had as much trouble as Lester in finding a job. So he spent his free time hanging out with his old friends, and eventually he was picked up for driving them to a drug deal. Gloria never did learn whether Johnny knew what was going down. She was sure he did not do drugs himself, "because he promised me he wouldn't, and I always check his clothes and bureau. He says he didn't know that the other guys were into that stuff." But she worried herself sick, spending hours with her sisters and with me and her church friends trying to piece the story together. As soon as Johnny was cleared, Gloria, whose husband was gravely ill, sent him back to low-country Georgia to live with her father, a minister, "because Daddy will see he gets his head together."

Aprill Ravenel, a single mother who is working as a secretary in a thriving engineering firm, wants her son "to be a responsible, productive adult, whatever he chooses to do in life." She worries constantly about his future. Looking at the world around her, she has trouble imagining what things will be like when Jahmil grows up, but she does think "It's going to be easier for a black female than a black male." She does her best to make him strong and responsible, nurturing him and insisting that he pick up his things and help with the dishes, but she cannot even say "I can empathize with what we call the 'plight of the black man,' because I can't." All she knows is that she has black male friends with master's degrees in accounting, "with degrees and experience and everything," who cannot find jobs. Aprill took Jahmil to see the film *Menace II Society*, the unrelentingly violent film about a group of black bullies, so he would understand that some people live that way. They themselves do not live in such an environment and do not normally see that kind of violence, but she wanted Jahmil to see it because she knows he confronts peer pressure that she cannot begin to understand. She also knows how easily one can get discouraged. And especially: "The black man can get discouraged."

Black or white, married women agree that, more than occasionally, the men they most love are, well, just plain impossible. More than once, out of the blue, a woman has said to me, "You know, the trouble with men is that they always want to be with you." And it matters not at all that she is echoing an oft-heard complaint that men file against women. Martha Miller, the teacher and graduate student from Baltimore, is devoted to her husband, Michael, an airline pilot, but thinks she is "lucky because he is gone as often as he is." But then, I would have trouble thinking of a woman I know, of any age, class, color, or ethnicity, who has a family and does not consider time alone in her own house a luxury. An old friend of my mother blurted out that her dream was to be alone, pull the shades, strip off her clothes, and eat a pint of ice cream without interruption. Michael, like many other husbands, wants companionship and attention at home—just to have Martha sit next to him to watch the news or something like that. "He really needs that." His desire for her company makes it difficult for her just to shut herself "in the other room and do schoolwork."

Martha recently confessed that one of her pet peeves was Michael's tendency to interrupt without apparent thought to what she might be doing: "It just kills me. I'm busy in the kitchen and he'll see something on television and he'll say, 'Hey, Martha, come here,' as if I'm not doing anything." But if the tables are turned, if he has work to do, "then you've got to leave him alone. You can't go near him." And I have yet to meet a woman of any race at any level of income or education who does not agree. Men just never seem to understand that women need privacy just as much as they do.

For as long as anyone can remember, women have had their lists of the ways in which men who claim to be serious adults behave like thoughtless boys. Martha Miller thinks her husband even shops like a boy. Every time she sends him off to the grocery store, he returns with vast supplies of jalapeño peppers, marinated artichoke hearts, and assorted exotic cocktail foods they will never use. (My husband laughs: "In case you haven't noticed," he says, "you're much more guilty of that than I am." He is wrong, of course.) Andrea Silvestri, who grew up in Detroit, chokes on her own laughter as she remembers a male friend who decided to cook a twenty-five-pound turkey for the two of them for Thanksgiving. Well, his brother was cooking a twenty-two-pound turkey and he was not to be outdone. So what if his brother was cooking for his family of six, plus assorted relatives? The point was who cooked the larger turkey, not whom they were cooking it for. Andrea saw a simple case of male competition. The boys were still at it.

Where women used to trade their inherited lore about the quirks of the men in their lives over sandboxes, pie-making, sewing, church sociables, and sickbeds, today they are just as likely to trade it over a computer workstation, a business lunch, an office meeting, or a commuter flight. Traveling a lot, I sometimes use my frequent-flyer miles to upgrade to first class, and I have learned that most of the other people in first are likely to have done the same. So, especially at peak commuting hours, first class feels a good deal like your basic old boys' club. Only these days, the club invariably includes a number of women, all of us just as tired at the end of a long day as the men. Not so long ago, I was drawn into conversation with two of my fellow passengers, a black woman who has been a major figure in a national educational organization and a white woman who was returning from a technical sales convention. Within minutes of finding out what the others did, there we were talking about husbands, gardens, kids, and elderly parents. And then we fell into what our husbands would or would not have remembered to do in our absence. The professional success and substantial salaries that had brought us together in the first place receded into the background, and, as we relaxed, we fell into conversational patterns that our mothers and grandmothers would have recognized immediately.

My traveling companions and I were doing nothing unusual. Countless women in all income brackets, like their grandmothers and mothers before them, patiently and impatiently share complaints about men's incorrigible thoughtlessness: Men talk through women's silences as if women had no private thoughts; men never assume their full share of domestic responsibilities; men flip the television channel in the middle of something you are watching. But like the many other women who complain knowingly of men's predictable failings, we could not wait to get home, and, to many people's amazement, each of us expected to have dinner waiting for us on the table. (I only hope that their husbands cook as well as my own.)

Deborah Tannen, in her book, *You Just Don't Understand*, delightfully captures the dramatic differences in women's and men's conversational styles.[3] Women, she demonstrates, effectively speak a different dialect—or what she calls "genderlect"—than men. Women communicate in a language of "connection and intimacy"; men communicate in a language of "status and independence." Small wonder, then, that communication between women and men can so often fail entirely. Reading some of her conversations leaves us not knowing whether to laugh or cry. We have all been there at one time or another. Women enjoy talking about the details of personal lives and motivations, men about news and sports. Women care that the people they are close to look at them when they are talking to them, men do not. Women just plain want their husbands to talk to them, but their husbands frequently prefer to remain silent. Remember Edith and Archie Bunker? How many of us have not prodded the man we live with to get his nose out of the newspaper or his eyes off the television screen and talk to us, or at least pay attention while we are talking to him?

The differences that Tannen finds in women's and men's conversational styles strongly resemble the differences that other observers have found in women's and men's tastes, their senses of morality, their patterns of behavior, their ways of thinking about the world. Tannen finds that these differences hold true for all classes, races, and ethnic groups and that the styles women mobilize in their interactions with men shape their interactions with other women. If anything, I suspect, the differences hold more true for groups with lower incomes and less education. When I visit Bensonhurst, the working-class Italian-American neighborhood in Brooklyn where my husband grew up, I always find it easier to talk to the women than the men, not because the men are the least bit indifferent, disrespectful, or unfriendly—quite the contrary—but because we women recognize that we have much in common that is special to us.

Similarly, Gloria Patterson and I, who come from radically different backgrounds, have had little difficulty in understanding the essentials of one another's experience. Yes, I am more affluent and have significantly more education, but from early on in our friendship, Gloria decided that those things made little or no difference. After all, she told me, "You and I are both Gemini, and that means we see things the same." So we traded notes about our parents and about our husbands' cholesterol, about clothes and lipstick shades, about the wear-and-tear of houseguests, and the pleasure of talking to our sisters. And once, after she heard me participate in a meeting with a group of men, she told me with genuine delight, "Oh, when you talked, they all shut up and listened." Her pleasure in what she regarded as a woman's triumph was grounded in her sense of what we as women shared.

Tannen's book must have struck a chord, for it was a best-seller. Many feminists, however, have dismissed her work with impatience. Feminists worry that the differences between women's and men's styles of talking, thinking, and relating to others reinforce men's power over women. In their view, the difference between the sexes cannot be separated from men's historical domination over women. Those who assume that difference cannot be separated from domination conclude that differences must be rejected and combated. When I remarked to my husband that most women feel that men do not talk to them seriously, he laughed, replying: "Men who do not talk to women seriously do not talk to men seriously either, except when business compels them to." And that is very much Tannen's point. For she has found that on most occasions women talk to men the way they talk to other women, and men talk to women the way they talk to other men. Tannen refreshingly suggests that we accept as given the asymmetry between women and men. How it arose and whether it is good or bad matter less than its existence. Women have always had to confront difference as a matter of attitude as well as biology, and that confrontation has shaped who we are. The differences between women and men that we intuitively recognize may come from nature, culture, or both. Beyond a certain point, where they come from matters little or not at all.

What does matter is that women and men have always shared the same world but on different terms, which are changing dramatically. As women have entered a "man's" world of politics and work, they have had to struggle both to adapt to the world and to get the world to adapt to them. In retrospect, it seems extraordinary how much of both has occurred within a few decades and yet how much remains to be done. But even as women become more assertive and confident and even as the men have, however grudgingly, begun to accommodate women's values and needs, most women's personalities have remained more similar to those of their foremothers than to those of the men they know. Feminists themselves tacitly acknowledge these patterns when they claim that women derive important strength from the ties and experiences they share with other women. But even as they make the claim, they deny that women and men differ in any essential way.

Although most feminists reject the idea of innate differences between women and men, recent research, largely conducted by women, confirms their importance in human development.[4] Hormones influence the development of fetuses from the beginning. What researchers do not yet understand is how much and in what ways those hormonal differences influence later development. After all, the women who are conducting the most sophisticated research are themselves accomplished scientists—hardly a traditional female occupation. Indeed, their findings confirm what most of us intuitively know about women and men. Yes, they are, in both specific and elusive ways, different. No, those differences do not predict the accomplishments of adults, nor do they justify any intellectual or professional discrimination against women.

The findings about sexual difference thus confront us with a paradox. We have no grounds to assume that women's moral sense differs from that of men, that women have different ways of knowing than men, or that women as a group are, in any way, less intellectually competent than men. Furthermore, we know that we live in a world in which women must be able to support themselves and their children decently. Justice and decency demand that women enjoy the same opportunities as men to realize their potential and reap the rewards of their labors. At the same time, we know that women, but not men, may bear and nurse children. And we have reason to believe that most women share a lore and culture of everyday life that differs from those of most men and that women experience sex differently than men. So we are left with the confusing knowledge that women are both very much the same as men and significantly different.

This knowledge confronts us with problems that most radical feminists resist, namely that the ways in which women and men share the world is richly and infuriatingly complex. It is a knowledge that challenges our imaginations and, above all, the ways in which we think about personal and public solutions to problems women face as women. For this knowledge allows no easy and equitable solutions. In denying its complexity, the warring claims of the religious right and the radical feminists only exacerbate the problems.

The differences between women and men become most evident in sexual relations. As women and men come to share more and more aspects of our rapidly changing world, especially in the workplace, sexual attitudes have been thrown into sharper and sharper relief. The differences, and the risks to which they have exposed women, have led to the charge that we live in a "rape culture," in which men automatically assume it is their God-given right to use and abuse women for their own pleasure.[5] Until recently, all societies, including our own, have taken men's brutality against women for granted. Over time, public tolerance of physical and sexual violence against women has steadily decreased, although the acts themselves may not have. As recently as thirty years ago, a cloak of silence muffled women's stories of abuse.

I still remember my shock when in high school one of my closest friends told me that her mother and father slept in separate rooms because when her father got drunk, which he frequently did, he became sexually abusive. I no longer remember if, at the time, I knew that such things ever happened; I assuredly did not know they happened in the families of the CEOs of major companies behind the walls of large houses in the Hamptons. Today, stories of male brutality have moved into the open. From the media and personal conversations, we all know stories of men who abuse, rape, beat, stalk, and kill the women who should most be able to trust them. We do not know how much of the story is new and how much just more openly reported and discussed.

When my husband was growing up in an Italian-American community in Brooklyn where "family values" included a large dose of physical violence, he frequently saw neighborhood women on the street, camouflaged by sunglasses that the weather did not call for. He added that the women of the few Jewish and Irish families in the neighborhood fared no better. Everyone, he tells me, knew that the woman was hiding the bruises of an especially acrimonious domestic dispute. But few commented and, under normal circumstances, no one outside the family would have dreamed of intervening. On the rare occasions the abuse exceeded community norms, the men of the woman's family and their friends took it upon themselves to punish the abuser.

Even now, most women do not find personal stories of violence and abuse easy to tell. The world is more receptive and less likely to "blame the victim," but women themselves often wonder what they have done wrong. Some women, like Gloria Patterson, walk out. Other women turn to therapists and social services to help them muster the self-confidence to break free. Sadly, for whatever mixture of psychological and economic reasons, some women just go back for more. Adult women have their own ways of coping, or not coping, with male brutality. Deena Wright, who had grown up in a crowded trailer and moved into another when she married, also tried to walk. Early in her marriage to Chris, a drinker who could never hold a steady job and tended to hit her when he was drinking, she left Berkeley County, South Carolina, for New York. Chris followed her, and after she became pregnant she decided to return to Berkeley County without him. Again, he followed her; again, she became pregnant; and this time she decided it was easier to let him stay. At least in Berkeley County she had friends and relatives to turn to.

Deena's case resembles that of many women, who find it difficult to free themselves of men, especially when there are children. Sharon Miller, a white dental hygienist in Toledo, Ohio, left her salesman husband when she caught him fooling around with other women. Her job permitted her to support their two kids, and, as the kids got older, she went back to business school at night. But she lamented to me that many of her friends were not faring as well. She especially worried about her friend Cheryl Polasky, who left her husband and then could not make ends meet on her job as a hairstylist. Eventually, Cheryl remarried, but this time she made up her mind to endure almost anything rather than face economic insecurity again—and the "anything" included looking the other way when her new husband showed too much interest in her fifteen-year-old daughter. Lorena Bobbitt notoriously returned her husband's physical abuse in kind, cutting off his penis to express her anger. None of these stories of male brutality are ones that many young women want to hear. The recent furor about acquaintance rape on campuses and the "Take Back the Night" vigils in which young women speak out about the abuse they have suffered or fear they will suffer are another matter entirely.

Feminists have consistently protested against the dangers to which sexuality exposes women, but recently, as in the furor over acquaintance rape, some feminists have intensified their campaigns. According to the alarmists, women's lives are dominated by sexual dangers—rape, acquaintance rape, sexual harassment. Few have been willing to draw the obvious conclusion that the sexual freedom, if not accompanied by some self-protective prudence, might contribute to the danger. After all, aren't we all in favor of sexual liberation? So feminists have intensified their claims that men are inherently dangerous. And many have begun to favor a variety of measures that would coerce or reform men out of their allegedly natural rapist tendencies.

On some days it is hard not to believe that our society has collapsed into an all-out war between the sexes. Each day brings news of yet another example of women who have been assaulted, raped, or murdered by strangers or kin. Television gets rich by terrorizing us with horror stories as readily as by selling us Tylenol. Like a tidal wave, the statistics that chronicle the violent abuse of women by men mount, drowning what remains of our notions of the civility— to say nothing of chivalry and protection—in which women were presumed to be swathed.

What do the numbers mean? Which ones can we trust? Has violence against women been steadily increasing? Or do we now describe as violent behavior that which would only recently have been taken as permissible or even normal? Has feminism forced into the open the violence once quietly practiced within the sanctity of homes? The answers are hard to come by. Even experts differ over whether sexual violence against women has increased or whether it is simply more likely to be reported. But if only the reporting has increased, then we are making some progress since women would not bother to report behavior that they did not expect the authorities to regard as criminal.

More often than not, feminists advance statistics about violence against women to promote a perception of women as the bloodied victims of men's war of conquest against them. But while the claims of victimization apply to some situations, they have been wildly exaggerated. Men are still almost twice as likely to kill women through spousal abuse than women are to kill men—but that means more women kill men than many have thought.[6] Scholars claim that women and men now engage in domestic violence in about equal numbers, although women may be less likely to initiate physical confrontations. And although men are more likely than women to molest children, women commit more than half of all child murders.[7] During the past few decades, the United States has become a terrifyingly violent society, but the worst manifestations of violence do not lie in the murder of women by husbands or boyfriends. Indeed, since the late 1970s, the number of women so killed has dropped by 18 percent.

Ironically, many of the preferred feminist solutions to the perceived problems of sexual violence against women resemble nothing so much as a restoration of the paternal authority against which feminists claim to be in revolt. But the authority they favor is not that of fathers over families, but of the government over us all. If men are naturally brutal, then their brutality must be forcibly reined in. Katie Roiphe, writing of the hysteria over acquaintance rape, has made the point clearly. And although she minimizes the sexual danger to which some women are demonstrably exposed, her basic point deserves serious consideration. The demand that the "authorities" protect women from men carries the depressing suggestion that independent, "liberated" women are not capable of taking care of themselves—or capable of showing the prudence to steer clear of the most dangerous situations. One of the abiding lessons of female lore has always been what today would be called internalization, namely the ability to develop personal standards of conduct and accountability—that is, to realize independence by taking responsibility for oneself, all the while knowing that some things will always be beyond control.

Recently Christie Denton, a young woman who had just graduated from the University of Wisconsin, came up to me at a reception to tell me how much she enjoyed my work. Grateful and flattered, I chatted with her for a while about her and her friends' views of feminism. And although she kept insisting that she agreed with me, it was not clear what the agreement meant. "Well," she said, "take sex." By all means, I thought. "You see," she continued, "my mother has the most unreasonable views. She does not understand anything." Without admitting that it struck me as possible that her mother and I might have more in common than Christie thought, I asked her to explain. "Well," Christie exploded, "can you imagine that my mother does not believe that a young woman has a right to be naked in a man's room with the door locked and still say no?" "Oh!" I responded, "imagine that." And, as gracefully as possible, I changed the subject. But my mind was reeling. Any woman always has a right to say no, but how could this intelligent young woman not understand that there were likely to be consequences if she exercised her right by engaging in heavy petting with a young man, going to his room, removing her clothes, initiating sexual foreplay, and then just saying no? Like Christie's mother, I could not help thinking that it would be more prudent if she said no before taking off all of her clothes. Feminists argue that women's sexual freedom represents a liberation from patriarchal male control, but young women like Christie apparently believe that sexual freedom means they can push sexual games to the limit, then change their minds, and, if the young men do not respect their no, turn to the college authorities or the police to punish him. This behavior, as Katie Roiphe has suggested, falls far short of taking responsibility for your own freedom.

It is not surprising that many women turn to romances and Gothic novels for stories that grip their imaginations. If the numbers who read those novels are any indication, many women, at some level, still entertain the fantasy of a strong, daring man who can literally sweep any heroine off her feet. We may be confident that most do not expect the men they encounter in the real world to resemble the heroes they meet in the pages of romance. As women know, the physical strength that can protect is the strength that can bully, batter, and abuse. But even women who know more than they want to about the dangers often cling, against evidence and reason, to the dream of the man who can make everything right and keep them safe.

The image of male strength, like the image of female nurture, springs from children's longing for the security and unquestioning love they expect fathers and mothers to provide. Even as they learn more about the realities of the world, vestiges of the myth persist. Young girls in Dorchester, who have seen the worst that male brutality has to offer and who have never lived with their own fathers, yearn to belong to one of the tough, successful neighborhood kingpins, knowing full well that he has a long history of knocking women around, may run with a gang and deal drugs, and probably will soon be dead or in jail. Even successful, professionally ambitious college women hope the right man will shield them from the worst bumps of the world. Thus one unusually bright young law school graduate, who excels at the fundamentally combative specialty of trial law, told me that she would never consider a man who did not exceed six feet in height. I hope she was kidding, but I do not think so.

Little girls grow up with stories of love and marriage. Even today, when they are learning to be tough and self-reliant, whether in school, at sports, or on the streets, the story lurks in the back of their minds, frequently encouraged by mothers, who want to see their daughters happily settled. More and more mothers also want their daughters prepared for economic independence and expect their unmarried daughters to be sexually active. Mothers still try to warn their daughters about the high risks of marrying the wrong man. And young girls still cling to the dream of a lasting relationship with a man.

Maria Ramirez, a Puerto Rican woman in her forties with grown children and working for a GED, has been happily married since she was seventeen. Talking of her daughter, a successful college student who encouraged her mother to go back to school, Maria insists, "I want her to have a happy marriage." But, as her grandmother used to tell her, "Marriage is a lotto." You can get a good man, you can get a bad one. And, above all, Maria does not want her daughter "to have to ask, What am I going to do now? How am I going to take care of my children?" Because, Maria told me, "Once you're in that trap, you're in it from generation to generation." Maria's classmates, all of whom live close to New York's dangerous streets, agree. They also agree with Gabriella Ortiz, who finally mustered the courage to break free of an abusive marriage, that "everyone wants their marriage to work out."

Most women cannot recognize the compelling story of women and men in what the feminist movement preaches. Today, as in the past, most women prefer to see men who beat up on women as exceptions—which they are—rather than the norm, or at least to see their own man as different. Young women especially want to believe that this old and recurring story will end happily for them. Many women mistrust feminism because it seems to force a choice between marriage and career, between relations with men and independence.

Women everywhere have taken pride in their ability to cope, including their ability to cope with difficult men. Today that sense of competence includes their ability to work outside the home and, if need be, provide for themselves. It also includes the confidence that they will be able to draw a line in their relations with men—to say and mean, "I will take so much and no more." Mothers and grandmothers have always helped women to draw those lines. When Gloria's husband hit her she drew the line, and the next time he crossed it she left him. Today, she advises her nieces and her daughter-in-law, Miranda. When Miranda complained to her that Johnny was taking an evening a week to drink with his buddies, Gloria responded, "Then you get a baby-sitter and go out with your friends. He ain't your father, girl." Gloria adores Johnny and wants the marriage to work, but she has seen enough to know that women, even young married women, must learn to stand on their own feet. The best time to begin managing your life with your husband is now.

Gabriella Ortiz divorced her abusive husband, although he supported her in comfort and she had never worked outside the home. Then, after she moved with her daughters to New York, she had trouble with a man she was dating. They had been going out for a year, and one night he had too much wine and after dinner asked suggestively, "What are we going to do now?" Gabriella answered that each of them was going to go home just as they always did. "And he blew up right there in the middle of Sixth Avenue and started calling me names and I said 'bye' and took a cab. And he got very offended and never called me again. 'Cause I just simply told him no, I just wasn't ready." Not liking her response, he exploded, "Who in the hell do you think you are? I have girls that are younger than you and better looking than you. . . ." She responded, "I am me, and you just go find one of those girls."

Gloria and Gabriella have not needed feminism to tell them that lines must be drawn, and they do not view the drawing of lines as a political issue. Neither of their mothers was perfect, but each communicated a strong sense of personal dignity and self-respect through innumerable stories, conversations, and shared activities— and just by being there when their daughters were young. Neither mothers nor daughters saw the need to draw lines as a justification for rejecting all men or for accepting only those mythical men who behave as if their masculinity has no legitimate claims of its own. For most women, the unflinching recognition of men's capacity for brutality, infidelity, and ordinary thoughtlessness coexists with an appreciation of men's virtues. No more than Aprill do they always believe they can understand their men, much less the pressures that are working on them. Like Aprill, they believe that they must decide what they will tolerate and what they will not.

Feminist theorists often attack love and marriage as a conspiracy that men have forced upon women to keep them docile, dependent, and in their place. But with eyes wide open, women have clung to love and sex as central, if risky, to a woman's life. They have not needed conservative theorists to teach them that life is risk, and, unlike too many feminists, they have no illusions that political programs can produce a risk-free life—at least not one worth living. Today, most of the barriers to women's participation in the public world have fallen, freeing women to create lives of accomplishment and independence. Yet even as they enter the public world as independent individuals, many remain attached to the traditional story, valuing it for its promise of economic security or for its promise of support in raising children. Young women especially value it as a story that promises companionship and stability in their lives—a buffer against the dangers and disappointments of the world.

Some women who have experienced the difficulties of the world look to marriage to rescue them. Deborah Kinler, who is in her early thirties and works full-time, is happily married, and her four closest friends, two of whom are single and two divorced, all want to be. Most of them, she says, "talk about it all the time. You know, 'when am I going to find the right man,' that kind of thing." Deborah worries that her friends are having trouble finding a man because, having been brought up with the idea that the man takes care of everything, they are too dependent, "and they really have nothing to offer a marriage." Deborah shares her friends' commitment to marriage, but thinks they are pursuing it in the wrong way. She believes they are so blinded by the dream that a man will rescue them—from a one-room apartment, from work, from themselves—that they neglect the talents and opportunities that might bring them independence and satisfaction later in life.

The appeal of marriage transcends differences of class, ethnicity, and race, just as it transcends specific women's deception, self-deception, and disillusionment. We all know that the myths of wedded bliss—the "they lived happily ever after" of domestic fiction and romance—are, well, myths. These days, single women, if they can support themselves, may live rich and satisfying lives. These days, increasing numbers of married women know that the story of love and marriage must be revised to take account of their working lives. These days, in fact, more women are choosing not to marry at all, on the grounds that men simply expect too much or are too burdensome. And yet, neither the changes that have engulfed our world nor the cynicism they often engender seem to have made a significant dent in most women's commitment to the promise of that story.

Feminists, who frequently argue that marriage and the family constitute the principal source of women's subordination, have been tempted to see the commitment to both as a form of escapism as, in some instances, it well may be. For generations, romance enshrouded and disguised the economic dependence that forced most women to marry, but romance has survived the collapse of that economic necessity. Through it all, most women recognize escapism for what it is and still regard the story of marriage and motherhood as central to their sense of themselves as women, much as it was for their mothers before them and is likely to be for their daughters after them.

NOTES

[1]Thus Carol Gilligan, whose best-selling book, *In A Different Voice: Psychological Theory and Women's Development* (Cambridge, MA: Harvard Univ. Press, 1982), claimed that women have a distinct sense of morality, signed an affidavit in support of Shannon Faulkner's suit against The Citadel. Her work, she insisted, should not be used to justify single-sex education—even as one option among others.

[2]Susan J. Douglas, *Where the Girls Are: Growing Up Female With the Mass Media* (New York: Times Books, 1994).

[3]Deborah Tannen, *You Just Don't Understand: Women and Men in Conversation* (New York: Ballantine, 1990), 42.

[4]Robert Pool, *Eve's Rib: Searching for the Biological Roots of Sex Differences* (New York: Crown, 1994). The real issue is not the existence of anatomical differences, but their consequences. See R. C. Lewontin, "Women Versus the Biologists," *The New York Review of Books* XLI, no. 7 (April 7, 1994): 31–35.

[5]Emilie Buchwald, Pamela Fletcher, Martha Roth, eds., *Transforming a Rape Culture* (Minneapolis: Milkweed Editions, 1993).

[6]In 1994, according to a Justice Department study, 62 percent of whites killed in spousal abuse were female, 38 percent male. Thus, among whites, for every two women (or slightly less) who are killed by a violent spouse, one man is. This may not be equality, but it is also not the unilateral victimization of women. And black women are even closer to parity than white. Among black couples, women account for only slightly more than half the spousal murder victims (53 percent) and men slightly less (47 percent). For an account of the

figures on domestic violence, see Katherine Dunn, "Truth Abuse," *The New Republic* (August 1, 1994): 16. On the general problem of feminists' abuse of statistics, see Christina Hoff Sommers, *Who Stole Feminism?: How Women Have Betrayed Women* (New York: Simon and Schuster, 1994).

[7]Dunn, "Truth Abuse."

Seven

WORK AND FAMILY

I f the popularity of television programs is any gauge, the heroine of the economic and sexual revolutions might well be Murphy Brown, the well-educated, upscale single woman who can embrace beckoning opportunities without worrying too much about costs. Murphy Brown has done it all and done it right. The Murphy Brown whose televised saga enchants countless Americans does not deserve either the opprobrium or the praise that has been heaped upon her. She embodies the dream of the talented, ambitious young woman who really does make it to the top. True, her marriage failed in record time, but then successful careers subject marriages to unbearable pressure, and she had chosen a man incapable of serious commitment. Once again unmarried, she wanted a baby, but her attempts at artificial insemination came to nothing. But then, she became pregnant during the brief period in which her ex-husband had unexpectedly reappeared, and they could not resist renewing their sexual relations. Their romance came to nothing—except that it left her pregnant. When her ex-husband made it clear that he was no more capable of commitment than ever, she decided to proceed with the pregnancy and raise the baby alone. So, is the saga of Murphy Brown the story of feminism triumphant or the story of one woman's decision not to have an abortion? Why not view Murphy Brown as a champion of the fetus's right to life?

Murphy Brown was never intended to represent opposition to abortion. Rather, she was intended to represent an abiding yearning for human connection—for some kind of family—among even the most successful and independent women. And if a Murphy Brown, who is normally too busy to be home for meals, much less cook them, wants that human connection, what of the countless women whose work is much less rewarding and demanding than hers? Murphy Brown can afford full-time help to care for her son, although even she has to cut back on her hours at work in order to spend more time with him. And now this contemporary heroine is even ready to try marriage again, but this time with her colleague, Peter, who promises to be a loving and loyal companion.

Cindy Dougherty, in her early twenties, was working as a technical editor for a large firm in Denver when she discovered her pregnancy. That very day she came home to find the man she was living with sitting in her apartment, doing drugs and drinking with eight of his friends. "He and his buddies were sitting on my bed smoking mushroom or something!" That was enough for her, although she subsequently discovered many other things about him she had never suspected. "I did not know who he was." She threw him out. Only much later did she tell him she was pregnant and then only because some day the child she was carrying would want to know. Cindy never doubted that she would continue the pregnancy, although she has multiple sclerosis and her doctors and friends pressured her to have an abortion. For the next three and a half years, she raised

Prudence, her daughter, alone. Then she met James, and a few years later they married. Looking back on those years, Cindy told me that raising Prudence alone had been difficult but not impossible. The real complications, she said, came when she tried to combine work, motherhood, and "a serious relationship with another adult human being."

In all the debates about women's roles as workers and mothers, the significance of Cindy's observation is too easily overlooked. Relations with other adults, especially husbands, do take time. The women who are living out the consequences of the sexual and economic revolutions are reminded of that truth almost every day of their lives. For most women, it does not ease the pressures to raise children alone. Ask any woman who has tried. Cindy found the responsibilities bearable when Prudence was an infant and toddler, primarily because she could do much of her work at home, sometimes late at night. But as Prudence began to attend day care and then school and as Cindy returned to graduate school, life got harder. For even the relatively flexible schedule of a graduate student did not always mesh easily with childhood illnesses, meeting school buses, or participating in the life of Prudence's school. And there was always a problem with money. Cindy could easily earn enough to support herself in modest comfort. Supporting a child was another matter.

In Cindy's case, the strains were exacerbated by her illness, but other single mothers, like Aprill Ravenel, a secretary in Atlanta, and Gloria Patterson, who has held a variety of jobs in the public schools and in private homes in New York and Atlanta, find them exhausting as well. Although Aprill and Gloria are both African-American, their backgrounds differ, and both differ from Cindy's. Yet, beyond all differences, these three women are drawn together by the problems that dominate each of their lives. For Cindy marriage to James made all the difference in the world. Yes, the adult relationship took time, but in return she gained the rewards of adult companionship and a partner to share the responsibilities of raising a child. Gloria feels the same about her marriage to Bill, whom she has known since her teens. Aprill has chosen to defer marriage until Jahmil is older, but she relies upon male friends to provide both her and her boy with companionship.

Before Cindy and Aprill were thirty, they had lived through many of the crosscurrents of the economic and sexual revolutions. Their experiences are no more typical than those of millions of women, each of whom has her own story of coping—or sometimes failing to cope. But it is very much an experience of our times. As a well-educated, middle-class white woman from Colorado, Cindy had lived with a man to whom she was not married, lived as a working single mother, and now juggles the demands of motherhood, work, and marriage. She has no regrets about any of her choices along the way, although today she, like Gloria Patterson, reflects wryly on how easy it is for a young woman like herself to choose the wrong man. And she is sure, as a working mother, that a companionable marriage is immeasurably better than the alternatives—and very much worth the time required to sustain it.

Aprill, who grew up in a large, close, churchgoing African-American family in Detroit, became pregnant her senior year in high school. At the time, she knew almost nothing about sex, which her mother and older sisters did not discuss with her. A "very private person," she never really opened up to anyone, even when the "pressure was really hitting me to have sex." When she became serious about one young man, she briefly took birth control pills, but when he left for college, she stopped. Then he came home for vacation, and "I think I probably had sex like two times. When I found out I was pregnant I couldn't believe it."

Rejecting both abortion and adoption, Aprill had Jahmil. For a while, she and her boyfriend were planning to get married: "You know, we loved each other, and we had done things in the wrong order, but eventually we were gonna get married and have a house with a white picket fence and a little dog." But six weeks before they were to get married, she canceled the wedding. "He was having an affair with someone else, and I found out." Deferring her plans to become a nurse, she now works as a secretary and word processor to support herself and her son.

Cindy's, Aprill's, and Gloria's lives have little in common with Murphy Brown's. Women like Murphy Brown—white women who have attended at least a year of college and hold professional or managerial jobs—may be the most rapidly increasing group of single mothers, but they are far from being the largest or most important.[1] Their story appeals to many radical feminists because it suggests that women prefer independence to the traditional story of marriage and family. But most single mothers are not upscale career women. They are poor, not least because being a single mother makes women poor. The dramatic growth in the number of single mothers affects women in every class, race, and ethnic group, especially the many who have never been married—up more than 60 percent during the past decade—and may never be. More than half of all African-American women and a third of Hispanic-American women now find themselves struggling to raise children alone, although usually not from choice and usually with disastrous consequences for their and their children's prospects. Single motherhood is the story of their lives with a vengeance, but normally not the story they aspire to.

For the Right, the increase in single mothers confirms the collapse of our moral fabric. But this charge amounts to little more than blaming poor single mothers for circumstances over which they have little control. Sensitivity to the plight of those whom the distinguished sociologist William Julius Wilson has called "the truly disadvantaged" has rarely been the strong suit of those who defend the traditional version of family values. The public discussion of Murphy Brown's single motherhood painfully revealed how completely the different sides in the debate continue to talk past one another. Vice President Dan Quayle opened with a broadside against the bankrupt values of a cultural elite that was shamelessly promoting single motherhood. Feminists countered that Dan Quayle should not be condemning other people's moral standards. Neither side understood that the American people, rightly or wrongly, do not perceive morality as the principal issue.

No longer seeing premarital sex as a moral issue at all, the vast majority of Americans will not condemn single motherhood on moral grounds. Why should Murphy Brown, an upscale, successful woman who earns more than most American families, not have a baby if she chooses? There may, in fact, be reasons, moral or other, why she should not, but they have little or nothing to do with her sexual life. Even Christian fundamentalists and neo-Evangelicals, who regard her behavior as sinful, are likely to leave her to God, remembering, "Judge not, lest ye be judged." They do not like single motherhood to be presented as a positive model of behavior, but they are also reluctant to condemn individual women. If they sometimes judge "welfare mothers" harshly, they do so primarily out of concern for the economic burden that welfare imposes upon taxpayers. Does any woman have a right to have children she cannot support? Does a woman have a responsibility to provide her child with a father? Does a man have a responsibility to live with his children and their mother? Needless to say, in a culture that primarily focuses on individual happiness and satisfaction, and in which adults disgrace themselves by worrying about who will nurture them, this is not a popular topic of discussion.

To complicate matters further, poor women frequently end up as single mothers because they like men and they like children. Many hope against hope that the man with whom they are having sex will marry them, and they see the coming child as someone who will love them. Poor single mothers embody the tattering of the traditional story of marriage and motherhood, but hardly the triumph of feminism. Upscale single mothers embody the newfound ability of some women to live the lives traditionally lived by men, although many of them are finding single motherhood difficult, and many, like Murphy Brown, eventually marry. Thus even upscale single mothers are casting doubt on the notion that women really want to raise children alone. Most American women hold fast to the possibility of a happy marriage. Most view the lives of poor single mothers as their worst

nightmare and view the lives of upscale single mothers as a repudiation of their highest ideals for themselves.

Most women want to anchor their lives in a network of human
connection—some form of family—which for most means marriage.
After three decades of steadily increasing sexual and economic independence, women still value marriage as an economic resource, even
when they do not look to a husband as their sole source of support.
Recent years have, nonetheless, taken a toll on marriage. In 1970, 70
percent of American women were married, but by 1993 only about
60 percent were, and 20 percent had never married at all.

The media gleefully announced that more women were remaining
single by choice, especially those in their twenties and early thirties
who had discovered they could support themselves and live as they
chose.[2] Yet most women, as even the case of Murphy Brown suggests, still prefer marriage to the alternatives. And probably, many of
those now divorced had expected marriage to be rewarding. Failed
marriages do not prove that women have given up on marriage, but
they do suggest that recent changes may have increased the strains.
Those changes have certainly destroyed many African-American
women's prospect of ever marrying, for the numbers of black men of
marriageable age who are unemployed, in prison, on drugs, or dead
have escalated.

Notwithstanding the increased strains on marriage, in 1990
women were more likely to trust the solidity of marriage as an institution than they had been in 1970.[3] Most people continue to marry,
and at least some of the women between twenty-five and thirty-four
who appear to have lost their enthusiasm for marriage are simply
deferring it while they establish careers. Some, like Murphy Brown,
are also discovering that the demands of marriage, not to mention
the demands of children and high-powered careers, pull strongly in
different directions.

Women like Murphy Brown, who are fighting their way to the top
in the "man's world" of business and the professions, have special
incentives to put their personal lives aside, at least for a while. But

so do some less affluent and highly educated women, whether because of ambition to better their situation or because of a personal distaste for emotional relations. Carla Uribe, a Hispanic-American woman who loves the dynamism of New York, has little interest in marriage, although she enjoys men and has two children. She is now completing her high school equivalency diploma while working as a secretary to support herself and the children. Carla knows little about feminism, but no feminist cares more than she about women's independence. Since her boy and girl were toddlers, she has taught both to be independent, but she regards her eleven-year-old daughter, the younger of the two, as the more responsible. "My daughter sees that she is really not going to need anyone but herself."

Carla's mother "always told me not to get married, and I passed that on to my daughter." Carla's mother figures that if you can love someone without the problems of marriage, fine, but you really have to be sure that you're ready for marriage. Her mother, who had once been married, spoke from experience and advised her daughter not to get married until she was about forty-five. Carla's children started day care when they were one or one-and-a-half years old. Now, thanks to her efforts, they both have scholarships to a boarding school in Pennsylvania. "I've always worked. I couldn't stay home and be a parent." She personally would go crazy if she had to stay at home, but "I give a lot of praise for the women who stay home."

Linda Maldonado, also Hispanic-American and working as an aide in a New York hospital while she completes her GED, has no children and "I don't want any." Yet she is very much attached to her nephews and her nieces, whom she regards as "spunky" and independent—occasionally too much so. Above all, she worries about the burdens that fall on her sister, a single parent who has to deal with everything alone, including finances. "She does it all. She has no life." As Linda sees it, her sister's "whole life revolves around" her thirteen-year-old daughter, Jessica. "It's all Jessica. She gets up at five. She goes to school. My niece has jazz; my niece has ballet." Linda's sister has always worked. She was married to Jessica's father, but he cheated on her, and she told him to get lost. He still wants her back, but she refuses. When asked, Jessica says, "I want to be like my mom. I don't need a man. I want to travel and see the world."

Young Jessica, like Carla, assumes that if a woman wants something she must be prepared to get it for herself. Their attitude speaks volumes both about the influence of feminism on the general culture and about the deteriorating prospects of lower-class men and families, especially if they are black or Hispanic. But many women, including many of Carla's and Linda's colleagues from the GED program, do not agree that marriage always demands more than it gives, much less that it means staying home. They all insist that no woman should count on marriage for economic support. Gabriella Ortiz, who grew up in a conservative Cuban-American community in Florida before moving to New York, recalls that "It took me about ten years to get out of a very sick marriage." When she left with the two children, her husband told her that she'd be back. "I told him, 'Just wait for me,' and I never went back." Gabriella agrees "that a woman should have her own career." She also believes "that women were created and men were created for each other, you know, companionship." But, she adds, whatever happens "you gotta keep going."

The attitudes of these African-American and Hispanic-American women in New York City strikingly resemble those of Southern-born black women like Gloria Patterson and Patricia Sanders in Atlanta and countless middle-class white women throughout the country. Yes, the sexual and economic revolutions have encouraged some women to defer marriage or not marry at all, just as they have compelled other women who might have preferred to marry to remain single. But during the past twenty years the real change in women's attitudes toward marriage has come in the kind of marriage they want. In 1974, half of the women who wanted to be married wanted a traditional marriage; by 1990, less than 40 percent did, and more than half wanted a marriage in which women and men shared responsibilities.[4] Today, the attitudes of women and men toward marriage are rapidly converging, doubtless in part because the economic revolution that has drawn more and more women into the labor force has corresponded with, if not caused, a decline in men's earnings. Under these conditions, increasing numbers of men see the advantages of a companionate marriage in which women and men share economic and domestic responsibilities.

On the face of it, David Moore, an African-American who works as a security guard in New York City, would seem an unlikely candidate to support such views. But, in conversation with me and the women of the GED class, he unhesitatingly acknowledges that these days "women are more independent," and he further insists proudly that their new independence does not make life harder for him. "I can do the things that I want and she can do the things that she wants. It's like sometimes you got to go with the flow." Doubtless, the uncertainties of employment have influenced his attitudes, for he elaborates, "Sometimes you won't be working; sometimes she won't be working. So it'll be harder on the other person. But in the long run the person has something to fall back on and a couple of skills, maybe like a secretary or maybe a hairdresser or maybe other skills." At this juncture, the faltering of David's newly raised consciousness moves Maria Ramirez to expand the list of female skills, firmly interjecting: "Construction worker?" David's grudging "yeah" suggests that he still has mixed feelings about women as competitors on the job, but it momentarily satisfies Maria, who cheerfully responds, "Thank you."

Whatever David's qualms about women's progress into "male" occupations, he has no trouble with the idea that when men and women share wage labor they should also share housework and child care, "cause I was raised by my mother. I was alone most of the time because she worked." Looking back, he thinks that the experience made him "more independent than some kids" and gave him some sense of the pressures on working women. David's remarks brought me back to one of my graduate classes in feminist theory at Emory. The question came up of whether men could be feminists, and some of the more "militant" women students expressed serious doubts. How could any man possibly understand the oppression women suffer? Suddenly a male student, Andrew Wilson, who normally retained a discreet, almost deferential, silence, spoke out passionately. Andrew's mother, who had been widowed at an early age, had worked and raised five children. No one, he insisted, barely controlling his anger, could tell him that he could not empathize with women, could not be a feminist. Night after night, he had seen his mother come home dropping with fatigue and on the verge of tears, collapsing under the strain of coping with the outside world, yet doing well by her children. He knew about women's issues, all right, and if feminism could not include him, then feminism was not really about women's issues.

Unlike Andrew, David Moore has never considered calling himself a feminist, but like many others he has learned that, if nothing else, social pressure requires respect for women's economic contributions and their right to equal pay for equal work. His conversion may be partial, like that of many of the men Linda Maldonado knows and who probably think they support these issues, "but when they're out there with their buddies they don't . . ." But such partial conversions represent a sea change that even David Moore's most suspicious women colleagues are not prepared to brush aside.

David's combination of old and new attitudes is becoming typical of American men. And it confirms that the new style of marriage does not always come easily for either men or women. Polls show that both women and men see persisting areas of potential conflict: in finances, the amount of time they spend together, the ways in which they communicate with one another, and child care. Time remains a terrible problem for everyone, especially for the baby boomers, who are now in their thirties and forties. For them, life is one mad dash, buffeted by pressures of rising careers, revised male-female family roles, demands of young children, and craving for leisure.

More than any other age group, the baby boomers are likely to be working and raising children and to feel squeezed for time. In 1991, almost half of the parents felt a "great deal" or "quite a lot" of conflict between work and family, and more than three quarters of those who report such conflicts believe that their personal life, children, and spouse suffer. More than half of working mothers and almost two thirds of working fathers feel they spend too little time with their children. An Omaha computer consultant, who, like increasing numbers of people, has taken a second job to help cover the growing gap between income and expenses, says, "My job requires me sometimes to travel and it's never really convenient when I do." He and his wife "split up all the housework and all the child care, and when one of us is not around it causes a lot of friction." Under these conditions, it is hardly surprising that one fifth of the baby boomers believe the demands and pressures of jobs sometimes seriously affect their relations with their children, and almost one quarter believe that their marriages or romantic relationships have suffered.[5]

The problems of juggling, as Cindy Dougherty suggested, may seriously strain the relations between husbands and wives. But difficulties notwithstanding, more than two thirds of the women and men polled in 1990 claimed to be firmly committed to the person to whom they are married, and they continue to rank "being in love" as the most important ingredient in a good marriage, closely followed by their spouse's sexual fidelity. People's sense of what makes a good marriage has changed little since the early 1970s, although they tend to value fidelity somewhat more and being in love somewhat less.[6] Most would marry the same person again. Yet a third of all women admit that either they or their husbands complain about the other's not having enough time for them.[7]

Married working women with children never have enough time for the most important things in their lives, much less the unimportant ones that help keep most of us sane. These are not lives that often permit a leisurely morning over a cup of coffee and a newspaper, shopping and lunch out with friends, a weekend away with a husband, or even a quiet talk with a child. What is truly astounding is how little men's and women's attitudes about the problems differ.

Although many women feel a special responsibility both for children and for making the marriage work, two thirds do not believe that they work harder at the marriage than their husbands do. Feminism has decisively contributed to a more equitable division of domestic labor, and we have come a long way from the days in which feminists were urging women to make their husbands sign contracts to cover the division of household labor. Indeed, it is precisely because so much has changed that feminist voices today strike so many women as shrill. Women have come to expect that the men in their lives will do a reasonable share of dishes, laundry, or child care, but they still refuse to see marriage only as a business deal.

We all know that, in most marriages, the division of domestic labor is not equal. Most of the married women I have spoken with, no matter what their age or background, do believe that they carry the main responsibility for household chores and family life. Even when husbands do a fair share of the work, wives are still likely to organize it and assign the tasks. That too is changing, although slowly. For those of us who have lived through the changes—who began in a world in which it was expected that the wife would assume most if not all of the domestic responsibilities—impatience still comes easy and may blind us to what has been accomplished. Not long ago, I received a letter from an accomplished woman academic remarking on a talk she had heard me give. For years, she had been struggling to balance career, marriage, and children, all the while frustrated that her husband, whom she loves, never seemed to do his full share of the work. But she was beginning to see that, although he might fall short of perfection, he had improved more than she ever could have imagined when they married. Her glass, which feminists had been telling her was half-empty, now looked at least half-full and getting fuller.

Half-full is a condition that might be improved upon, but these days, increasing numbers of married women insist that they are reasonably satisfied with the amount of time they must devote to household chores and with the way in which those chores are shared. True, both married and single men, as well as single women, are even more satisfied, which suggests that married women believe they pick up more than their fair share of the pieces. But the differences are not great. The greatest difference reflects the presence of children. Not surprisingly, single-mother heads of households are most likely to feel that they have more to do than is fair or they can handle. And married women feel significantly more burdened by the division of household responsibilities when they have children than when they do not.

Regardless of race, ethnicity, and class, men readily agree that women do more of the work, and they are consistently happier than women with domestic arrangements. Tellingly, the women who are least happy with their own domestic burdens are upscale women, who presumably are pursuing careers, and women with daughters, who presumably expect more help from daughters than the daughters are providing. The main point remains that, for most women, children rather than men decisively increase the work. Thus a feminism that focuses exclusively on the burdens that fall on the woman as wife strangely ignores the greater burdens that fall on her as mother. Mothers are hard pressed to manage without help, which some receive from husbands or other family members and which others receive from hired help. Poor single mothers frequently have no such recourse. And, however unintentionally, a feminism that applauds single motherhood mocks their plight.[8]

Feminist views on marriage and children primarily reflect the experience of upscale women who are engaged in demanding careers and who frequently marry men with equally demanding careers. The most painful strains in these families come from the struggle for the time to do what each parent "must" do. And often, what people with careers "must" do turns out to be precisely what they want to do: stay late at the office, take on another client, write another book or article, take another business trip. The problem is not necessarily that the parent who is caring for the children and the house suspects the other of wasting time or even carrying on an affair. Rather, both parents want the freedom to give the maximum amount of uninterrupted time to the work that brings them professional advancement and personal satisfaction. Both want the right to be so busy that they must be spared the responsibilities of everyday life.

Companionate marriage is bringing a welcome new balance to the lives of women and men, but it does not easily meet the pressing needs of children. Increasingly, women and men agree about the tension between their work and those needs, but they primarily agree in not knowing what to do. Seeing no easy solution, they remain pulled between a nagging sense that any child would do better with a mother at home and the conviction that women should work. When pollsters pose the same question in different ways, the tensions emerge clearly. Thus, in one 1989 Roper poll almost two thirds of all women and men said that children would do best if the father had a job and the mother cared for the children at home, and then said that their children would do just as well if both parents worked. If the answers seem contradictory or confusing, they are. But they do wonderfully capture our collective uncertainty about how to combine opportunity for women, economic stability for families, and the crying needs of children. And they show that the real struggle is not between women and men, but between children and work.[9]

The real losers in these conflicts are the children. An administrator at a private school in New York City told me with great sadness of Angela Johnson, a ten-year-old female pupil whose single mother had recently had a second child. Angela was adjusting well enough to the work, but seemed inexplicably tired, withdrawn, and somewhat sad. The teachers and staff were having trouble in understanding the problem, when one day the school received a panicky call from her mother. "Where," the mother demanded, "is Angela? I must speak to Angela." The administrator who answered the phone replied that Angela was in class, and they would have her call back in half an hour. Half an hour did not satisfy the mother, who insisted that she must speak with her daughter at once. The administrator, still unwilling to pull Angela out of class, asked what the problem was. The baby, the mother replied, seemed to be running a fever, and only Angela knew where to find the thermometer. Suddenly, everything made sense. At ten, Angela was not only going to a new and demanding school, she was effectively raising the baby with which her mother could not cope.

Peggy Orenstein, while working on her book, *Schoolgirls*, spent more than a year following the lives of two young women in their early teens. Superficially, the girls, April Welch and Becca Holbrook, could not have been leading more different lives. April, African-American and poor, had grown up as the daughter of a single mother who was unsuccessfully struggling with an addiction to crack cocaine, to which a boyfriend had introduced her. Her subsequent attempt at rehab had failed, and, before April finally left, she had taken up prostitution to support her habit and stolen April's small stash of money. Becca, in contrast, was the daughter of white middle-class parents, both of whom had good jobs. But notwithstanding dramatic differences in circumstances, the two girls shared a sense that no one was paying attention to them, and, especially, that their mothers were asking too much of them. Their anxieties about their lives, which in Becca's case manifested themselves in anorexia and thoughts of suicide, led both to perform far beneath their capabilities at school, where teachers seemed unable or unwilling to help them.

No more than Angela's mother did April's and Becca's mothers understand how they were contributing to their daughters' insecurities and undermining their chances to succeed. Indeed one is tempted to believe that, in different ways, all of these mothers were looking to their daughters to mother them. For Angela and April, the experience obviously produced a strength beyond their years. Angela did mother her baby sister, and April did call Social Services to persuade them to place her with her great-aunt and uncle, who have a stable marriage and a comfortable home. But the strengths are not necessarily appropriate to their years and often take a toll in later years. Becca, who enjoyed material security, almost crumbled under the weight of listening to her mother's complaints about her father's continuing demands for sex.[10] Her case shows that the daughter of a comfortably situated working mother may not perceive her mother as any less demanding or any more there for her than the daughters of the single mothers.

It is tempting to attribute many of these young women's problems to the vagaries of personal circumstance and psychology. Feminists insist that the problems of individual women are always, in some measure, social or political problems, and they frequently blame the "sexism" of the schools for adolescent girls' lack of self-confidence. Yet they are reluctant to discuss the extent to which daughters' problems are influenced by the lives their mothers are leading. Conservatives, in contrast, are quick to blame mothers, whom they reproach for failing in their moral and maternal obligations. But conservatives are reluctant to acknowledge that we live in a culture and an economy in which it is becoming increasingly difficult for even the most devoted and responsible mothers to provide as much as their daughters legitimately need.

If we step back from the details of the stories and the personalities of the women, we are left with a pattern of absent mothers. And the prevalence of the pattern across lines of race and class has at least as much to do with our culture and our economy as with the personal failings of individuals. This is not a question of "individual responsibility." Angela's, Becca's and April's mothers have all suffered emotional damage that makes it difficult to respond to their daughters' needs. Most mothers have suffered one or another form of emotional distress that makes it difficult for them to respond fully to their daughters—as have most mothers throughout time. But some cultural norms and social constraints offer us greater opportunity to see the work of mothering as an admirable way to make peace with a difficult past than others. And our culture now accords mothering diminishing respect, while our economy makes serious mothering difficult for many women and impossible for others.

Feminists tend to see any talk of women's responsibilities to mother as a male plot. Early on, they launched a broadside attack on Mother's Day, and recently they have been promoting a substitute, "Take Our Daughters to Work." It is reasonable to conclude that feminists intend to free women from motherhood. But that is not the whole story. Some feminists are quick to defend the rights of mothers, especially single mothers and divorced mothers who are fighting for custody of their children. Many even defend the right of welfare mothers to stay home with their children. But the moment husbands enter the picture, everything changes. Wives, we are told, must be free to work as much as their husbands. So feminists can hardly complain when American women conclude that feminists see married women's responsibilities to children as another form of male oppression.

Most women, however, do not see motherhood as a form of male oppression and more often than not agree with men about the best solutions, although experience is leading both women and men to change their views about which solutions are best. By 1991, the percentage of both women and men who wanted one parent to remain at home to raise the children had increased, while the percentage that wanted both parents to work full-time outside the home had decreased. But the majority rejected both alternatives. Today, most people prefer that both partners have at least some work and spend at least some time caring for children. Their desire to have one parent at home does not mean that they favor a return to the 1950s or want to strip women of their independence. It reflects a growing concern for the well-being of children and families. In fact, women and men largely agree that fathers who stay home could be just as good parents as mothers, although they are more likely to see a mother at home as ideal.[11]

Feminists have sorely misunderstood the importance of motherhood to most women. Working mothers are much less likely than working fathers to see work as the most, or one of the most, important parts of their lives, and most would prefer jobs close to home with flexible hours and higher pay for the time worked. Half would prefer not to work at all while their children are young.[12] And if their main concern remains their children, they also worry that a full-time job gives them too little time for their spouse.[13] These attitudes reflect hard experiences and a sense of responsibility, not a repudiation of women's independence. Experience has apparently taught such women that independence must mean the freedom to meet the responsibilities they have chosen, not freedom from any responsibility at all.

Women's attitudes toward the balance between work and family vary according to their circumstances and their prospects, but in general women still feel bound to children in a way most men do not. And child care experts like Burton White confirm their instinctive sense that children do best when their primary caretaker is a parent or grandparent.[14] Women with children under six feel especially torn: About half of them prefer to stay home at least until their children go to school, and another half prefer to work. And then there are the many who work out of necessity, for whom the preference to stay home is an unattainable luxury. As children grow up, women feel less torn, and two thirds of those with children six or older would prefer to be working. But clearly few if any mothers of young children find the choices easy. And no less clearly, men sympathize with and share their anguish.

not an easy choice...

However much women and men agree about what would be good for children and families, women live the conflicts in a way men do not. Most women want to be good mothers, and many come to believe that good mothering requires more time than is possible when you work full-time. For poor women, who know all too much about the dangers that threaten their children and who do not regard their jobs as especially fulfilling, the desire to stay home comes easily. But for them, to work or not work is no choice at all. They must work. The lower a woman's income, the more daunting the difficulties. Their husbands, if they have husbands, do not earn enough to support a wife at home and two or more children, much less to buy a house. They cannot even be sure of steady employment. Under these conditions, it is hardly surprising that men as well as women so easily agree that a woman must be able to support herself or bring money into the household. The cost of even modest day care is rising, and the availability of grandmothers and neighbors is declining. Working single mothers must depend upon the children themselves, boys as well as girls, and must encourage their children's independence. Increasingly, working married mothers must do the same. All of the women in the Lehman GED class except Maria Ramirez, whose husband, a senior postal worker, can support the family, are working at a job that does not require a high school diploma—that is, for low, if not minimum, wages.

Like poor women in every part of the country, economic hardships top the list of their problems, but for these women the responsibility of caring for children weighs especially heavy. Although some had grown up in the Caribbean islands and some in New York City, all agree that the world they knew as children is disintegrating. In the islands, everyone assumed responsibility for their kids. Amanda Thomas said that her mother had taken care of her children, "but if they were outside they were watched by the neighbors." All the middle-aged people "were watching the kids. They felt like they were their own children."

Not everything was perfect in the islands. Carolina Watson, who now lives in the Bronx, reminded her friends that early sexual activity, sexual abuse, and even incest were problems there as well, "but they cover it up. It is kept quiet. They don't talk about it. But they know." Nodding heads suggested that her colleagues from different backgrounds understood exactly what she meant. Terrible things went on, but they went on within the context of a community that helped people to cope with the worst effects. The victims had relatives and friends to turn to in an environment in which people looked after one another. Even those who had grown up in New York agreed that things had changed for the worse. Some changes have been good. They applaud the new tendency to bring abuses out in the open and favor more open communication within families and especially among mothers and daughters. The changes they dread are those of the outside world, notably drugs, violence, graphic displays of sexuality, and a culture that seems to be tearing their children away from them.

Linda Maldonado, who grew up in the Bronx, where she still lives, insisted firmly, "My mom raised me. My mom raised me with morals." But today her nephews and nieces are living in a different world. She is full of admiration for their spunk, independence, and intelligence, but she worries: "Kids today are more advanced, they're exposed to a whole lot more on the street. You can only teach them certain things." And everything you try to teach them runs up against peer pressure, which, in her judgment, influences them a lot more than anything an adult can say or do. They are learning "to defend themselves when they're out there in the real world." Linda suspects that kids today, in their own way, also have a community. "Their neighborhood is where they grew up, they're familiar with it, they know. You know, they look out for each other, they have their own survival techniques." But she, like the others, worries that in learning to survive they are hardening too young—that they are, in some way, being cut adrift.

These women primarily register the breakdown of community as the proliferation of external dangers to their daughters (and sons): violence, explicit sex, and early pregnancies. But if they are supremely conscious of the triumph of a world without morals, they especially resent and fear a world that is making it increasingly difficult for them to be good mothers. It would be hard to find more ardent champions of "family values," although few if any enjoy the luxury of owning snug, single-family homes, or even the luxury of being able to devote themselves full-time to their children.

In essential ways, upscale professional women are spared the worst of these problems, if only because their incomes permit them to live in safer neighborhoods and to hire more help. Most also enjoy more choice about whether to work when their children are young. But most also live with intense—sometimes wrenching—conflicts about how to reconcile responsibilities to children with work. It is common these days for young professional women to start with the assumption that the proper help and schools will take care of the problems. Many return to work after the birth of a first child. Brooke

Mason, a talented and successful corporate manager and accountant for an engineering firm in Atlanta, returned to work six weeks after the birth of her first son, coming to the office for three days and working from home the other two. "So it's been wonderful." But after the birth of her second child, she decided to stay home for a few years. "I just feel like I've stretched my abilities as a human being, or stretched my limits as a human being. Trying to be the best wife, and the best mother, and still being the best employee I can be."

All of the women I spoke with who had decided to stay home while their children were young felt that their choice had benefited their marriages as well as their children. Jennifer Carlson, whose husband, Niel, is a physics professor at a large Midwestern state university, left an excellent job as a curator at the university museum just before the birth of their first son. Now that their two boys, Ezra and Adam, are both in school, Jennifer has returned to work part-time. But during her years at home, she assumed all of the household responsibilities, including management of their money. When I asked who makes the decisions, she immediately responded, "I make them." Work had prepared her to enjoy the responsibility. On most things, she does not even consult him. She trusts herself to make the decisions, although they do discuss the very big ones. Occasionally, it makes her nervous to have to hire someone to do major jobs around the house. "But I usually use my own network," especially women friends in the neighborhood. When Jennifer was growing up, her mother did not do the kinds of things or make the kinds of decisions that Jennifer now takes for granted, although later in life, as Jennifer's father became increasingly infirm, she began to. Jennifer thinks the new responsibilities have been a source of confidence for her mother, as they are for her.

Jennifer's affectionately tolerant attitude toward her husband's general domestic incompetence resembles that of Carolina Watson of the GED class. Carolina regards her husband as her "best friend," but does not think highly of his abilities as a domestic manager. She does respect his skill as a worker and is happy about his earnings. But, as she cheerfully says, at the end of each week, he comes home and "paycheck put down." She takes care of the bills. Carolina, like her husband, works because otherwise the family could not make ends meet. Thanks to Niel's salary, Jennifer can afford not to. She believes, "There's a certain quality of life that we both want—order and calm—that you just can't have . . . we can't live at a frenzied pace." Both of them value that calm more highly than any money she could make.

In one business and law firm after another, other young mothers are doing the same, possibly agreeing with Brooke that, confronted with a hard choice, "I realize that at the end of my life I'd rather have been remembered as a great mom and a great wife rather than a great forecaster." The choice was not easy. She and her husband "needed some of the income," and she wanted "the ability to come in and see an adult face." She also just plain loved her work. But none of her responsibilities would give, they just got "squished into a smaller time frame at work" and then there was "a screaming child at home." And Brooke, like so many "traditional" women before her, loves the screaming child at home.

Even when things go well, the pull between family and work can drive working mothers to distraction. When they go badly, the pressures and, above all, the feelings of guilt may become almost too much to bear. A young mother who thought she had provided her oldest son with a loving, responsible caretaker told me of her anguish in discovering that the woman she thought she could trust had probably been terrorizing and perhaps abusing him. With much attention from his parents and help from a therapist, the boy recovered from his fears. The young woman persisted in her career. And she hired a loving, full-time nanny who also took care of her infant daughter and, as the children have started school, has remained with the family to be available in case of illness and to greet both children when they come home. On good days, that mother delights in the abundant, heartwarming evidence that her boy has emerged unscathed. On bad days she still struggles with the haunting sense that if only she had been there . . .

She could not have been there. Her family needed her income, and she had as much right as her husband to pursue the career for which she is superbly gifted. But her sense of her responsibilities as a mother sinks its roots in the experience of her mother and grand-mothers before her. Even if she is as talented, or more talented, than the men with whom she works, she lives out a different story. She would never want to trade her sense of professional success for her sense of herself as a good mom. She wants both, and, in her case, has both. But then, she works at a college, across the street from her house, and knows that in an emergency she can be home in five minutes.

Most high-paced professional careers do not provide such flexibil-ity, and child care arrangements are rarely, if ever, perfect even for well-to-do women. So, caught between the unyielding demands of work and the compelling needs of children, a surprising number of upscale women are still choosing to stay home while their children are young. When Beth Cooke married Crawford, an ambitious and successful stockbroker, she was running the dynamic consulting firm that she had founded and built. Having grown up with three ener-getic brothers, Beth cut her teeth on the rough-and-tumble of com-petition, and she enjoyed every aspect of running her business. There was no doubt about Beth's ability to support herself and any children she might have. There was every reason to expect that if she chose, she could make as much money as Crawford. Thus her friends and associates, who knew her talent and ambition, were stunned when, after the birth of their first child, she announced that she planned to stay home. Worse, she told me sadly, most of the women were downright nasty about it, and many no longer have time for her. Beth has never looked back. For, as she said to me in dead earnest and without a trace of self congratulation, "I said to myself, There is nothing in my life that I will ever do that is as important as rearing this child." Of course, she added, "We feel the loss of my income, and I hate that my choice means that Crawford has to work harder." He fully supports the decision, telling me that rearing their child was also the most important thing he would do in his life. They have agreed that they can best care for their daughter, and the son who followed, by dividing the labor along what approximates traditional lines.

Beth and Crawford can afford that choice. They will not be as wealthy as they would have been had she continued to work, but they are comfortable. For many other couples, the choice for either parent to stay home is simply not viable. Without two salaries, and sometimes more if one or both must take a second job, the rent will not be paid, the children will not have shoes. The many couples who can barely afford it but still choose to have one parent stay home at least for a while are saying that children do need more of their parents than can easily be squeezed around two full-time jobs. Meanwhile, feminists and conservatives persist in rebroadcasting simplistic positions that woefully misperceive the realities of ordinary people's lives.

For the women of the GED class at Lehman College, a woman's work does not flout traditional values: It provides their necessary foundation and the conditions for transmitting them to the next generation. Throughout history, women have combined work with motherhood. Contemporary American society is exceptional in making the combination so difficult and in tacitly suggesting that women should choose between the two. Most women simply cannot. Only the cruel or the ignorant could charge working women with selfishly choosing "careers" and self-realization over the interests of their families. Only the ideologically blind could assume that they have embraced a feminist agenda that presents men and families as their oppressors. In defiance of all slogans, they are, in an increasingly hostile environment, struggling to live their ideal of family values.

Feminists who condemn women who choose to stay home are arrogantly denying to other women the right of choice they claim for themselves. In the name of what values do they dismiss devotion to children as capitulation to sexism and patriarchy? By any reasonable standard, the rearing of children is the most important thing that individuals—or, for that matter, societies—do. And the evidence is mounting on all sides that, especially in a society as complex and dangerous as our own, that rearing takes time. Many of us who grew up well-off in the 1950s under the anxious supervision of restless, educated mothers understandably came to believe that we might have benefited from a little less mothering. Perhaps. But for all of our complaints, most of us did not, in the end, do badly. And even to us, a little less mothering primarily meant a little less supervision. It did not mean a mother who was never there when we came home from school, a mother who was always too tired to talk, a mother who could never help with homework or attend a meeting with a teacher, a mother who could never watch a Little League game—a mother who did not know us well enough to know when things were going wrong.

NOTES

[1]*The New York Times,* July 14, 1993.

[2]Thomas Hargrove and Guido Stempel, "More Women Single and Happy About It," *Scripps Howard News Service* (July 29, 1993); Paula Ries and Anne J. Stone, *The American Woman 1992–93* (New York: W. W. Norton, 1992); *The 1990 Virginia Slims Opinion Poll: A 20-Year Perspective of Women's Issues, A Study Conducted by the Roper Organization* (Storrs, CN: Roper Organization, n.d.). While the vast majority of unmarried women between eighteen and twenty-four want to marry, only a bit more than two thirds of those between twenty-five and thirty-four do.

[3]*1990 Virginia Slims,* 43. In 1990, 60 percent of the American women who were married and living with their husbands believed that marriage as an institution was weaker than it had been in the past; in 1970, after the early experience of the sexual revolution, almost three quarters believed marriage was weaker than it had been in the past. In 1970, 71 percent of men thought marriage was weaker; in 1990, only 62 percent did.

[4]Roughly the same proportion of men agreed with them: 50 percent of men and 53 percent of women. *1990 Virginia Slims,* 45.

[5]Conflict between work and family: 43 percent of baby boomers, 35 percent of all parents. *Gallup, 312, September 1991.*
[6]*1990 Virginia Slims*, 48.

	being in love	sexual fidelity
1974	90%	79%
1990	87%	85%

[7]"Relations Between the Sexes," *The American Enterprise* (September/October 1993): 91. The survey was taken by E.D.K. Associates for *Redbook*, March 7–15, 1992.

[8]*Harris* 861011, February 18, 1987.

[9]"Seeing Eye to Eye on Family Roles," *The American Enterprise* (September/October 1993): 92. The survey was taken by the Roper Organization for Virginia Slims, July 22–August 12, 1989. The reverse of these numbers is that a third of both women and men thought that both parents should have jobs and share care for the children when they were home, a third thought that children would do better if their mother did not work, and a third claimed to experience considerable conflict between their job and their family.

[10]Peggy Orenstein, "Children Are Alone," *The New York Times Magazine* (July 24, 1994): 18–25, 32, 40, 44. The article was taken from her book, *School Girls: Young Women, Self-Esteem, and the Confidence Gap* (New York: Doubleday, 1994).

[11]*Gallup*, 312, September 1991; and on the fathers as good parents, "Seeing Eye to Eye on Family Roles," 92.

[12]*Harris* 861011, February 18, 1987.

[13]*Gallup*, 312, September 1991. These findings are almost identical to those that emerge from an earlier Harris poll. *Harris* 861011, February 18, 1987.

[14]Burton L. White, *The First Three Years of Life*, rev. ed. (New York: Prentice Hall, 1985).

Eight

WHAT MOMMY
TRACK?

When Cheryl Polasky, the hairstylist in Toledo, left her husband, she felt an incredible sense of freedom and power. For years, George's drinking and open playing around had been undermining her self-confidence. The worse he behaved, the more worthless she felt. She did not believe that she could muster the courage to say "enough." During the first months after she left, it was almost as if she had taken the kids on vacation. Their new apartment was more cramped than the house they had lived in with George, but the absence of his bullying made it feel even larger. Cheryl knew it would be difficult to make ends meet, but she did not want Laurie and Junior to feel deprived and assumed George would meet his child-support payments. He did not. When the weather turned cold the children started to get sick. So long as they only got colds, Cheryl sent them to school as usual.

Then Laurie came down with strep throat and had to be kept home. Cheryl missed most of a week at work. The small salon where she worked did not pay her for the days she missed, and she lost the tips.

By Christmas, she had lost two full weeks of pay, and the bills were beginning to pile up. She could not bear not to give the children presents for Christmas. After New Year's she decided she would have to cut out Laurie's ballet lessons, and she could not imagine how she could possibly get Junior the new athletic shoes all his friends had. Her sense of freedom and power began to evaporate. Then on one of her rare evenings out, her friend Sharon and her boyfriend introduced Cheryl to Charlie. The next day, Charlie called and asked her to go bowling. Since the children were with George, she accepted. The next day, he called again and suggested that she and the children go out for a burger with him. They did, and Charlie could not have been more attentive to them all. By the end of the summer, Charlie had started to pressure Cheryl to marry him. Cheryl knew she did not completely trust Charlie, although she could not say precisely why. It was just a nagging, uncomfortable feeling that he was never quite straight with her. And she hated his love for pornography and X-rated movies. But her economic difficulties were making her frantic, so she said yes. Six months after the wedding, Sharon gave her bad news: Fourteen-year-old Laurie had tearfully told Sharon's daughter that she did not like the way Charlie kept running his hands over her. Cheryl froze. "What," she asked Sharon, "can I do? I cannot make it on my own. There is no way I can support two kids!"

During the fall of 1994, the country was chilled by the widely publicized story of Susan Smith, a young South Carolina mother who strapped her two boys into their car seats and pushed the car into a lake. Her reasons remain obscure. No doubt, Smith was emotionally unstable. She had been dating a young man from an affluent local family, and, in one version, she had come to believe that he would not marry her because of her children. The young man insisted that he never said any such thing, but she may well have believed the children stood between her and her dream for a secure future. Among the many tragedies of this bizarre story, surely the most troubling remains the possibility that Susan Smith believed that she would never have the future she wanted unless she was freed from responsibility for her children. Many other single mothers face similar conflicts, although most do not seek freedom from children. What they do seek is the freedom to care for their children properly.

Women's ties to marriage stretch, bend, and sometimes break. Their ties to children usually remain iron-cast. Yet, the United States stands out among industrialized nations as the one in which women do best and children do worst. Our society is unmistakably failing its children, who are increasingly being left to cope alone with a world that adults find daunting. American parents spend 40 percent less time with their children than they did only a few decades ago—down from thirty hours a week to seventeen.[1] Divorce and remarriage play an important role in these patterns, but so does the economic pressure for both parents to work full-time. The poorly understood consequences of the economic and sexual revolutions are playing themselves out in the lives of children, who, as often as not, are being left to their own resources.

It is easy to attribute the most glaring problems to poverty. Between 20 and 30 percent of American children live in poverty, and perhaps as many as half of all African-American children do. Yet the proportion of poor children has decreased since World War II. And, although the number started to creep up again during the 1980s, it remains much lower than when the grandparents of today were children. The most alarming aspect of children's poverty today may well be its cause. Most poor children are poor because they live in households headed only by a woman, and the poorest children are likely to live with a mother who has never been married. Half of all poor children live in families headed only by a woman, and almost 70 percent of African-American children are born to single mothers.

In absolute terms, many more white children than black live with single mothers and grow up in poverty, and their numbers are rising, but the proportion of black children remains consistently higher, and it, too, is rising.[2] The single best explanation for the poverty of children is the absence of marriage, and 73 percent of children who grow up in a single-parent household will experience poverty at some point during their first ten years.[3] The visible tip of this iceberg of misery is the notorious "welfare problem," which no one seems able to solve. But the unfolding horror vastly exceeds welfare, for many single mothers earn a little too much to qualify for Aid to Families with Dependent Children (AFDC) and can barely keep their heads above water.[4]

Poverty alone does not begin to account for the problems of American children, nor are only poor children troubled and disoriented, as we saw in the stories of Becca and Aprill. Many of the most distressing symptoms of children's and adolescents' discomfort cut across class and racial lines. You do not have to be poor to feel yourself abandoned. Children and adolescents may well feel abandoned when, by ordinary criteria, they are not. Childhood and adolescence are proverbially unsettling and even tempestuous periods. But the distress that our young people are registering can no more be explained by purely personal problems than by family income.

→ Whether economic, psychological, or both, the needs of children are being ignored because no one can agree about how they should be met. Conservatives charge that children are being abandoned by mothers who prefer to work. Feminists angrily counter that fathers have as much responsibility to care for children as mothers. Thus conservatives avoid the obvious truth that most women must work. Feminists avoid the no less obvious truth that, however much things have changed, most women do remain bound to children, and children do curtail women's freedom of mobility and action. It is, to be blunt, difficult to reconcile the needs of children with feminist demands for women's freedom. Children, by their nature, restrict the freedom of their parents.

Not so long ago devotion to children was widely recognized as an important responsibility. Today that rhetoric has virtually disappeared. We do not publicly celebrate mothering as valuable and difficult work. We do not even celebrate it as praiseworthy service. No wonder women who decide to stay home with their children simmer with resentment against women who do not. They feel as if they were being told that they themselves do not work. Worse, the work they have chosen to do is too often treated by other women as if it were menial—as if menial work itself should ever be considered degrading. Thus, during a recent television debate on *Firing Line*, even Betty Friedan, who increasingly emphasizes the importance of families, portrayed mothering—I trust inadvertently—as the demeaning work of serving meals.

However unintentionally, both conservatives and feminists reinforce the message. Conservatives talk as if they wanted to imprison women within motherhood; feminists talk as if they want to liberate women from it. When conservatives stress women's attachment to children and wax eloquent about its rewards, their words ring hollow since they fail to appreciate the painful difficulties of most women's lives. Thus congressional conservatives remain reluctant to pass legislation that encourages business to make minimal accommodation to mothers' needs. What is getting lost in the increasingly shrill exchange of abuse between feminists and conservatives is the notion that the bearing and rearing of a child might well be the most important and rewarding thing that most women—or men—do in their lives. Perhaps not always the most fun; assuredly not what pays the rent; almost invariably demanding and more than occasionally frustrating. But important, as Beth Cooke, who gave up her thriving business to stay home when her children were young, understands, is something altogether different, and many, if not most, women throughout history seem to have agreed with her.

Beth's quiet, sure statement that raising her children is the most important thing she will do in her life invites us to think seriously about what we mean by important: a "power" lunch; yet another meeting; making a sale; sealing a deal; winning a legal case; removing an appendix; discovering a cure for breast cancer; winning an election; serving in the army; averting a global nuclear holocaust? The list could be extended indefinitely, and I, for one, do not pre-

tend to know the answer. Nor am I endorsing the sentimental notion that no human activity can be more important than raising a
single child. But our actions offer a better guide than words to what
we really view as important. And, by that standard, children do not
rank high on the agendas of either the feminist or conservative political movements. Yes, feminists claim that their support for abortion,
day care, and other programs represents support for children, but
they display no patience with those who claim that children need a
parent at home, especially if that parent is likely to be the child's
mother. Yes, conservatives oppose abortion and support the idea of
mothers at home, but they have no interest in paying for the children who are not aborted or subsidizing their mothers to stay home.

Feminists insist that during the Reagan and Bush administrations,
women lost ground. But when they speak of a period of backlash,
they neglect to mention that, during the same years, the women for
whom they most clearly speak made equally impressive gains. Some
feminists sincerely deplore the widening gap between social classes
that unfolded during those years, but they have shown little understanding about what less fortunate women really need. Specifically,
feminists' ideological effort to free women from families rather than
strengthen their ties to them reveals a breathtaking disregard for the
principal cause of poor women's poverty. Their blindness is all the
more remarkable since the women who profited most during the
Reagan-Bush years belong to the two-career, upscale families that
most dramatically benefited from the rise in women's salaries. But
then, how can feminism cope with the unpleasant possibility that
some women, like some men, have done well while other women
and children have not?

Although many upscale career women share poor women's goal of
caring for their children, feminists assume that poor women share
the goals of upscale career women like themselves. Such unwar-
ranted assumptions have cost feminism supporters even among upscale career women. More important, they have had serious consequences for public or private policies to support working mothers.
Feminists who do consider the needs of mothers normally insist ei-

ther that men must assume an equal share of the responsibility for children or that the state must step in to support women and children. Within limits, both initiatives are necessary, and both are, in some measure, occurring. Men are doing more, and the state is providing some services and support, although many are now being cut and neither, as feminists insist with a measure of truth, have been doing enough. But the real problem concerns what we need and expect them to do.

✳ We gain nothing by romanticizing motherhood. Not all women want to care for their children, and many who love their children find that caring for them conflicts with other things they also want. Decent women may shortchange children's needs to meet the demands of a job. Lonely women may shortchange children's needs out of their own longing for love or just some social life. Desperate women may shortchange children's needs out of addiction.

Many women who do not believe that a woman's personal fulfillment dictates a choice between her children's life and her own rapidly discover that motherhood conflicts with other aspects of their lives. Consider Terry Romano's situation. When she was thirty-four, Terry became the proud and doting mother of her first child, Veronica. Until about the sixth month of her difficult pregnancy, Terry had had a job she loved, working for the local of a transportation union in Brooklyn, but her employers provided no maternity benefits of any kind. As her pregnancy grew increasingly difficult, they cut off her medical benefits entirely. A few months later, she and Veronica were both thriving, and she would happily have begun to go back to work. Not possible. Her employers—a labor union!—provided no day care, and none was readily available in her neighborhood in Staten Island. As for so many New Yorkers, getting to and from her job required an hour and a half of travel. Her husband, who earned considerably more than she, worked even longer hours.

Left with no choice, Terry decided that she would have to stay home for at least a year or two. Luckily, the Romanos could afford it, although barely. She tried to persuade her union employers to take her back part-time, but they refused. "I have my friends there. I like the work. I like being there. And then there's money coming in. And, you know, my brain would function a little better." Terry had married at twenty-nine, many years after most of her cousins and friends from Brooklyn had married and had children. Having spent a number of years not sure that she would ever marry, much less have children, Terry considers herself lucky. And she delights in her exuberant daughter. "You know, I love her so much, I just love her to death." But being alone with her child "every day, all day" is not always easy and occasionally leads her to "lose patience a little bit. What was I going to do? I couldn't be away five days a week. You know, where am I to put her? She's so young, and you get very nervous."

Terry gave considerable thought to the possible solutions. She would have been happy to work part-time, to work at home, or to share her job. If her employer had had on-site day care, she could have taken Veronica with her. Later in our conversation, Terry comes back to having lost her job. It eats at her. She believes that in not making it possible for her to stay, the union office lost money and, above all, lost loyalty. "They had everything to gain and nothing to lose." Terry does not have a "career," but she did have a job for which she had developed expertise. She and her husband will survive the temporary loss of her income, although it may have an adverse effect on Veronica's education later in life. Presumably, she will find another job. Meanwhile, she has lost her first real opportunity to develop skills and seniority. She has lost her benefits. And she feels that her mind is stagnating. But to keep the job, she would have had to leave her infant daughter for as many as twelve hours a day, and she would have been too worried to enjoy and concentrate on her work. Left with no compromise, Terry chose motherhood over work.

Where Terry Romano had a choice, single mothers like Aprill Ravenel normally have none. Even the most successful, upscale career women, who have larger incomes and more resources than either Terry or Aprill, find the choices difficult. Even married working mothers whose husbands participate actively in what sociologist

Arlie Hochschild calls "the second shift" more than occasionally feel as if their lives were running out of control.[5] But career women normally gain rewards from their work that may make them underestimate the pain of hard choices for less successful and affluent women. In 1994, the magazine *Working Mother* reported that seven out of ten women it polled felt good about themselves and their lives. Their survey was based on telephone interviews with one thousand women, five hundred chosen at random, "five hundred selected as career-committed, that is, women who are highly educated or consider their jobs to be careers."[6]

One does not have to be a mathematical genius to understand that if half of the respondents to a survey have been selected because of their commitment to their career, their attitudes will shape the results. Two of the women admitted that much of their satisfaction with their lives comes from their being able to afford excellent child care and to count on the support of their husbands. Both also insisted that their commitment to work makes them better mothers. Thirty-five-year-old Nancy Masloski, who works as a tax examiner for the State of Maine, told *Working Mother*, "Family life is important to us, of course," but she believes her two sons benefit from the knowledge that she and her husband "have lives outside of the home and that those lives make us happy, too." And Lisa Simon, an office worker who loves her job, insisted, "I'm happier when I'm working. It makes me a better mother."

Not all women agree that being away from young children for ten or twelve hours a day makes them better mothers or makes their children happier. Sylvia Hewlett, who earned her doctorate in economics at Harvard in 1973 and went on to an enviable job at Barnard College, assumed that she was one of those who could "have it all." She had her first child easily, without missing a beat. But her second pregnancy was more difficult, and there was no maternity leave. To follow her doctor's recommendations, she would have to resign. Not likely. "Ten years of hard, grinding work had gone into this career of mine," she writes, "and I was only eighteen months away from tenure. Could I really give up the possibility of lifetime job security?" She agonized but decided to stick it out. A few months later, after she had gone into early labor, the twins she was carrying were born dead. She recovered and, just over a year later, had a healthy child. "But losing those babies . . . permanently changed my priorities."[7]

Hewlett did not abandon her career, but she left Barnard to take a job at a policy institute and specialized in advocacy for families with children. Then, the week of her fortieth birthday, she resigned even that "plum of a job" because no adult can "carry on with business as usual" and meet the needs of growing children. Hewlett forcefully advocates generous family-support policies but has come to believe that "they only get you partway there." An ambitious and accomplished scholar and administrator, she is not telling other women to sacrifice ambition and accomplishment. Indeed, as her own children have grown up, she has returned to her own career as vice president for economic studies at the United Nations Association and as a writer, but she is arguing that children need—and deserve—sustained parental attention. And she is arguing that children who do not get that attention are much more likely to get into trouble, including drugs and alcohol, that might have been prevented.

Hewlett has no interest in dishing out blame, especially to other women. She knows how difficult the decisions may be. Nor is she pretending that a woman can temporarily put her career aside and, when the children no longer need her as much, pick up where she left off. They cannot. Cathy Gerhold took ten years away from her promising career with a Pittsburgh law firm to raise her two children, and when she returned could find only a $25,000-a-year job as a law clerk. Like Hewlett, she is happy about her choice, but she also believes that "I'll probably never achieve the pay scale or the prestige I would have had if I'd kept working those ten years." Anne Bernstein, chairwoman of the maternity and medicine task force of the American Medical Women's Association, says Gerhold's experience is typical. If a woman takes an extended leave, the professional establishment "immediately takes for granted that you're not dedicated to your career."[8]

In careers and the professions, "dedicated" normally means to the exclusion of everything else. Women like Hewlett and Gerhold do consider their careers important, they simply consider "being there" for their children more important. Some women who make that decision consider it appropriate to return to work when their youngest child starts school, others when their youngest leaves for college, others at some point in between. Most agree there is no "right" time, since different children and mothers have different needs, and sometimes fathers can step in to pick up the slack. When the insurance company for which Gloria Patterson's husband worked closed, he had had trouble finding another job, but he could be home in the afternoons when Jackson, their twelve-year-old son, returned from school. And although Bill did not take unemployment easily, both he and Gloria told me that the "being there" had everything to do with Jackson's consistently making the honor roll.

Sadly, for too many parents "being there" remains an unattainable luxury. Conservatives who preach family values and women's responsibilities to children are rarely talking about most middle-class, much less poorer, people's lives, and they do not ease the plight of the children by condemning their working mothers as selfish. The feminist response, which even many nonfeminist women echo in their hearts, is why should it always be the woman? Why do we not condemn working men as selfish for not staying home with the kids? We will not begin to develop viable solutions to these problems until we acknowledge that no ideological formula can answer the legitimate questions that working people in a variety of situations are asking. Above all, the scapegoating of mothers is neither fair nor helpful.

The first step is to sort out the questions. First, do children need a parent at home and, if yes, which parent and for how long? Usually, the question is rephrased, Should women stay home with children? But the rephrasing throws us back into the debate over women's rights and responsibilities: Are women entitled to the same careers as men? Do women have a special ("natural") responsibility to children? Buried in both questions is the one that will not go away: Are women and men the same or different? Today most people believe that the only sensible answer is both. And the "both" explains their apparently contradictory beliefs that the ideal solution for families would be to have the mother stay home with the children while they are young, that fathers can parent as well as mothers, and that children will do just as well if both parents work as they would do if one did not. These attitudes do not divide women from men. Rather, they capture both women's and men's knowledge that the needs of families conflict with corporate life, and their instinctive recognition that, in our society, the interests of women are especially likely to conflict with the needs of children. Yet the needs of children, especially babies, are necessarily nonnegotiable.

Penelope Leach has passionately argued that we are ignoring the needs of babies.[9] In Leach's view, no baby can have too much love; no baby makes demands that should not be met. The more a baby is held, cuddled, and attended to, the better the baby will do. And the responsibility of meeting those demands naturally falls to the baby's mother, for the mother's sake as well as the baby's. Both mother and baby, having been linked together in pregnancy, need time to separate gradually. That gradual and mutual separation also builds new bonds between them so that, throughout a child's early life, its mother will truly be unique. Thus, in the lives of babies and young children, mothers and fathers are neither the same nor equal. Leach regards fathers as tremendously important, but, if truth be told, she barely disguises a certain tolerant condescension toward them. The mother, in her view, must make every effort to draw the father into the intimacy that binds her to her child so that he will feel a part of things—will not feel too painfully excluded.[10] As the child grows up, the father's role should expand and eventually become as important as the mother's in everyday care.

Few feminists accept Leach's emphasis on a mother's unique role in the life of a child. They impatiently insist that the importance of mother-child bonding is an invention of male psychiatrists and psychologists, who emphasize gender differences to protect men's advantage over women. They find the news no more welcome when it comes from a woman. Once you admit that mothers have a unique role, you are forced to concede that they have a special responsibility. But if you make that concession, what becomes of fairness—or women's equal opportunities in the labor force? They evaporate, leaving women frustrated, bored, and at risk to be left when the men whose children they have raised tire of them.

Married and single mothers alike will tell you that children do curtail a woman's independence and, in a moment of candor, may even tell you that there are always moments at which any mother would give anything to be free of the constant demands on her time and attention. I still vividly remember one afternoon when I was nine and my brother eight. We were walking with my mother and, all of sudden, she said, with an edge of desperation in her voice, "Don't hang on me!" Something in her tone shocked me, although at the time I could not begin to understand her feelings. Today, even though I have no children of my own, I understand. The hours I have spent with nieces, nephews, and godchildren and, especially, the many conversations I have had with mothers have given me at least a taste of what it feels like to have someone who always needs something of you, always wants your attention, and cannot just be told to go away.

The claim that children are men's as well as women's responsibility cannot be overemphasized, but many feminists still remain uncomfortable with it. Their attitude reminds me of my mother's, who, when she found me especially provoking or incomprehensible, would say impatiently, "You are your father's daughter." From the perspective of the war between the sexes, it is sometimes more convenient to regard children as a burden that men impose upon women and sometimes more convenient to insist that they are women's alone. But from the perspective of women who are raising children alone, that battle makes no sense at all. For good reason societies throughout history have tried to make men accountable for the children they father. Without some assistance from fathers or extended families women normally find the care for children a heavy burden. And even with the assistance of fathers, working women frequently have less time to devote to their children than they want or their children need.

→ We know that children need time, which is another way of saying they need emotional stability and continuity. The most substantial research confirms that the single most important element in a child's development remains a stable emotional relationship with one person. There is no rule that beyond infancy the person need be the mother. There is even no rule that the person need be either of the child's natural parents. Grandparents have frequently played that role, especially in the black community. The rule is that the child needs a loving, constant, and reliable person—a person to whom the child may safely become attached and against whom he or she may define her own personality. Thus do countless children delight in some form of the game of throwing a ball and watching it return. "Come back" ranks at the top of a child's priorities. It is at once command, wish, and statement of fact: You must come back, I want you to come back, you will come back.

Historically, mothers have been more likely than fathers to be the person who is there and comes back, and that likelihood has shaped the expectations of both women and men. Feminists are right to insist that those expectations may change. The trouble with their claim that men can "mother" as well as women is that it has normally taken the form: "Women may not be forced to mother." And the moment you put the emphasis on what women may no longer be forced to do, you transform the job they may not be forced to do —in this case mothering—into a punitive burden from which everyone should be freed.

The feminist determination to free women from mothering also reflects a reaction against the romanticized, Hallmark card view of mothers as all-giving, all-understanding, all-forgiving saints. No one, they correctly say, can be expected to live up to those standards of self-abnegation and sacrifice. But, then, notwithstanding the fantasies of fairy-godmothers, that is not what most children want. And it is assuredly not what the best psychologists recommend. All children need is what the British psychoanalyst D. W. Winnicott has called "good enough mothering."[11] But good-enough mothering brings us back to the problem of time. It has become fashionable to speak of "quality" time as an adequate, or superior, replacement for the mere "quantity" of everyday time. Just because many women no longer have the option of spending long stretches of everyday time with their children, we are not obliged to deny the value of those long stretches. For the repetitive—even dull—activities of everyday life provide parents and children a unique opportunity to come to know one another.

For the last thirty years, Felice Schwartz, founder and president of Catalyst, a nonprofit organization that works with business to promote change for women, has insisted upon women's need for a distinct pattern of employment. Schwartz ignited what is now known as the "mommy track" debate with an article in the *Harvard Business Review* in which she forcefully argued that the world of paid employment, which was created by men for men, makes no—or inadequate—concessions to the facts of women's lives.[12] She points out that women who work in prestigious corporations and law firms live with the same kinds of tensions as women who work for the minimum wage. Schwartz noted that many are leaving the workforce, at least while their children are young. One such woman, the reporter Julie Rose, wrote an article on Schwartz in which she evoked her own experience. Two and a half months after the birth of her daughter, Rose returned to her exciting and demanding full-time job as a budget policy analyst for the Texas legislature. Returned, she notes, "with great relief." She remembers the infancy of the daughter whom she "adored" as "the most tedious and demanding" days of her life. Back at work, however, she found her thoughts constantly turning to the child at home, and as time passed "I felt even more keenly the conflict between work and home." During one frenetic two-day stretch, she spent thirty minutes with her one-and-a-half-year-old, and only when her husband brought the child to her at the legislature.[13]

When Rose's husband was offered a good job in Massachusetts, she agreed he should take it, knowing that she would be leaving a job she loved and would not make a full-time commitment to another. "Instead, I eagerly committed myself to my children." No more than Hewlett does Rose regret her choice. She simply recognizes that for women "who seek both career and motherhood, something usually has to give." Rose believes her experience typifies that of millions of women and illustrates Schwartz's argument that companies need to take account of the differing experiences of women and men. The "dismal" facts are, she insists, that most women have babies, and most babies sooner or later interrupt careers. "The facts are not fair." Men who want families do not face the same choices as women. But then, men do not give birth.

Like Penelope Leach, Schwartz insists that maternity is more than having a baby. Nursing, bonding, and childrearing absorb women's physical and emotional energies, triggering new emotions with which they will wrestle for the rest of their lives. Motherhood changes women's sense of who they are. Most young career women do not foresee the impact that maternity will have on their identities and lives. Recently, a young woman friend in a New York publishing company told me with evident outrage about a female co-worker who had just returned from maternity leave. "I am not sure she's going to last," my friend exploded. "There she is, all the time hanging on the phone. It's the nanny this, and the baby that, and then she has to leave early to see what's going on." She did not last. For her, like many new mothers, the pull of home eventually won. Taking the pull of home as natural and beneficial, Schwartz advocates putting women on a special track that allows them to return to work after spending some time at home while their children are young. These days, she even advises them to tell prospective employers about their plans to have children, since a growing labor shortage puts women in an excellent position. "There's not a company in the country that isn't eager to attract and retain the best women."[14]

Schwartz has come under feminist fire. NOW and the National

Women's Political Caucus, joined by the ACLU, delivered a blistering attack, and even Betty Friedan has referred to Schwartz's views as "dangerous" and "deplorable." The radicals have called her "a traitor to the women's movement." Feminists cannot forgive Schwartz for betraying the dream of women's equality with men. But Schwartz focuses on what many women want, not on what radicals presume they should want. And she has found that even highly successful women frequently want to spend much more time with their young children than the sixty-hour weeks required by the corporate fast track will permit.

Time alone will tell whether Schwartz has correctly assessed the untapped possibilities of the labor market for returning and part-time working mothers. She has scored impressive success in increasing women's presence in corporations, not least by helping corporations to become more hospitable to women. The polls show that married women and especially working mothers remain as eager as ever for part-time work and flexible work schedules. So, despite feminist disapproval, Schwartz has a good sense of what millions of women want. Less clear is the willingness of employers to meet their needs, although some are trying. IBM, for example, permits its female employees to take a three-year maternity leave. The leave is unpaid, but the women who take advantage of it are guaranteed that they may return to their jobs.

Meanwhile, we are left to ponder the feminist charge that Schwartz has betrayed women.[15] How? By claiming that women want to be mothers? By claiming that mothering takes time? Or perhaps by suggesting that men are not as good mothers as women? In fairness, many feminists would probably insist that they mean none of those things. But since they do not much like to talk about any of these questions, we are left to ponder what they might mean. Perhaps their reluctance is itself the point. Feminists have single-mindedly focused the discussion on women's opportunities to equal men in income and status. And however much they talk about transforming the climate of the workplace, they assume that it should shape the lives of women as it has always shaped the lives of men. We are thus left with the depressing conclusion that feminists expect children to fit into the nooks and crannies of women's lives, the way women have traditionally fit into the nooks and crannies of men's. But when motherhood is demoted from the center of women's lives to a parenthesis, children are demoted as well.

Working mothers understandably bristle at the idea that their choices may hurt or disadvantage their children. Few want to put their own needs before those of a young, vulnerable person who depends upon them. But nagging fears that their children might prefer to have them at home help to account for the passion with which they insist that their working ultimately benefits their children—that their children are perfectly happy. No woman wants to be called a bad mother, much less to feel guilty about being less attentive than she might be. Few, if any, issues evoke as much resentment and hostility among women as the decision to work or not to work while children are young. And since our society does little to support either working mothers or mothers who remain at home, it offers fertile ground for women to resent women who make one choice rather than another. These tensions among women obscure the real horror, namely that with rare exceptions, the nature of our economy is preventing both groups from really having a choice—and that children continue to be the real victims.

Most working mothers find it difficult to stay home for more than a year or two; some cannot afford to stay home even that long. Their ability to care for their children demands cooperation and support— from husbands, from employers, and from society. But even when husbands cooperate fully, as increasing numbers do, the support of employers and society remains decisive. Ruth Trescott, who is about the same age as Terry Romano and who, although married, does not yet have children, shares Terry's concerns about child care. Ruth has recently begun work at the ACXIOM corporation in Conway, Arkansas. In the Conway office, where about eight hundred people work, ACXIOM "has on-site day care and visible women in their senior management." The new vice president of corporate marketing, brought in from New York University Law School, is a woman: "Very outspoken. Very different, because she's from New York—in Arkansas." Overall, Ruth thinks as much as 50 percent of the workforce is female, including her three immediate supervisors. "Yet if you tried to discuss if these are feminist issues, or are they employee issues, they would really get offended at the use of the word 'feminist.' They wouldn't know what you meant by that."

Since most of ACXIOM's employees, except for the top management, who are brought in from New York and Chicago, come from Conway, "There are a lot of marriages in the corporation." Ruth knows that some people might see that as a problem, as almost incestuous. "But it also has meant flexibility, because the men were working with their wives and they couldn't ignore the problems of family." Working with their wives and their friends from down the street or the PTA, "They knew of their problems and they couldn't put them in a separate category of women whose issues don't concern us."

A number of her male coworkers whose wives work elsewhere bring their children to ACXIOM day care. The men are responsible for the children, "bringing them in every morning and picking them up and taking them home." Employees at ACXIOM often work late, so if the wife hasn't finished her computer run, "the husband just goes and picks up the kids and goes home." In Conway, where there are a limited number of good jobs and living costs are very low, the company has been able to substitute benefits for hard cash. Ruth wonders what will happen when two of her immediate bosses, both women, have children. Both are "obviously rising up the corporate ladder," but children will confront them with difficult choices about day care, "since staying in Conway for the day care might "cut into their career tracking." So, she reflects, "they're going to have to make some choices and have to have some options available to them if they want to keep the positions that they're in right now."

Ruth knows that she is making substantially less than she would elsewhere, especially in a big city like New York, Chicago, or Atlanta. She believes that if she performs well at her job, she will get raises every year—"forever"—as well as opportunities for stock options. She knows she is settling for less salary than she is worth on the market. "But I can't give up the future potential of having a place where I would feel comfortable with the day care. And it really is a wonderful day care." Thinking of it, she smiles warmly: There is one caretaker for every five children, and they have separated the facility into small classrooms. "In fact, there's a waiting list."

Ruth credits ACXIOM's strong day care and treatment of women employees, but she also believes that the attitudes of her coworkers have been shaped by life in Conway, Arkansas. "This whole definition of career is a yuppie thing." A lot of women in this small town in Arkansas have always had jobs. "Maybe your mom was a secretary at the elementary school or worked at the church office two days a week. It's only when it becomes a career that it becomes a thorny issue. When everybody had a job, everybody pitched in, everybody worked." The question is not whether women will work, "It's just what and how. Who's going to take care of the kids, who's going to pick up the dry cleaning, who's going to sleep? Who's going to take the kids to Little League on Saturday morning and those kinds of issues."

Among the people whom she and her husband, an engineer, know well, "one father is staying home with the daughter and working on his dissertation while the mother's teaching at the college." Another father who teaches at the local high school and whose wife works for an accounting firm in Little Rock takes the children to and from day care because she has a forty-five-minute commute and must leave the house by 7:00 A.M. He feeds the children breakfast and gets them to day care by 8:30. Yet another couple, Sophie and Ethan, who have a two-year-old daughter, have worked out their lives so that she can spend the summer in New York at drama school while he is at home with their child. "They're making it work. And this family, in particular, is very politically conservative and also very religious. They don't drink, they're very active in the Methodist Church in Conway." Sophie and Ethan have found a way "to make all that work for them" without compromising any of their principles. "Again, if you said the word 'feminism' to Ethan and Sophie, it wouldn't mean anything."

The same kinds of attitudes seem to prevail among the people she knows less well at work. In part, she thinks, it comes back to ACXIOM's hiring husbands and wives; in part, it comes back to the quality of life in a small town in which families have always been working units. "But then, it is Arkansas." She does not mean that as a put-down. "They just aren't as cosmopolitan. They are really good, hardworking, family kind of people." Right now, six women of forty people on her floor at work are pregnant. "It comes up at lunch. It comes up when we have baby showers in the boardroom. The men are, by virtue of being on that floor, all part of that." The men respect the women when they are good at their jobs. "And they must not have much trouble with taking authority from women, because, like I said, the three bosses in our division are all women."

Some of these attitudes can be attributed to the technical nature of their work: "Either you can do it or you can't. It doesn't matter whether you're attractive or not—not when you have to get the job done." And because so many of the employees are married to each other, "There is more of a familial kind of attitude toward work." And because it is such a small town there is always a good chance "that you will meet people, like I say, at the store or at the church or in the PTA." She does wonder what will happen if the company moves to St. Louis or Chicago. Would a move to a big city make things worse for women? "Or do you always assume that the larger city and more urban setting is better for women? That you have all these progressive men . . . Maybe that's not so true anymore."

In many ways the lives of Ruth's coworkers and friends in Conway resemble those of many working couples of different classes and races throughout the country. They take for granted that women will have to work and that men will have to share the responsibility of raising children. Their values strongly resemble those of the working-class and lower-middle-class Italian-American community that Terry Romano grew up in, but their circumstances make it easier for them to work outside the home and pay close attention to their children. Ironically, the poverty of their state has, at least for the moment, spared them the worst features of contemporary urban life.

Ruth, who enjoys the cosmopolitan bustle of big cities, does not view Arkansas as perfect: "It is very interesting to watch this happen in Arkansas, which has every stereotype of poor education, poor economic class, racial problems forever." It was also fascinating to watch the Arkansan response to the national furor over Hillary Clinton's remarks that she was not one of those women who baked cookies and served tea. Arkansans had already been through that debate when Bill Clinton became governor. "So, she wants to work. Our wives work. It's a poor state. Everyone has to work." Perhaps the executives at ACXIOM understood that, in this environment, good day care was more important than higher salaries. Certainly Terry Romano would have thought so.

We may safely assume that the women of Arkansas have pretty much the same range of frustrations with their husbands as other women throughout the country. We may also assume that, like Maria Ramirez and the other women of the GED class, they value women's independence. Their advantage over many other American women comes in the support they receive to combine work outside the home with family life—in their ability "to make it work for them." These women would never call themselves feminists, in no small part because from what they know about contemporary feminism they see little in it of use to women who value their marriages and their children.

Sadly, too few companies provide the kind of day care ACXIOM does, but throughout the country, fathers of all classes and ethnicities are helping to make things work for their families. Only a few years ago, when I should have known better, I was stunned to hear a group of men, who work for the physical plant division of Emory University, talk openly about their domestic responsibilities. A white Southern-born man somewhat impatiently queried the white middle-class female expert in sensitivity training who was leading the discussion: "How do you expect me to watch CNN every night? By the time I have had dinner, done 'my' dishes, and helped to put the kids to bed I only have time and energy left for my bath." This man had fully accepted some parts of what had conventionally been viewed as "women's work" as his own. One of his African-American colleagues, who also assumed a variety of domestic responsibilities, drove home the need for women and men to work together to keep a family going. What he did was all very well, "but if anything happened to my wife I would be up shit's creek." And he painted a poignant, if whimsical, picture of his having to take the kids to McDonald's every night.

In New York, the women of the GED class are raising their daughters to be able to earn a living and raising their sons to expect to help around the house. As a divorced mother whose husband had taught her all she needed to know about thoughtless men, Gabriella Ortiz took her son's domestic education as seriously as her daughters'. "I taught my son to iron when he was nine. He knows how to cook. He knows how to clean. So he won't depend on anybody." And Maria Ramirez notes with pleasure men's new relations with their children: "I admire the younger men these days, the way they are with their children." Previously, some of the men would not even walk down the street alone with their children. A few months later, her words echoed in my mind during a conversation with Alicia Cobb, the elegant white wife of a successful lawyer. She, too, was commenting upon the way in which men of her class had changed. Her father, she wryly noted, could not be trusted to boil water, and Tom, her own husband, was only a little more experienced in the ways of kitchens and children. But these days, while driving to work, she sees fathers waiting with their kids at the school bus stop. "Why, Tom did not even know where the school bus stop was!"

We might expect that men whose wives work would come to understand the unfairness of women's performing the entire "second shift." And women's work does account for many of the changes in men's attitudes—many, but not all. Men whose wives earn more than they are still less likely to pitch in with kids and household labor, doubtless because they believe that the balance between women and men has, in their case, shifted too far. But some men adjust well. When Alison Michaels, who trains employees of major firms in computer programs, received a spectacular offer from a company in St. Louis, Missouri, she and her husband, Jonas, agreed she should accept it, and they should move from Utah, where they had both grown up. The St. Louis firm was offering her a salary that was more than double their combined salaries in Utah. During their first year in St. Louis, Jonas stayed home to ease the transition and, especially, to be available for their seven-year-old son, Joshua. At the end of the first year, he was ready to go back to work himself, but he never resented the arrangement, and he was delighted that Alison earned enough to make it possible.

Other men whose wives are not working at all contribute a lot around the house.[16] The issues concern balance—or, if you prefer, fairness. Increasingly, men are treating women as people rather than servants and expecting to share in the work necessary to keeping life going. And most working women still spend the equivalent of a second full work week in their care for children and the needs of their family. This is what Arlie Hochschild calls "the second shift."

These changing attitudes register women's attainment of a measure of the independence that Maria Ramirez wants for her daughter. So, whether they are working for wages at the moment or not, their husbands are more likely to appreciate the need for some equity in the domestic division of labor. The new attitudes are clearly visible among academic couples. One of my senior male colleagues said with a mixture of appreciation and regret, "You simply cannot have department meetings at the end of the afternoon or in the evenings anymore." He explained that he did not only mean that there were now women in the department, although when he started there had been none. He meant that too many of the men were leaving in the middle of the afternoon to take care of their kids. These days, fathers are as likely as mothers to bring their kids to campus with them. An economist in Boston, who in his early forties has built a highly successful career, told me that this year his wife, who is finishing a doctorate in psychology, is doing a demanding internship that requires her to leave before her children go to school in the morning and not to return until after dinner is prepared at night. So he is assuming more responsibility for their two children's car pools, meals, and homework, as well as housework, errands, and laundry.

Some fathers have not adjusted as rapidly as others, although more may be doing so than we suspect. Increasingly, domestic arrangements reflect agreement rather than conflict between partners, although they remain a major source of conflict. Many couples find the years after the birth of a second child especially difficult, for that is when both financial and domestic pressures increase. And the period after the birth of a second child is when the most divorces occur. In the measure that generalization is possible, the central issue for men seems to be that they feel good about their own position. Participation in the second shift comes less easily to men who make less money than their wives and may have reason to feel that traditional roles have been reversed rather than equalized. But growing numbers of men understand that women have gained a new independence and that women who choose not to work for wages or to work part-time while their children are young are in fact making a choice and could, under other circumstances, reverse it.[17]

In the end, the choices that women and men make about the sharing of responsibilities for earning an income and for child care are private, and couples find their own balance. The Family and Medical Leave Act now permits men as well as women to take twelve weeks unpaid leave a year to assist with the birth or adoption of a child or the care of an elderly parent or seriously ill family member. The government thus officially recognizes that men as well as women have pressing family responsibilities that may not always mesh with the demands of full-time employment. But the dedicated rearing of children is not simply a passing crisis. For a given number of years, it becomes a way of life. It may be combined with paid labor, especially as children grow older, but more often than not, those who attempt to combine it with full-time labor find that something suffers. After the birth of her first child, Judy Woodruff moved from her top position covering the White House for NBC to the *MacNeil-Lehrer Newshour* because the constant travel would now be too much. Explaining her decision, she said, "I have come to terms with the fact that I cannot be all things to all people, or all things to myself."[18]

With each passing year, the number of upscale women who are making similar choices is steadily growing. Between 1983 and 1991, the number of professionals who chose to work part-time grew by almost 30 percent, although the workforce grew by only half that amount. And a third of all part-time women workers have children thirteen or younger. As Felice Schwartz predicted, more companies are accommodating them by offering them new assignments or helping them to restructure their old ones. While remaining professionals, although on a reduced schedule, such women are normally paid at the same rate as previously and retain their benefits. Some even succeed in advancing their careers while on a part-time or flexible track. None make as much money as they made before they decided to stay home, and even after they return full-time they almost never catch up. And some never regain a foothold on their previous career track at all. Thus for many women, although not all, motherhood puts professional accomplishments and standing at very high risk.

When we consider the lives of women and children, the feminist hostility to the "mommy track" seems puzzling at best, irresponsible at worst. It reflects the revolutionary fervor that insists that the world should be entirely transformed—right now—in accordance with the revolutionaries' theories and dreams, to say nothing of prejudices. Even so, it remains difficult to imagine what the radical feminists intend, unless they simply want men to stay home so that women may work. What their various scenarios lack is any sense of who will really take care of the children, unless, of course, you assume that children do not need much attention beyond that which can be provided by servants.

The attitudes of upscale women, especially feminist policy makers, do matter if only because of their influence over our public discussion of policies. They have, for example, been more concerned with tax deductions for domestic labor (which benefit working women) than tax deductions for children (which benefit mothers who stay home), and they have preferred public support for day care (which permits parents to work full-time) than public support for part-time workers (which permits a parent to spend more time with children). For if parents' decisions about the appropriate division of labor are largely private, the conditions under which those decisions are made are inescapably public. Most women would ask nothing better than to be able to follow a "mommy track," but they do not have the option. Many do not have men with whom to share the responsibilities, and many more have no opportunity to restructure their jobs or reduce the hours they devote to them. If they can find part-time work, it is at minimal wages and without benefits. Almost none have access to high-quality, on-site day care, and many cannot afford quality day care at all. Yet frequently these women do regard their children as the most important thing in their life. Their problem is not lack of commitment, but their inability, despite often heroic efforts, to meet that commitment.

Notes

[1] Sylvia Ann Hewlett, *When the Bough Breaks: The Costs of Neglecting Our Children* (New York: Basic Books, 1991).

[2] Marian Wright Edelman, *Families in Peril: An Agenda for Social Change* (Cambridge, MA., Harvard Univ. Press, 1987). Experts quarrel over the meaning of these statistics. See, for example, Charles Murray, *Loosing Ground: American Social Policy 1950–1980*, tenth anniversary edition (New York: Basic Books, 1994); William Julius Wilson, *The Truly Disadvantaged: The Inner City, the Underclass, and Public Policy* (Chicago: Univ. of Chicago Press, 1987).

[3] Patrick F. Fagan, "Rising Illegitimacy: America's Social Catastrophe," *F.Y.I.* (Washington, 1994). The report is available from the Heritage Foundation, 214 Massachusetts Ave., N.E., Washington, DC 20002-4999; David Ellwood, *Poor Support* (New York: Basic Books, 1988), 83–84.

[4] Valerie Plakow, *Lives on the Edge: Single Mothers and Their Children in the Other America* (Chicago: Univ. of Chicago Press, 1993).

5Arlie Hochschild with Anne Machung, *The Second Shift* (New York: Viking, 1989).

6*Working Mother* (May 1994): 42.

7Sylvia Ann Hewlett, "Tough Choices, Great Rewards," *Parade Magazine, Atlanta Journal and Constitution* (July 4, 1994): 4–5.

8Meredith K. Wadman, "Mothers Who Take Extended Time Off Find Their Careers Pay a Heavy Price," *The Wall Street Journal* (July 16, 1992): B1.

9Penelope Leach, *Children First: What Our Society Must Do—And Is Not Doing—for Our Children Today* (New York: Knopf, 1994).

10Leach, *Children First.*

11D. W. Winnicott, *The Maturational Process and the Facilitating Environment* (London: Hogarth Press, 1972, c. 1965) and *Playing and Reality* (London: Tavistock Publications, 1982).

12Felice N. Schwartz, *Breaking With Tradition: Women, Work, and the New Facts of Life* (New York: Warner Books, 1992). Schwartz did not use the term mommy track in her original article, "Management Women and the New Facts of Life," *Harvard Business Review* 67, no. 1 (January/February 1989): 65–76.

13Julie Rose, "From Career to Maternity," *Washington Monthly* 24, iss. 7–8 (July–Aug. 1992).

14From a speech Schwartz gave, cited by Ellen Hopkins, "Who Is Felice Schwartz and Why Is She Saying Those Terrible Things About Us," *Working Woman* (October 1990): 118. Title 7 of the Civil Rights Act of 1964 gave women the right not to be questioned about their plans to become pregnant.

15According to Julie Rose, "From Career to Maternity," 53, Friedan charged Schwartz with "retrofeminism." In *Backlash*, Susan Faludi incorrectly claimed Schwartz had seen the error of her ways and "recanted." The most heated response to Schwartz came in 1989 at the time of her *Harvard Business Review* article.

16Hochschild, *Second Shift*; Karen D. Pyke, "Women's Employment as a Gift or Burden? Marital Power Across Marriage, Divorce, and Remarriage," *Gender and Society* 8, no. 1 (March 1994): 73–91.

17Pyke, "Women's Employment as Gift or Burden?"

18Cited in Barbara Kantrowitz and Pat Winger, "About the Mommy Track," *Working Woman* (February 1993): 51.

Nine

WOMEN IN THE
CULTURAL WAR

ost feminists regard "family feminism" as a contradiction in terms. When Betty Friedan, in *The Second Stage*, proposed that feminism should now attend more closely to families, radical feminists exploded with outrage. Ellen Willis pronounced it "a step backward" and "less a prescription for the feminist dilemma than a symptom of it." In her view, feminists would be mistaken "to imagine that the women's movement can concede the right's moral assumptions and retain any credibility for its political agenda." For feminism "is not just an issue or a group of issues; it is the cutting edge of a revolution in cultural and moral values."[1] According to Willis, Friedan "would destroy feminism in order to save it, and beat the Moral Majority by joining it."[2] Notwithstanding Willis's blast, Friedan deserves credit for trying to compel feminism to rethink its direction and priorities.

By rejecting her effort, radical feminists announce that they see the needs of women as incompatible with the needs of families and especially children.

The conservative emphasis upon "family values" has made it easy for feminists like Willis, Catherine Stimpson, and Susan Faludi to view any reference to families as capitulation to a conservative back-lash that aims to strip women of the independence for which they have been fighting. But their attack on the feminist Friedan makes clear that they do not have much patience for any burdensome fam-ily ties. Thus feminist denunciations of "family values" as a right-wing ploy to subordinate women suggest that families necessarily subordinate women to men. But men are not the real problem. To-day's American men, like men of all times and places—and women too—are quite capable of angling for advantage and even of bully-ing. Most, however, are adjusting to women's growing indepen-dence, albeit some more gracefully than others. In *The Feminine Mystique*, Friedan claimed that women were suffering from "the problem that has no name," namely boredom, restlessness, and a diffuse dissatisfaction with their lives. Trapped in the suburbs, the women she was describing were deprived of meaningful work and cut off from the larger world for which their educations had pre-pared them. Under the impact of the economic and sexual revolu-tions, that problem dissipated. For the past thirty years, women, including married women and mothers, have become a vital force in our economy, political life, and society. Yet neither women's revolu-tionary gains nor their prospects for making more have impressed feminists, who complain even more loudly that women remain far from true "equality" with men.

Today, women's "problem that has no name" is children. Chil-dren, not men, restrict women's independence; children, not men, tend to make and keep women poor. Few but the most radical femi-nists have been willing to state openly that women's freedom re-quires their freedom from children. Yet the covert determination to free women from children shapes much feminist thought and most feminist policies even, and especially, those policies aimed at having the government assume a large part of the responsibility. Thus, disagreement about the relation between women and children explodes into the angry cultural war between feminists and conservatives, although many Americans who are not palpably conservative are joining the anti-feminist side.

At the center of the confrontation lies the problem of women's special responsibility for children. Most feminists emphasize women's claims to equality, while most conservatives emphasize the realities of sexual difference. Most feminists minimize the importance of marriage, while most conservatives dwell upon it. Both sides feed the nightmares of the other. Responding to conservative rhetoric, feminists argue that marriage primarily serves men's determination to control women and keep them dependent. Responding to feminist rhetoric, conservatives argue that feminists intend nothing less than the destruction of the family, and the intimacy and privacy it affords.

Conservatives celebrate women's special responsibility for children as natural; feminists dismiss it as an oppressive myth. Those who remain uneasy with both extremes face difficult questions. Are there any differences between women and men that explain why the responsibility for children must fall more heavily on women? If so, how may we protect women's necessary economic independence? May we assume that, in general, children benefit from the focused attention of their own parents or of close family members, and that making it possible for them to enjoy such attention should rank as a national priority? If so, what policies would best serve children's needs, and should they be provided through public or private means? Almost everyone now recognizes the problems, but we cannot agree on solutions, especially if they cost money. The money presents a serious problem, but we could probably raise it if we agreed about the value of what it was to be spent for. We do not.

The conflict has surfaced most sharply in the debates over abortion, which offer a mirror of our moral and political paralysis. The noisy incompatibility of the extreme positions has forced the majority into a live-and-let-live agnosticism, which says, in effect, "I may believe it is wrong, but I have no right to impose my beliefs on you, nor you a right to impose your beliefs on me." In most instances, the preference for maximum tolerance of different views is healthy, and in some instances we do not have enough of it. But, in the case of abortion, it is disastrously inappropriate. After all, we do not normally regard the taking of a human life as a mere matter of personal preference. The real debate concerns the moment at which our society regards abortion as the taking of a human life: At what point do we regard the fetus as a human being?

Scientific evidence helps but cannot alone provide a solution. Strong evidence suggests that before the age of twenty-four weeks, no fetus is likely to survive outside the womb, no matter how much medical technology is brought to its assistance. From then on, almost any fetus may. But even stronger evidence confirms that, from the moment of conception, the fetus is a form of human life, albeit a very primitive one. Long before a fetus can survive outside the womb, it looks like a miniature baby and has the potential to develop into a human being. Scientists nonetheless argue that its humanness—that which differentiates human beings as members of a species from all other species—lies in its verbal and intellectual abilities, which are located in the cortex of the brain and which do not develop until the twenty-fourth week. Medical technology has not significantly increased the ability of infants born at twenty-four or fewer weeks to survive, and there is scant prospect of its doing so.[3]

Even the six-month-old fetus requires massive assistance to survive outside the womb. A fetus of three or four months, although it does embody potential life, cannot. These facts suggest that an abortion of a third-trimester fetus closely resembles the taking of a human life, whereas the abortion of a first-trimester fetus does not. No doubt, the respect for the life of a first-trimester fetus reflects a deep moral conviction about the sanctity of life, which in itself deserves respect. But respect for the conviction does not require that we ground our public morality in it. By the same token, those who favor third-trimester abortions may argue that they do not regard any fetus as an independent or morally responsible human life and, accordingly, regard the moral claims of the mother to control her own body as superior to the claims of the fetus she is carrying. Again, respect for this conviction does not require that we ground our public morality in it. The two convictions clash over which embodies our most sacred conception of life—the unformed fetus or the woman. They clash over which constitutes the true victim of an unplanned pregnancy—again, the unformed fetus or the woman.

With respect to abortion, as with much else, we should be doing our best to respect and evaluate both claims upon our moral sympathy. Our decision has implications for our understanding of the claims of morality upon the common life of our society. Respectful attention to both claims would suggest that the line for legal abortions be drawn at the fourth or fifth month. My own preference would be for the third or fourth, although Pope John Paul II makes a compelling argument that, with respect to life, the drawing of lines is inherently difficult. Others may disagree. But at least this is a public discussion we could hold, for it acknowledges that we regard the legality of abortion as a moral concern. It might even help to move us away from the cynical compromise of economic convenience and sexual liberation that shapes so much of our discussion of public affairs. For Americans who reject the extremes are not insensible to the moral issue. Rather, they are appalled by calls to a morality that turn desperate women into murderers or, alternatively, celebrate selfishness as a high moral value.

The disposition of abortion relates directly to our other policies (or lack thereof) for women and children. Let us not forget that in *Casey* an ostensibly conservative Supreme Court found the main justification for its reaffirmation of *Roe v. Wade* to be economic. If women must work, then they must not be burdened with more children than they choose—or are prepared to support. The Court could hardly have affirmed more clearly that it did not regard abortion as a moral issue. And one might plausibly argue that its failure in this regard has strengthened the hand of those who oppose the public funding of abortions for poor women. Yet, from the strictly economic perspective, the failure to fund abortions for poor women remains something of a puzzle. After all, state support for them and their children costs incomparably more than the abortions they are being denied. Republicans have nonetheless had to yield to their conservative flank on the funding question. So out of respect for economic convenience, we find ourselves permitting abortion for those who can afford it and simultaneously asserting religious convictions to prohibit abortion for those who cannot. What kind of morality is that?

Both feminists and conservatives apparently believe that the recognition of abortion as a matter of public morality will automatically lead to its prohibition. Yet absolute prohibition is clearly not what most Americans favor, and their resistance hardly proves them amoral. Some on the religious right will never accept anything short of a total prohibition. Others may learn to live with a compromise, provided it respects their convictions. Respect for religious opposition to abortion under all conditions does not require that abortion be totally prohibited. It requires that abortion be publicly regarded as a matter of moral concern. It is noteworthy that Pat Robertson, among others, is now counseling the foes of abortion to concentrate on moral suasion rather than try to force their views politically on a skeptical public.

Feminists have been reluctant to acknowledge abortion as a matter of moral concern out of a legitimate fear that, in acknowledging the claims of morality, they automatically cede the ground to their opponents. So, although their defense of legal abortion has its own moral fervor, they have grounded their arguments in the political language of rights, the natural and constitutional grounding of which remains obscure. Fundamental moral concerns, notably the defense of human life, can never be left entirely to the private decisions of individuals, for they are the products of community life and define a society's deepest sense of itself. In suggesting that our society draw a line around meaningful human life that excludes the first four months of a pregnancy, I am not suggesting that moral principles can ever be defined by votes, much less by the cynical convenience of individuals or political factions. Rather, I am suggesting that our society must reconcile acceptance of early abortions with time-honored moral standards, most notably respect for human life.[4]

As Professor Stephen Carter of Yale Law School has argued, American society, political institutions, and laws have always been grounded in the Judeo-Christian tradition. More than 150 years ago, Joseph Story, one of our greatest Supreme Court justices, demonstrated that Christianity shaped the development of the common law from the beginning and thereby provided the groundwork for the individual liberties we cherish. One need not be a Christian to appreciate, value, and benefit from that achievement. But the abiding role of that tradition in defining our shared moral principles is that we have always made room for expansion and contraction in our definition of specific moral issues. Thus, slavery was once viewed as morally acceptable but came to be rejected as an enormity. In our own time, the dual revolution has severed the bonds between morality and female sexuality. Women's new sexual freedom has spearheaded the emergence of what Carter calls our "culture of disbelief." We have become leery of binding moral principles lest they ride roughshod over the diversity of our people's beliefs and values —or perhaps out of laziness and self-indulgence. In a period of rapidly changing social attitudes, the possibility of finding a common ground seems especially daunting. Our public discussions pit the needs and responsibilities of women as independent beings against our inherited moral convictions. If we repudiate rigid adherence to the letter of those convictions, must we end in a rejection of all moral standards? Or can we rethink the convictions to accommodate women's new independence and still retain a moral baseline? Bluntly: Does a common morality depend upon the subordination of women? Does the liberation of women require the abolition of a common morality? If either or both views prevail, we shall end by casting aside children and placing our common social prospects at high risk.

Throughout most of our history, it was possible to assume that women and children would be privately cared for by the men under whose guardianship they fell. Frequently men failed in their duty, but the public services that developed to compensate for those private failures treated the women and children they served as exceptional. Today, when men in record numbers leave women and children to their own resources, women and children who require public support are no longer exceptional. Some conservatives may want to turn the clock back, but the growing numbers of women and children without adequate private resources testify that the clock cannot be turned back.

So is the solution to abandon the children? Our sterile and deadlocked discussions of abortion suggest the possibility. Certainly, the feminists' reluctance to regard abortion as a story about children and reverence for life points in that direction. But then, so does the conservatives' reluctance to regard abortion as a story about women who do not have the resources to support the children they bear and cannot readily assume that others will step in to care for or adopt the children. Willy-nilly, these two positions have combined to free us from our obligations to women and children. It is as if we were, however unintentionally, treating the children as extensions of women's sexual freedom rather than as the future of our society. And because society has been so reluctant to meet its responsibilities to children, it has sent a message that for women to prosper they must be freed from children as well. Feminism has seized upon this message, arguing that to hold women responsible for children is to punish them by restricting their freedom and independence. Conservatives, who normally express concern for the sanctity of life and the needs of children, want poor women not to have them unless, of course, they are married. In contrast, feminists, who normally want women to be able to lead independent lives like men, defend poor women's right to become single mothers.

The thorny case of "welfare mothers" illuminates the problems. No more than others do I pretend to have a solution, but some basic elements seem clear. Overwhelmingly, children do better with two parents than one. The psychological arguments are complex, since, as we have seen, children primarily need a sustained relationship with one adult, but most of us also know that even psychologically a second parent gives a child some breathing space. If all of a child's love and discipline come from one person, the child is likely to vacillate between compliance (pleasing) and revolt (defiance). For good or bad, the child's identity is tightly bound to the one parent. A second parent permits the child to negotiate the bonds of love and authority and encourages the development of an independent sense of self. Two parents give the child a space in which to choose and, by choosing, to define himself or herself.

William Julius Wilson and Deborah Prothrow-Stith, a specialist in public health, have effectively argued that, especially for young black men, a father offers an essential role model.[5] Perversely, feminists have resisted that argument, sometimes out of the conviction that children need nothing that mothers cannot provide, sometimes out of the conviction that men are so naturally abusive and violent that children would be better off without them. Above all, many feminists resist arguments that evoke the significance in children's development of salient sexual differences between women and men and frequently argue that the differences we see are created by social institutions rather than by nature.[6] Their reluctance to insist upon the importance of fathers is all the more distressing since, in other situations, they are quick to insist that for mothers to pursue their own lives fathers must take up their share of child care. The grim situation of welfare mothers may, however, yet prompt some, especially if they hold public positions, to change their minds. Recently, Donna Shalala, Secretary of Health and Human Services in the Clinton administration and a leading feminist, announced that it was simply "wrong" for women to have children outside marriage.[7] The official feminist position, nonetheless, continues to be primarily driven by two convictions: first, that women should not be forced to marry in order to have children, and, second, that children do not need relations with parents of both sexes.

Whatever the social and psychological benefits of fathers, their economic contributions cannot be disputed. If middle-class families normally need two (or at least one-and-a-half) incomes to survive, how much more so do the poor? The abiding, and often insurmountable, problem for women on AFDC remains their inability to cover even basic expenses. And since they tend to have their children young, frequently before high school graduation, their prospects for completing enough education to get and keep a decent job are virtually nonexistent. These days, the American public is reluctant to support women and children who are widely perceived as living at the expense of others, yet most of these women cannot support themselves, much less their children. In most cases, their lack of education condemns them to minimum-wage, dead-end jobs without benefits of any kind. Those who can get a job have to work full-time and more to put food on the table and a roof over their children's heads, which will leave them little or no time left to devote to the children, who, sooner or later, will be left to the streets. And if the children see no prospects for a different future, they will, likely as not, end up repeating the one they know.

Conservatives insist that if people would only marry before having children, in most cases everything would take care of itself. It is true that many mothers who earn the minimum wage or a little more do manage when they can count upon a husband's wage and his help with the children. Unfortunately, the escalating number of single mothers cannot simply be attributed to women's unwillingness to marry and, hence, to a willful moral failure. Our culture of violence and sexual license has much to answer for, and doubtless some of the women who are having babies at very young ages could defer sex or use contraception to refrain from having children until they had completed at least some education and job training. But even if they did, it is not clear that they would find men to marry, much less that the men would themselves be able to find jobs or that the marriages would last. The unemployment figures for young black men run more than double those of any other group, including white men of the same age. Between the early 1960s and the late 1980s, the percentage of black men, at all levels of education, who held no job during the calendar year tripled, and for the period 1985–87 it almost tripled that of whites. Since the 1960s, the number of black men who earn enough to support a family has been steadily declining.[8] Experts now project the chilling statistic that more than half, and even up to three quarters, of black men between the ages of fifteen and forty will soon be on drugs, in prison, or dead.

The story for inner-city black men is uniquely dramatic, and a persistent racism does not by itself account for the impending catastrophe, for increasing numbers of whites have grim prospects. Thus the figures for white illegitimate births are relentlessly overtaking those for blacks. In 1994, the U. S. Departments of Labor and Commerce issued a joint report that chillingly depicted the inexorable development of a growing class of unskilled laborers.[9] Liberals and conservatives hotly debate the evidence of increasing impoverishment, and I shall not attempt to assess it here. What remains indisputable is that the transformation of the global economy has destroyed the world in which one might plausibly assume that most men could earn enough to support a wife and children. Even the comfortable middle class is feeling the increasing pressure of an economy in which full-time jobs may disappear overnight and in which too many jobs do not carry health insurance or other benefits.

During the past thirty years, we have seen a massive erosion of the private support for children without any substantial increase in public support to take its place. During the same period, the wages of unskilled jobs have failed to keep pace with inflation, and many skilled and semi-skilled manufacturing jobs have disappeared.[10] This crisis of employment has primarily affected men, who normally held the jobs that have disappeared. And during the past decade, while men's economic position has been weakening, the wages of women have increased by almost 10 percent. These numbers bring us back to the problem that an economically viable family will normally depend upon the incomes of two adult workers, and a wage-earning mate is precisely what poor single mothers lack. Marriage may help to solve the problem in the future, but it is not a practical solution for most of those currently dependent upon welfare. And for marriage to help, prospective husbands must have some education and prospects of employment.

Meanwhile, conservatives, who want mothers to stay home with their children, want welfare mothers to work, and feminists, who want most mothers to work, want welfare mothers to be able to stay home with their children. These paradoxes testify to a larger consistency in both conservative and feminist thought. For conservatives look to the workings of the market, whereas feminists look to public expenditure. Their differences with respect to welfare policy have implications for society as a whole. Welfare mothers may be anomalous, but the policies that work best for them are policies that work for society as a whole.

Welfare policies are, by definition, remedial, and they are expensive. They are designed to correct a situation that should never have occurred in the first place. Unfortunately, we have no reason to believe that all women who find themselves in that situation can or want to be helped. So the immediate, practical decisions must ultimately turn upon some judgment about our commitment to and prospects for saving the next generation. To put it differently: Even a disproportionately high expenditure would be justified, if we could be assured that it were for one time only—that is, if it were accompanied by a viable family policy for society as a whole.

But who could give such assurances under present conditions? Extensive "temporary" programs have a way of quickly becoming permanent, especially since the government bureaucrats who enforce them have a vested interest in saving their own jobs by keeping programs going and even expanding them. The widespread resistance to taxes to pay for social projects arises less from presumed callousness toward the poor than from a strong sense that the programs do not work or that, if they do, they are kept in place long after they are needed.

Since feminists bristle at family policies and conservatives bristle at both feminism and taxes, the contours of a "family-friendly" policy have been slow to emerge. Such a policy must start with the assumption that children fare best in an intact family with a mother and a father who can provide for their basic needs, including considerable parental attention. It is a measure of our times that, as I write this sentence, I know many will regard it as provocative, if not bigoted. Thirty years ago it would have been regarded as a truism—so obvious as not to be worth saying. Today, it must be said, although in saying it I do not mean that children may not thrive in any number of family situations. It must be said because without some clearly articulated basic expectations, we will have no constructive policies at all. But then, since the goal of our policies should be to protect and foster children's development, our basic expectations need have no implications for how childless adults live their lives and with whom, if anyone, they choose to live them.

As both feminists and conservatives know, all policies carry implicit or explicit assumptions about the kind of society they wish to promote. The assumptions are rarely made explicit when the policies are advanced. As a result, ordinary Americans may not recognize the larger implications of policies that, on their face, look sensible and humane. Take tax policy. Most of us never progress much beyond resentment of higher taxes and support for the deductions we ourselves may claim. But the availability of one kind of deduction frequently limits the availability of others. In recent years, working women have been able to claim a deduction for day care. Good. It seems unreasonable that a woman who must work should suffer a crippling reduction in the pay she takes home because of the expense of providing care for her child. But during the same period, the deductions that parents could claim for children did not rise at all, and, given inflation, they actually declined. In 1995, the Republicans declared for an additional $500 deduction per child, but at least some Democrats are resisting since President Clinton claimed that it gives too much to the rich. And the feminist leaders, who influence the Democrats, have sided with President Clinton. But until the deduction is passed, we will have a tax policy that favors working mothers over mothers who stay home.[11]

Or take the question of federal guidelines for day care centers. Who could object to our government's requiring that those entrusted with the care and development of the nation's children meet the highest standards? We all want children to have facilities that meet the highest standards of cleanliness and safety. We all agree that children will do better when day care providers do not have to supervise too many children at one time. We all want such centers to provide the maximum amount of education appropriate rather than leave children parked in front of a television set. In fact, we all want day care to approximate as closely as possible the care that a child would receive from its own parents in its own home. Unfortunately, what we want costs money. And, notwithstanding lingering fantasies of maternal devotion, day care managers cannot afford to be philanthropists. They pass the expense along to their clients in increased fees. These expenses may not much trouble upscale women, who can afford to provide the best for their children at a high price, but they exceed the budgets of poorer women, who also want the best for their children and face incomparably greater difficulties in providing it. As we have seen, in forty-five states, all-day day care for two children would cost more than AFDC mothers receive for all their living expenses.[12]

As recently as 1987, only about one quarter of full-time working mothers with children under five used day care centers for their children's primary care, although upscale college-educated, African-American, and single mothers were somewhat more likely to than others. Thus, formal day care especially appeals to the affluent and the poor. And it is a necessity for many single mothers, who, of course, are frequently poor. Upscale working mothers may favor formal day care because they work long hours, because they place a special value on the educational component, or because they do not often have nonworking relatives or friends nearby. Poor working mothers may use it for similar reasons. But most working mothers still prefer the informal care provided by friends or family members in their own homes.[13] So, once again, the ideal of the majority differs significantly from the practice of the very affluent and the very poor.

The debates about day care are almost as extensive and heated, although not as well publicized, as the debates about welfare. With day care as with welfare, feminists and conservatives tend to split over whether they favor public or private solutions. The conservative preference for private solutions, however admirable in principle, will not work for women who have no private resources to turn to. A single mother like Aprill Ravenel, who lives far from her family and works full-time to support herself and her son, has no alternative but to turn to organized day care for her basic needs. Aprill, like Gloria Patterson and many other African-American women, also turns, when possible, to her church and, especially, to the men's groups within it. Wherever Aprill turns, she cannot do it alone. And since conservatives are not offering to support her in minimal dignity so that she may stay home to care for her son, she must work.

When eleven million American children need some form of child care for all or part of the day, we cannot afford to look the other way. But that is what we seem to have been doing. During the past decade the quality of child care has declined, and it is becoming harder to find. The Child Care Action Campaign in New York City is forcefully calling attention to the problems and urging employers to play an active role in providing child care for their employees.[14] Infants and toddlers need what most parents want them to have, namely warm, loving attention within a setting that resembles a family as closely as possible. Older children, beginning at age three or four, benefit from child care that provides the beginnings of education and a foundation for what the children will learn when they go to school. And although good child care is expensive, it more than repays its costs. Companies that offer child care find that their employees are consistently more productive and loyal. Children who receive the advantages of educational child care perform better in school. Even the best child care cannot substitute for the sustained attention of parents, and children who are simply turned over to child care from an early age are more aggressive, more antisocial, and less respectful of authority than those who are not.[15] But quality child care offers a valuable supplement to the efforts of family members and helps women to balance the claims of family and job.

In 1990, single mothers headed one quarter of all households in the United States, and, for black Americans, the figure rose to more than one half. No moral pronouncements about the superiority of private care for children can withstand these figures without risking public exposure as punitive, indifferent, contemptuous, or hypocritical. Conservatives who continue to preach the moral superiority of the world of the *Donna Reed Show* are not talking about the world we live in. And if you do not talk about a world people recognize, they may be expected to ignore you. A just and humane society must embrace standards that the majority of its people can, if with effort, meet, or it must support its people so that they can meet those standards. Without one or the other, people may well decide, as many seem to be deciding, that moral standards are beside the point. If conservatives wish to encourage private virtue and responsibility, they need to provide social conditions that permit people to act virtuously and responsibly.

The feminist preference for extensive public day care has an inexorable logic. Feminists assume that mothers, whether married or single, prefer to work and need day care to do so. They have a vested interest in the idea that children will do as well or better without their mothers as with them. They also have an interest in the expansion of public programs, which provide women with jobs—jobs with benefits. In 1980, women already held 70 percent of the social service jobs in the government sector.[16] And although the jobs do not pay as well as many in the private sector, they are considerably more secure. In this respect, the welfare state is becoming a women's preserve.

Jobs and salaries play an important, if largely hidden, role in these debates. We are accustomed to dividing federal expenditures according to the program on which they are spent: so much for the military, so much for fighting crime, so much for social services, and so forth. We are even conscious of the tendency of federal agencies to allow their suppliers to jack up the cost of goods. But we are rarely reminded of how large a share of public expenditure goes into non-military salaries and benefits for the more than 2.8 million nonmilitary federal and 17 million state and local employees. At best, we know that programs are difficult to cut, in part because the cutting of programs inevitably entails the cutting of jobs. Since the beginning of the republic, patronage and spoils have loomed large in political struggles, and now more so than ever. Even when administrations change, social service jobs remain difficult to cut, and today a large share of those jobs continues to go to women. The protection of public employment, however important to individuals and their families, should not dictate our public policies. After all, when President Clinton downsized the military, to the applause of feminists and the Left, he cut many thousands of jobs.

If we start with the needs of children, the failure of the private sector may well justify the existence, or even expansion, of publicly funded social service programs. But it is one thing to turn to the federal government to see people through a crisis, as was done during the Great Depression, and another to regard dependence upon federally funded social service programs as a positive good. Many personally admirable and socially responsible left-wing feminists forcefully insist that the failures of federal supports for women and children may be attributed to the demeaning conditions imposed upon those who use them. Feminists like Valerie Polakow argue that the United States should long since have followed the lead of the European welfare states in making support for women and children universal like Social Security, rather than dependent upon the indignity of proving need.[17] The United States remains one of the few industrialized countries not to provide universal child allowances. Western European countries also provide statutory housing allowances, health care benefits, maternity benefits, and subsidized child care as a matter of course. Consequently, the benefits are seen as a "right" or entitlement rather than a stigmatized form of public assistance. Thus welfare, with its aura of dependence and deviation,

plays a much smaller role than in the United States.[18] Unfortunately, those social entitlements are placing increasing burdens on
their national budgets and, as has already happened in the United
Kingdom, even the generous policies in France and Sweden are in
danger of being cut back.

The argument that assistance to poor women and children should
be freed from stigma and humiliating reminders of dependence is
cogent and humane. Those who defend "Christian values" should
have no trouble with it, at least not if they read the crystal-clear
words of Jesus. The price paid by children who are publicly labeled
"poor" is incalculable, beginning, as Gloria Patterson furiously reports, with the school free-lunch line, which stigmatizes the children
who use it. But the feminists who favor universal federal programs
leave out important aspects of the story. The countries that provide
so well for women and children are also countries that place significant limitations on abortion, which none of them defines as a
woman's "right."[19] They are countries in which women have not had
the same economic and professional success that many women have
enjoyed in the United States. In some, notably Sweden, the number
of single mothers has increased substantially, so that their "family"
policies are permitting, if not facilitating, the disintegration of
the two-parent family. Some, notably post-unification Germany,
strongly discourage abortion and are edging women out of the labor
force. In sum, European countries provide benefits in a social-corpo-
ratist framework that limits the freedom of individuals.

The feminists who favor a significant expansion in our public entitlements along European lines clearly do not favor limitations on
individual freedom, least of all their own. They must, accordingly,
assume that we can have the benefits without the price that European women pay. If they were prepared to trade abortion as a
woman's "right" for the support of children as a woman's "right,"
they would at least have ground upon which to open a discussion
with conservatives. For one may consistently maintain that limitations on abortion and support for children are both issues of public
morality—both commitments to the sanctity of life and the preemi-

nent importance of the next generation. There are conservatives as well as people on the Left who have corporatist or "communitarian" sympathies, but neither dominate their own political club, and they disagree with one another about what an American communitarianism might look like.

In the struggle to balance individual freedom and community authority, Americans have always preferred maximum space for individual freedom. The response of public opinion to the debates over health care clearly revealed that although Americans began by favoring a national health care system and universal coverage in principle, their growing worries about costs, restrictions, and quality led to a significant decline in their support. And in November 1994, Republicans swept into Congress, largely on the basis of promises to cut federal programs drastically. Many Americans understandably favor reduction of federal programs, which seem to be getting more expensive and less effective by the day. Nor have programs for working mothers and children proved significantly more effective than others. But neither the cost nor the failure of federal programs means that we can complacently do nothing, letting the children fall where they may.

We should keep in mind that a reduction in the size and power of the federal government cannot in itself solve the problems under discussion. Rather, it transfers them to the states and, through the states, to the cities, counties, and communities, where the debate over the relation of government to individuals will have to be fought. The feminist movement, by its romantic attachment to the federal bureaucracy, has left itself without a program for the terrain on which it will now have to fight. And the Right will now have to confront a struggle within its own ranks between those who think the market can solve everything and those who, though generally pro-market, are by no means sure that the market alone can restore family stability.

The strong preference of the majority of Americans for some kind of informal day care, preferably in a private home with a relative or friend, suggests that most people do not want to send children, especially the very young, to public institutions. If, in other words, they turn to some kind of day care center, they do so because there are no appropriate family members at home. And the day care they prefer is normally a small group of children in the home of a woman they know. No, she may not have the latest educational toys and almost certainly has not been trained in a school for teachers or social workers. At nap time, she may put one child on a bed, another on a couch, still another on a blanket on the floor—much as a mother might do. But parents do not turn to her to be an expert or even to know the nutritional value of each graham cracker. They turn to her because they trust she will come to know and care about their child—will make their child feel loved and "at home." Strange to say, that is what the experts say the child above all needs. And yes, one may imagine that "she" could be a man.

Most working parents want their children to have the closest possible approximation of what they themselves would provide if they were not working, but none of our public policies help them. In many solid working-class neighborhoods, women who work irregular shifts, whether in factories or as waitresses or nurses, frequently provide that kind of care for one another's children. Here and there, some upper middle-class women are doing the same. Sometimes they do it free, sometimes they charge. And sometimes those who charge do so because they are temporarily out of work or have an elderly parent or a retarded or disabled child who needs them at home. Our tax laws do nothing to support their activity, and most of the day care providers probably do not declare the income. They cannot declare themselves a small business, since they could not meet federal day care standards. But then, they cannot declare business expenses, and the friends whose children they watch will have difficulty in claiming child care deductions. Our public policies, in other words, do nothing to support—and even discourage—these private arrangements that most Americans prefer and most closely resemble what parents would do themselves if they were not working, or if they were only working part-time.

For most women—and perhaps more men than we know—part-time work emerges as the key, at least while children are young. And, while we are creating a wish list, three-quarter-time work with some benefits might wonderfully ease the lives of parents of school-age children. For it is good for most children to know that after school there is someone to come home to—someone who will notice if they are not there. Our economy makes part-time work difficult, except at minimal wages, and our government does almost nothing to encourage it. (We will turn to the Family and Medical Leave Act of 1993 in a minute.) In recent years, business has come to appreciate the advantages of part-time work, as is evident in the rapidly growing tendency to hire contract rather than full-time workers, even for many skilled and some professional jobs. But the advantages business appreciates are those of the bottom line: the chance to reduce wages and, especially, to throw off responsibility for benefits.

Perhaps more than any single other thing, working mothers want respectably paid twenty-or thirty-hour-a-week jobs with benefits. Many working mothers need benefits and a continuing record of responsible work as much as they need the income itself. For the benefits insure them against disaster, and the employment record ensures their continuing development as workers. Hence, benefits ensure their ability to return to appropriate full-time work when their children are grown. Women's need for part-time work does not rank high on any feminist agenda, as may be seen in the hostile response to the mommy track. For feminists hold tightly to the egalitarian dogma that women must be free to work as long and intensely as men. Most women do not share their view and would welcome a viable program of part-time work. The real problem with part-time work for mothers (and those fathers who choose it) does not lie in the feminists' "principled" opposition, but in the continuing tension between business and the government. And, as we need to remind ourselves now more than ever, government is we the people. If we firmly demand part-time work for mothers of young children as a top national priority, if we are willing to pay taxes to support our conviction, and if we could have any confidence the taxes would be well spent, we would probably get what we want. Those are big "ifs."

Americans cannot agree how much responsibility for social policies should fall to government and how much to the private (market) sector, which includes large and small businesses. The Family and Medical Leave Act of 1993 (FMLA) illustrates our uncertainties. The act guarantees to employees of businesses with more than fifty full-time employees the right to take twelve weeks of unpaid leave during any calendar year to recuperate from illness or injury or to care for a new baby or an ill family member. It supplements, but does not replace, existing benefits, including available medical insurance and maternity leave.

FMLA clearly reflects the views of feminists, who above all seek to equalize opportunities and responsibilities between women and men. It also reflects the views of the many American couples who want marriages in which women and men share economic and domestic responsibilities. But it offers little to single mothers and nothing to the many women and men who do not work for large businesses, or who work for them only on a contractual basis. It does not provide paid leave, and it does not guarantee part-time work for the mothers of young children. It offers nothing to less affluent and less educated black men, for whom regular jobs of any kind are disappearing. It is too soon to tell how FMLA is working even for those it should benefit, and some employers have refused to abide by it. But it is the law, and the government is preparing to deal with those who are flagrantly resisting. Even the government can do little, however, when a company nominally observes the law and still finds ways to fire those who take advantage of it. In the happiest cases, some companies are complying, as illustrated by the Georgia woman who retained her job through a second pregnancy and was allowed to do some of her work at home.[20]

FMLA has met with qualified feminist approval because it is gender neutral—that is, it does not assume that women are more likely than men to take advantage of it. In practice, women are more likely than men to take advantage of it, and many companies have been reluctant to acknowledge that men, too, may have pressing domestic responsibilities. Those problems can be worked out if women and men privately decide that they are willing to forgo twelve weeks of the man's income in order for him to assume a fair share of family responsibilities. Under the best conditions, however, we are left with no federally guaranteed maternity leave and no benefits for part-time workers. And under the worst conditions, large companies may accelerate their practice of hiring contract workers, thus relieving themselves of responsibility to observe FMLA and to provide other benefits as well.

As a government initiative, the costs of which will be borne by the private sector—specifically by large businesses and their employees—FMLA differs markedly from European entitlement programs, which are entirely funded by the taxpayers. Faced with the challenge of family policies, Americans have preferred to fund them privately. The European programs, as conservatives insist, do not simply return tax dollars to citizens in the form of services. They redistribute income, ensuring that affluent citizens will disproportionately help to meet the needs of the less affluent as a matter of social duty—not charity. They thus insist that the health of the national community requires that the basic needs of all citizens be met. We have done the same with Social Security, but not with other programs. Where the Europeans assume that support for the common good will enhance the lives of all citizens, we seem to assume that the maximum independence for citizens will produce the greatest common good. Traditionally, Americans, including and perhaps especially feminists, have deeply believed in the maximum freedom for individuals. But beyond that conviction, we clearly harbor serious doubts about whether we can agree on the nature of the common good.

Even our modest steps toward a responsible family policy betray the continuing tension between feminists and conservatives about the nature of the common good. More often than not, that tension results in a deadlock that produces nothing or very little. Feminists do not want a family policy that takes women's roles as mothers for granted. Conservatives do not want a family policy that strengthens the federal government or places financial burdens on business, which they credit for job creation. Thus feminists defend mothers who depend upon public support, and conservatives defend mothers who stay home full-time. Neither offers much to the vast majority of working mothers, who work precisely because they believe in family values.

Most Americans have not given up on family values. According to a recent poll, a majority believes that the government could strengthen families by providing high-quality day care for families in which both parents work, requiring employers to allow parents to take leave to care for a new baby or sick child, passing stricter laws to regulate violence and sex on television and in the movies, and relying on families rather than schools to teach religious and moral values to children. But only a quarter believe that tax incentives to help mothers of small children to stay home and not work will strengthen families.[21] The message is clear: Americans assume that most mothers have to work and deserve some support from the government. No less clearly, they do not want the government to take over their role in teaching their children values. In their ideal world, a mother would take a leave from her job for up to a year after the birth of a child, return to the job without penalty on a part-time basis during the child's early years, and gradually move back into full-time work. During the same years, a father would have the flexibility to spend time with the children, including the option to take a leave when a child or his wife was ill. Both parents would have time to participate in their children's homework and moral education, not to mention the PTA and Little League.

A morally responsible and realistic family policy for the United States should start from the assumption that when we talk of working women we are talking of mothers, and that when we talk of mothers we are talking of working women. For the typical woman worker is a mother or is likely to become one, and more than half of all mothers work. Meanwhile, men are privately assuming a growing share of domestic responsibilities, including child care. We cannot effectively legislate those changes in attitude and social behavior, nor should we, if only because our attempts to do so invariably penalize the many mothers who have no men with whom to share responsibilities. Nor can we restrict support for mothers to married mothers on the grounds that two-parent families are preferable for children. We should take the two-parent family as the norm and devise policies that encourage people to observe it, but we cannot sacrifice one or more generations of children while we wait for their parents to comply. The costs to the common good will be incalculable—perhaps irreversible.

We must start with a double attack that simultaneously respects the needs and sensibilities of women who work outside the home and of those who do not. And, in the measure possible, we should try to fund our programs indirectly rather than directly, by tax breaks and incentives rather than by adding more employees to federal and state payrolls. Indirect financing has the special advantage of encouraging people to work together within local communities to promote the values in which they believe. Some programs may have to be directly funded by state and federal governments, but we should turn to them only as a last resort.

What the federal government can do is to enact a substantial enhancement of the tax deductions that parents may take for children. We thus register our commitment to children as a national priority and simultaneously ease the financial pressures on women (or men) who choose to stay home while their children are young. Next, we need to encourage the development of policies for maternity leave, preferably that permit women to leave work a month before their child is due and stay home with it for nine months or a year after birth. Maternity leave poses real problems, and different states may develop different models. Maternity leave does cost money and does inconvenience business, but we have seen that large companies like IBM can provide it, and the case of ACXIOM in Conway shows that they can provide quality day care as well. Everywhere, the problems are more difficult for small businesses than large. For example, someone must take over for the woman during her absence. But if it proves onerous to guarantee that a woman return to the job she left, she should be guaranteed one comparable to it. In this day of expanding contract, part-time, and temporary labor, even small businesses should be able to hire a replacement without having to promise a permanent job. And the federal government can support local initiatives by paying a proportion of the woman's salary as unemployment compensation is now paid. We should also have a provision for a maternity IRA to which a woman could start contributing as soon as she starts to work—and to which her husband or partner could also contribute—and upon which she could draw without penalty during her child's first four years. These funds would equally benefit working and nonworking mothers, for they would permit working mothers to extend their maternity leave or hire child care and would permit nonworking mothers to contribute to their families while they are not earning.

Day care presents a different order of problem, but it too could benefit from a fresh perspective. Private day care centers primarily benefit upscale families in which the woman works at a demanding and well-paying job and poor families, whose children receive subsidies. It is not clear that they need concern the federal government any more than private schools now concern it. After all, upscale parents normally have their own very high standards of what they want for their children, and their ability to pay for it normally gets them what they want. If the market for these exclusive institutions were to drive up the salaries of day care workers, so much the better since most day care workers are notoriously underpaid. At least for the foreseeable future those salary increases would primarily benefit women, and, in the long run, they might attract some men. Upscale parents may bristle at the increase in costs, but they can afford it. In the best of all possible worlds, upscale day care centers would also offer scholarships to the children of less affluent parents, as many private schools do. The respect for the "privacy" of these private institutions would also create some space for churches to create day care programs that would reflect the values of their parishioners and might more easily keep down costs by enlisting volunteer labor.

A word on religion and the churches. It is easy to forget that, until the past few decades, the American people never understood the separation of church and state to mean that religion must be, or indeed could be, excluded from our national life. I do not wish to plunge into that subject here and shall restrict myself to a simple point. Wherever we draw the line, we should recognize that churches (broadly understood to include churches, synagogues, mosques, and the ethical societies of nonbelievers) are institutions vital to the health of our society. We have to give them room to breathe—to participate fully in our community life, even as we carefully rein in their occasional political excesses. They need and deserve disinterested encouragement to contribute to solving the day care center problem, just as they do for their central role in combating the despair and hopelessness that is destroying the ghettoes and steadily creeping into the suburbs. Most Americans do not want schools to replace the family in teaching values to their children, and more often than not they welcome the assistance of their church.

Many churches already offer day care programs, and an impressive number even offer a "mother's day out" for nonworking mothers. Their initiative should be encouraged by granting tax incentives to small businesses to contribute to their support. Small businesses cannot be expected to provide on-site day care for their employees, but they can be encouraged to contribute financially to the availability of quality day care within their neighborhoods, at churches, local YWCAs, and other community institutions. Large businesses normally can afford to provide on-site day care, although too few do. But as the example of ACXIOM again shows, some are beginning to discover the advantage of doing so, and the ACXIOM employees in Conway value day care highly enough to accept somewhat lower wages. Other businesses in which employee demand is strong, and qualified employees are difficult to find and retain, may be expected to do the same. My own university established an excellent day care center only when it became clear that the university hospital was having difficulty in attracting and retaining nurses—a large group of professional female employees, many of whom could not work without good day care for their children. Too often, professional women do not wage a strong fight for day care, preferring to turn to private arrangements. One accomplished feminist scholar told a group of graduate students in women's studies that day care was not a problem at her institution. Presumably, she did not remember, or had never noticed, that at her university, as at all others, the vast majority of female employees are secretaries or physical plant workers.

With respect to state and federal programs, the issues of cost are of an entirely different magnitude but nonetheless command attention. We should expand and strengthen the Head Start program, which especially appeals to poor African-American women. The program is admittedly expensive, and not everyone agrees about its value. There are limits to what any program can do for children who do not have a stable environment at home. Head Start nonetheless provides opportunities to those who have few or no private resources, and those who complain about its "failures" do not normally pay much attention to how the children would have done without it or propose alternatives. Even the critics occasionally admit that the "failure" of Head Start may primarily reflect the disintegration of families or our public schools. But since Head Start is a public educational program, it is only natural to transfer its operation and development to the states. Communities that have Head Start programs should also have Head Start boards, analogous to school boards, which represent the parents they serve as well as the local community. And both small and large businesses should receive tax incentives to contribute to the cost of operation. Some measure of local funding and control will help to ensure that the program genuinely serves the needs of the community.

For the moment, we may assume that the various formal programs will serve roughly one quarter of American children, while the remaining three quarters will continue to be cared for in informal, private arrangements. Maternity leave, maternity IRAs, and adequate support for part-time workers, reinforced by the FMLA, will make it possible for more mothers, with or without the assistance of fathers, to provide more of their children's primary care themselves.

And if working women enjoy more flexible schedules and full-time mothers enjoy more respect, there is likely to be even more informal sharing of child care among friends and neighbors. To encourage these arrangements, which are comfortable for children as well as parents, we should make sure that our tax laws permit women to declare child care income and deduct child care expenses without penalty, up to, say, $2,000 per year. We should, in other words, offer more indirect subsidies for child care to women with modest incomes than we do to upscale women.

Many of the policies I have proposed explicitly assume that women have primary responsibility for children, especially when they are very young. Most feminists reject those assumptions out of a commitment to equality between women and men. But most women are not living lives that could conform to those feminist principles. It may mark me as a woman of a transitional generation. I am prepared to believe that younger women will prove me wrong, but I do believe that, for the foreseeable future, the care for young children will remain more of a woman's responsibility than a man's. And I fail to understand how we will improve the prospects of most women and children by deferring desperately needed supports until that fabled day of glory when equality will somehow prevail. Beyond that, I remain unconvinced that most women really wish to relinquish their special bonds with children. Children more than occasionally drive mothers to distraction, and even the most devoted mothers desperately need some time off from their children. Mothers are people too, although children frequently forget it. And some mothers may not be well suited to being mothers at all. Contrary to conservative sentimentality, mothering, especially in a society as dangerous and complex as ours, does not always come naturally.

But then, that is the point. Society cannot expect women to become mothers if it does not value and support what mothers do. So long as we treat the work of mothering as if it were servants' work— and smugly demean servants' work—we virtually guarantee that the more talented a woman is the less likely she will be to choose to become a mother. Both feminists who want to free women from mothering and conservatives who want to condemn them to it implicitly treat mothering as servants' work. The real tragedy for women, however, lies elsewhere.

These days, most of us live very long lives. Both scholarly and popular literature abound with advice on the sense of purpose and renewal to be gained by changing careers once, perhaps more, during the course of a life. I recently traded notes with a college classmate from the West Coast. We were talking about the kind of life her daughter, a sophomore in college, wanted to lead—about the ways in which young women's prospects and expectations differ from those we had when we were starting out. Today, my friend, a successful psychologist for Kaiser Permanente, works full-time and earns more than her husband (as do I). Musing over how each of us had gotten where we are today, we suddenly found ourselves agreeing that, along with having attended a woman's college and married a strong man, one of the most important aspects of our careers had been the luxury of having a few years off before we began to work full-time. Those years, we agreed, had allowed us to solidify our marriages and personal lives and bequeathed us a fund of energy that sustains us in our adult lives and careers.

From this perspective, what a pity it would be to have women throw away the possibility of enjoying their children for a few years, before returning to work—provided we guarantee that they can return. Many young women no longer enjoy the luxury of taking a few years off, even to bear and rear children. Conservatives, ignoring the economic pressures, are too quick to charge them with selfishness and a betrayal of family values. Feminists, in contrast, assume that they have a right to full-time work and, if the pressures mount, then it is up to men or the government to pick up the slack. In strange ways, both the conservative and feminist positions encourage the notion that our real problem is the war between the sexes. For conservatives, women are failing men; for feminists, men are failing women. Meanwhile, everyone is failing the children, and the majority of Americans, who do worry about children, recognize neither the

conservative nor the feminist picture. Yes, they know there is competition and, occasionally, violence between women and men. They
also know that there is more than a little cooperation and a sincere,
loving attempt to make things work.

Neither government nor social policy can alone settle the competition between the sexes as it plays itself out in private lives. Within
the bounds of the law, women and men must be trusted to settle
their own lives. Family violence is a serious problem, and, as Roberta
Cooper Ramo, president-elect of the American Bar Association,
forcefully insists, it especially harms children. But the first challenge
of family violence is to define and punish those manifestations that
law and common sense brand as criminal, not to seize every opportunity to have the government intrude into our family lives. When
the bounds of law are exceeded, the police and the courts must step
in. The spousal and child abuse that our society defines as criminal
do, by definition, require police action. They are pathological. Some
conservatives sweep the pathological under the rug, implicitly treating it as if it were normal. Some feminists label it normal, implicitly
suggesting that all relations between women and men are inherently
violent. But if we agree to call the pathological normal, we lose the
possibility to call it criminal and thereby exonerate ourselves of responsibility for combating it.

Americans have not normally viewed the personal relations between women and men as appropriate matters for state control, and
now is not the time to begin. But the care for children, which has
also been regarded as a private matter, poses altogether different
problems. Our failure to meet the needs of children, and the needs
of the women who bear them, is costing us heavily and promises to
cost us more. There is no easy way to support children without also
supporting their parents, especially their mothers, and that is a burden we have to shoulder together. We may also need institutional
settings for children whose parents cannot cope. Contrary to the
left-wing outrage at the idea of reviving orphanages, they may work
much better for children than inadequate families, and many children appreciate them much more than many people suspect. But a

good boarding school or orphanage costs much more than support for families.

It saddens me immeasurably to think that my views may seem threatening or oppressive to younger women, especially those I teach. But even as I am saddened, I remember the voice of the ambitious young law school graduate who had just returned from a visit to Honduras and told me with awe of the women she had met. "Oh," she said, "they do love their children. Nothing had prepared me for women who find children so rewarding." And then I remember the voice of my Italian-American sister-in-law. Jo was listening to me interview a group of younger women about the difficulties of combining children and work. She herself has not worked since her first pregnancy, and the younger women asked her if being at home with the children had not bored and frustrated her. "Oh, no," she replied, "I loved talking with my children."

These are not the words of a woman who thought she had been condemned to servant's work. These days, that ability to enjoy one's children has become a rare and precious freedom that too few women enjoy and too few people recognize as freedom at all. Yet it remains the embodiment of the "freedom for"—for willing service, for love, for renewal—without which there is no freedom at all. And if that were not enough, it remains the work that, if freely and lovingly done, will assure our society's future.

NOTES

[1]Ellen Willis, "Betty Friedan's 'Second Stage': A Step Backward," *The Nation* (November 14, 1981): 494. Catherine R. Stimpson claimed that the book "dismays me" in her review, "From Feminine to Feminist Mystique," *Ms.* (December 1981): 21. Betty Friedan, *The Second Stage* (New York: Summit Books, 1981).

[2]These words are taken from a letter Willis wrote to *The New York Times*, quoted by Megan Marshall, "What Women Want in the 1980s," *The New Republic* (January 20, 1982): 31.

[3]Harold J. Morowitz and James S. Trefil, *The Facts of Life: Science and the Abortion Controversy* (New York: Oxford Univ. Press, 1992).

[4]On these questions, see Mary Ann Glendon, *Abortion and Divorce in Western Law: American Failures, European Challenges* (Cambridge, MA: Harvard Univ. Press, 1987), and Elizabeth Fox-Genovese, "Feminism and the Rhetoric of Individual Rights, I & II," *Common Knowledge* 1, nos. 1 & 2 (Spring & Fall, 1992).

[5]William Julius Wilson, *The Truly Disadvantaged: The Inner City, the Underclass, and Public Policy* (Chicago: Univ. of Chicago Press, 1987); Deborah Prothrow-Stith, with Michaele Weissman, *Deadly Consequences* (New York: Harper Collins, 1991).

[6]See, for example, the essays in *Between Feminism and Psychoanalysis*, Teresa Brennan ed. (London & New York: Routledge, 1989), Toril Moi, "Patriarchal Thought and the Drive for Knowledge," 191. On the social creation of perceived differences, see, for example, Susan Moller Okin, *Justice, Gender, and the Family* (New York: Basic Books, 1989).

[7]See Carol Jouzaltis, "Unwed Mothers a Common Target in Welfare Debates," *Chicago Tribune* (July 18, 1994): 3.

[8]Christopher Jencks, *Rethinking Social Policy: Race, Poverty, and the Underclass* (Cambridge, MA: Harvard Univ. Press, 1992), 156; Wilson, *Truly Disadvantaged*, 82.

[9]Charles Murray, "The Coming White Underclass," *The Wall Street Journal* (October 29, 1993); Catherine S. Manegold, "Study Warns of Growing Underclass of the Unskilled," *The New York Times* (May 26, 1994).

[10]Louis A. Ferleger and Jay R. Mandle, *A New Mandate: Democratic Choices for a Prosperous Economy* (Columbia, MO: Univ. of Missouri Press, 1994).

[11]Allan C. Carlson, *Family Questions: Reflections on the American Social Crisis* (New Brunswick: Transaction Publishers, NJ, 1991).

[12]Christopher Jencks, "What's Wrong With Welfare Reform," *Harpers* 288, iss. 1727 (April 1994): 20.

[13]Lawrence M. Mead, *The New Politics of Poverty: The Nonworking Poor in America* (New York: Basic Books, 1992), 121–22. Slightly more than one third of college graduates and slightly less than a third of African-American and single mothers did.

[14]Child Care Action Campaign, 330 Seventh Avenue, 17th Floor, New York, NY 10001.

[15]Andrew Peyton Thomas, "Can We Ever Go Back?" *The Wall Street Journal*

(August 9, 1995): A8, and his book *Crime and the Sacking of America: The Roots of Chaos* (Washington, D.C.: Brassey's, 1994).

[16]Frances Fox Piven, "Ideology and the State: Women, Power, and the Welfare State," in Linda Gordon, ed., *Women, the State, and Welfare* (Madison, WI: Univ. of Wisconsin Press, 1990).

[17]Valerie Polakow, *Lives on the Edge: Single Mothers and Their Children in the Other America* (Chicago: Univ. of Chicago Press, 1993).

[18]Linda Gordon, *Pitied but Not Entitled: Single Mothers and the History of Welfare* (New York: Free Press, 1994), Polakow, *Lives on the Edge*. For the European background, see also Sheila Kamerman, "Women, Children, and Poverty: Public Policies and Female-Headed Families in Industrialized Countries," in *Women and Poverty*, Barbara C. Gelpi and Nancy M. Hartsock, et al., eds. (Chicago: Univ. of Chicago Press, 1986): 41–63; Sheila Kamerman and Alfred J. Kahn, *Child Care, Family Benefits, and Working Parents* (New York: Columbia Univ. Press, 1981).

[19]Mary Ann Glendon, *Divorce and Abortion in Western Law*.

[20]*Atlanta Journal and Constitution* (August 9, 1994), E1.

[21]NBC News/*Wall Street Journal* Poll, conducted by the polling organizations of Peter Hart (Democrat) and Robert Teeter (Republican), June 10–14, 1994, published in *The Polling Report* 10, no. 13 (June 27, 1994).

SELECTED BIBLIOGRAPHY

Becker, Gary S. A *Treatise on the Family*. Cambridge, MA: Harvard Univ. Press, 1981.

Carter, Stephen J. *The Culture of Disbelief: How American Law and Politics Trivialize Religious Devotion*. New York: Basic Books, 1993.

Chodorow, Nancy J. *The Reproduction of Mothering: Psychoanalysis and the Sociology of Gender*. Berkeley, CA: Univ. of California Press, 1978.

Craig, Barbara Hinkson, and David M. O'Brien. *Abortion and American Politics*. Chatham, NJ: Chatham House, 1993.

Dworkin, Ronald. *Life's Dominion: An Argument about Abortion, Euthanasia, and Individual Freedom*. New York: Knopf, 1993.

Elshtain, Jean Bethke. *Democracy on Trial*. New York: Basic Books, 1995.

Fox-Genovese, Elizabeth. *Feminism Without Illusions: A Critique of Individualism*. Chapel Hill, NC: University of North Carolina Press, 1991.

Friedan, Betty. *The Feminine Mystique*. 20th anniversary ed. New York: Dell, 1983 (orig. ed. 1963).

Furstenberg, Frank, Jr., and Andrew J. Cherlin. *Divided Families: What Happens to Children When Parents Part.* Cambridge, MA: Harvard Univ. Press, 1991.

Gelb, Joyce, and Marian Lief Palley. *Women and Public Policies.* Princeton, NJ: Princeton Univ. Press, 1982.

Gilligan, Carol. *In a Different Voice: Psychological Theory and Women's Development.* Cambridge, MA: Harvard Univ. Press, 1982.

Ginsburg, Faye D. *Contested Lives: The Abortion Debate in an American Community.* Berkeley, CA: Univ. of California Press, 1989.

Glendon, Mary Ann. *Abortion and Divorce in Western Law.* Cambridge, MA: Harvard Univ. Press, 1987.

Glendon, Mary Ann. *Rights Talk: The Impoverishment of Political Discourse.* New York: Free Press, 1991.

Goldin, Claudia. *Understanding the Gender Gap: An Economic History of American Women.* New York: Oxford Univ. Press, 1990.

Goldscheider, Frances K., and Linda J. Waite. *New Families, No Families? The Transformation of the American Home.* Berkeley, CA: Univ. of California Press, 1991.

Gordon, Linda. *Pitied but Not Entitled: Single Mothers and the History of Welfare.* New York: Free Press, 1994.

Hewlett, Sylvia Ann. *A Lesser Life: The Myth of Women's Liberation in America.* New York: Warner Books, 1986.

Hunter, James Davison. *Before the Shooting Begins: Searching for Democracy in America's Culture Wars.* New York: Free Press, 1994.

Hunter, James Davison. *Culture Wars: The Struggle to Define America.* New York: Basic Books, 1991.

Jenks, Christopher. *Rethinking Social Policy: Race, Poverty, and the Underclass.* Cambridge, MA: Harvard Univ. Press, 1992.

Jencks, Christopher, and Paul E. Peterson, eds. *The Urban Underclass.* Washington, DC: Brookings Institute, 1991.

Kahn, Alfred J., and Sheila B. Kamerman. *Child Care: Facing the Hard Choices.* Dover, MA: Auburn House, 1987.

Kamerman, Sheila B., and Alfred J. Kahn. *Child Care, Parental Leave, and the Under 3s: Policy Innovation in Europe.* New York: Auburn House, 1991.

Kassian, Mary A. *The Feminist Gospel: The Movement to Unite Feminism Within the Church.* Weaton, IL: Crossway Books, 1992.

Klein, Abbie Gordon. *The Debate over Child Care, 1969–1990: A Sociohistorical Analysis.* Albany, NY: State Univ. Press of New York, 1992.

Lasch, Christopher. *The Revolt of the Elites and the Betrayal of Democracy.* New York: Norton, 1995.

Lawson, Annette, and Deborah L. Rhode, eds. *The Politics of Pregnancy: Adolescent Sexuality and Public Policy.* New Haven: Yale Univ. Press, 1993.

Litan, Robert E., Robert Z. Lawrence, and Charles L. Schultze, eds. *American Living Standards: Threats and Challenges.* Washington, DC, 1988.

Luker, Kristin. *Abortion and the Politics of Motherhood.* Berkeley, CA: Univ. of California Press, 1984.

McFate, Katherine, Roger Lawson, and William Julius Wilson, eds. *Poverty, Inequality and the Future of Social Policy: Western States in the New World Order.* New York: Russell Sage, 1995.

MacKinnon, Catharine. *Only Words.* Cambridge, MA: Harvard Univ. Press, 1993.

Maloy, Kate, and Maggie Jones Patterson. *Birth or Abortion? Private Struggles in a Political World.* New York: Plenum, 1992.

Mansbridge, Jane J. *Why We Lost the ERA.* Chicago: Univ. of Chicago Press, 1986.

Mathews, Donald G., and Jane Sherron De Hart. *Sex, Gender, and the Politics of ERA.* New York: Oxford Univ. Press, 1990.

Mensch, Elizabeth, and Alan Freeman. *The Politics of Virtue: Is Abortion Debatable?* Durham, NC: Duke Univ. Press, 1993.

Mezey, Susan Gluck. *In the Pursuit of Equality: Women, Public Policy, and Federal Courts.* New York: St. Martin's Press, 1992.

Micael, Robert T., John H. Gagnon, Edward O. Laumann, and Gina Kolata. *Sex in America: A Definitive Survey.* Boston: Little Brown, 1994.

Newman, Katherine S. *Declining Fortunes: The Withering of the American Dream.* New York: Basic Books, 1993.

Newman, Katherine S. *Falling from Grace: The Experience of Downward Mobility in the American Middle Class.* New York: Free Press, 1988.

Okin, Susan Moller. *Justice, Gender, and the Family.* New York: Basic Books, 1989.

Orenstein, Peggy. *School Girls: Young Women, Self-Esteem, and the Confidence Gap.* New York: Doubleday, 1994.

Palmer, John L., Timothy Smeeding, and Barbara Boyle Torrey, eds. *The Vulnerable.* Washington, DC: Urban Institute Press, 1988.

Polakow, Valerie. *Lives on the Edge: Single Mothers and Their Children in the Other America*. Chicago: Univ. of Chicago Press, 1993.

Pope John Paul II. *The Gospel of Life [Evangelium Vitae]: The Encyclical Letter on Abortion, Euthanasia, and the Death Penalty in Today's World*. New York: Times Books, 1995.

Posner, Richard. *Sex and Reason*. Cambridge, MA: Harvard Univ. Press, 1992.

Rosenblatt, Roger. *Life Itself: Abortion in the American Mind*. New York: Random House, 1992.

Schwartz, Felice N. "Management Women and the New Facts of Business Life," *Harvard Business Review* 67, no. 1 (January/February 1989): 65–76.

Skocpol, Theda. *Protecting Soldiers and Mothers: The Political Origins of Social Policy in the United States*. Cambridge, MA: Harvard Univ. Press, 1992.

Solinger, Rickie. *Wake Up Little Susie: Single Pregnancy and Race Before Roe v. Wade*. New York and London: Routledge, 1992.

Tannen, Deborah. *You Just Don't Understand: Women and Men in Conversation*. New York: Ballantine, 1990.

Wilson, James Q. *The Moral Sense*. New York: Free Press, 1993.

Wilson, William Julius. *The Truly Disadvantaged: The Inner City, the Underclass, and Public Policy*. Chicago: Univ. of Chicago Press, 1987.

Winnicott, D. W. *The Maturational Processes and the Facilitating Environment: Studies in the Theory of Emotional Development*. London: Hogarth Press, 1972; orig. ed., 1965.

Wolgast, Elizabeth H. *Equality and the Rights of Women*. Ithaca, NY: Cornell Univ. Press, 1980.

Wolgast, Elizabeth H. *The Grammar of Justice*. Ithaca, NY: Cornell Univ. Press, 1987.

INDEX

Abortion, 10, 13, 17, 25, 68, 99, 109, 173, 204
  and contraception, 70–71
  debates over, 78–81, 87–95, 102–5, 229–33, 234
  and Europeans, 244
  legalization of, 72–73, 81, 82, 88, 89, 231, 232
  as moral issue, 29, 76–77, 89–90, 232, 244–45
  for poor women, 102–7, 231–32, 234
  pro-choice on, 11, 12, 16, 25, 61, 73–74, 87, 91, 92, 103
  pro-life on, 25, 73–74, 87, 91, 94, 103
  restrictions on, 59, 76–77, 107–8, 230–31
  and single women, 75–76
ACLU, 215
Acquaintance rape, 162, 164
ACXIOM corp., 216–20, 251, 253
Adolescence, 202
"Adultery," 96, 97
Affirmative action, 19, 130

African-Americans, 18–20, 22–24, 26, 48, 49, 61, 66, 69, 75, 78, 136, 153, 174–76, 178, 201, 221, 241–42, 254, 259
  See also Blacks
Age of Innocence (Wharton), 51
Aid to Families with Dependent Children (AFDC), 19–20, 27, 65, 120, 128, 202, 236, 240
AIDS, 95, 100–2
Anorexia, 39–40, 57, 187
Appearance, 38–39
  See also Clothes

Babies, 210, 214
Baby boomers, 68, 75, 94, 182–83
Backlash (Faludi), 226
Baird, Zoe, 124
Barnes, Jonathan (pseud.), 70–71
Beatty, Megan (pseud.), 93
Beauty Myth, The (Wolf), 24, 39
Beauvoir, Simone de, 39
Before the Shooting Starts (Hunter), 90

Bernstein, Anne, 208
Birth control, 65, 66, 70, 76, 100
    See also Contraception
Blacks, 24, 28, 29, 66, 122, 133,
    155, 170, 178, 202, 235–37,
    248
    See also African-Americans
Bobbitt, Lorena, 162
Bowles, Ron (pseud.), 142–43
Breast implants, 39
British, 139
    See also United Kingdom
Brown, Selina (pseud.), 153
Bunker, Archie & Edith (fictional
    characters), 115, 157
Bush administration, 131, 204
Business Week, 133

Caggiano, Mary (pseud.), 19–21,
    28–29
Career women, 111, 151, 195, 204
    See also Professional women
Carlson, Jennifer (pseud.), 193,
    194
Carmichael, Mara (pseud.), 25–
    26, 28
Carter, Stephen, 88, 233
Catalyst (organization), 213
Catholics, 10, 88, 231
Chastity, interest in, 60
Child Care Action Campaign, 241
Child pornography, 99
Children
    failure to meet needs of, 256–
        57
    incentives for having, 92–94
    and "mommy track" debate,
        213–16
    and motherhood, 202–3, 205–9

nonnegotiable demands of, 11
poverty of, 201–2
prospects for, 234–38
responsibility for, 183–85, 209–
    13, 223–25, 228–29, 255
and sex, 99–100
and tax policy, 225, 239, 246,
    247, 249, 250, 252, 255
vs. work, 186–90
of working mothers, 123–26,
    204
    See also Day care
China Beach (TV series), 18
Christianity, 233
Churches, importance of, 253
Citadel, The, 36–37, 38, 170
Civil Rights Act of 1964, 226
Clinton, Bill, 31, 102, 220, 239,
    242
Clinton, Hillary Rodham, 127,
    220
Clothes, 38, 40–56, 58
Cobb, Alicia (pseud.), 221
College women, elite, 66–72
Communication, 157
Communitarianism, 245
Companionate marriages, 95, 181,
    186
Congress (U.S.), 245
Conservatives
    and abortion, 234
    and common good, 249
    and family values, 148, 228
    vs. feminists, 151–52
    and motherhood, 188, 202–4,
        255–56
    and sexual differences, 229
    and tax policy, 238–39
Contraception, 63, 66, 68, 85, 100
    and abortion, 70–71

See also Birth control
Cooke, Beth (pseud.), 195–96, 203
Cosmopolitan, 53
Cuomo, Mario, 90

Darwinian theory of evolution, 79
Davis, Anslie (pseud.), 120
Davis, Tanya, 32
Day care, 123, 124, 128–29, 190, 216–20, 225, 239–42, 245–46, 250, 251–54
Democrats, 239
Denton, Christie (pseud.), 164–65
Dieting, 39–40
Discrimination, 117, 132, 138
Divorce, 72, 81–82, 95, 96, 114, 115, 151, 189, 201, 223
Donna Reed Show, 242
Double standard, 63, 95
Dougherty, Cindy (pseud.), 173–76, 183
Douglas, Susan, 40, 150
Dressing. *See* Clothes

Economic revolution, 110–39
and equality, 134–36
history of, 114–18
problems of, 123–34
and sexual revolution, 110–11
stories of, 118–23
threat of, 114
Equality, of pay, 128, 134–36, 138, 139
Equal Rights Amendment (ERA), 15, 16, 77
Erotic Silence of the American Wife, The (Heyn), 97

European welfare states, 243–44, 249
Evans, Lisa (pseud.), 26, 28
Everly Brothers, 61
Extramarital sex, 64, 95–97

Faludi, Susan, 29, 31, 226, 228
Family
and human connection, 178
ideal, 81
middle class, 135, 236
policy, 238–39
and sexual liberation, 96
size, 68
violence, 257
vs. work, 118, 172–98
Family values, 148, 161, 196, 227–28, 249–51, 256–57
Fantasy, 151, 165
Farrell, Maggie (pseud.), 83–84, 110
Fathers, importance of, 235–36
See also Working fathers
Faulkner, Shannon, 36–38, 170
Federal programs, 242–45
See also Aid to Families with Dependent Children; Welfare
Feldman, Don (pseud.), 67, 70
Feminine Mystique, The (Friedan), 14, 111–12, 228
Feminism
and abortion, 10, 12, 13, 17, 29, 59, 76, 234
agenda of, 12, 32
"backlash" against, 145
and censorship, 99
and common good, 249
vs. conservatives, 151–52
and day care, 241–42

and discrimination, 132
diversity in, 30–31
and economic revolution, 10,
    111–12, 116, 135
failure of, 28–33
and families, 28, 30, 32, 228,
    238–39
and federal programs, 244–45
and femininity, 36
and FMLA, 248–49
goals of, 29
and household chores, 184
impact of, 16
and inner city, 24–26
irrelevance of, 33
litmus test of, 12, 59
and male brutality, 145, 147–49
meaning of, 11, 16
mistrust of, 9–11, 17–18, 167
and "mommy track," 224
and motherhood, 202–4, 212,
    255–56
and pay equity, 128
perception of, 32–33
and sexual dangers, 162–64
and sexual freedom, 58–59, 90
and single mothers, 185, 234
and vulnerability, 144–45
and welfare, 27–28
See also Radical feminists
Feminists for Life, 12
Femininity
appeal of, 52–53, 54
and clothing, 43, 45
ideal of, 40
importance of, 38
as mask, 39
traditional image of, 35, 56
as trap or bond, 36

Fetus, 73, 88, 89, 91, 92, 107,
    152, 159, 173
first-trimester, 230
and hormonal differences, 159
third-trimester, 230
vs. woman, 231
Fidelity, value of, 183
Firing Line (TV show), 203
FMLA (Family and Medical
    Leave Act of 1993), 223,
    247, 248–49, 254
Folk wisdom, 149
France, 244
French, Marilyn, 115
Friedan, Betty, 14, 30, 111–12,
    116, 203, 215, 226–28
Fund for a Feminist Majority, 12

Geraldo (TV show), 22, 40–45,
    50, 58
Gerhold, Cathy, 208–9
Germany, 243–44
Goldfarb, Lucy (pseud.), 67–68,
    70, 83, 84, 110
Grandparents, role of, 212
Grayson, Dawn (pseud.), 121
Griffith, Melanie, 52

Harvard Business Review, 213
Haucly, Victoria, 32
Hawn, Goldie, 147
Head Start program, 254
Health care, 245
Hedstrom, Janis, 32
Hewlett, Sylvia, 207–8, 209, 214
Heyn, Dalma, 97
Hill, Anita, 29, 32
His Girl Friday (film), 111

Hispanic-Americans, 82, 122, 176
HIV, 100
Hobson, Polly (pseud.), 101
Hochschild, Arlie, 207, 222
Holbrook, Becca, 187, 188, 202
Holly, Buddy, 142
Honduras, 258
Honesty, as value, 65, 81
Hooper, Dora (pseud.), 25
Hormonal differences, 159
Houck, Judge, 37
Housewives, 121–22, 196–97, 203
Hunter, James Davison, 89, 90

IBM, 215, 251
Infanticide, 79, 91
Infidelity, and women's liberation, 96–97
Ireland, Patricia, 29, 96

Jobs, important role of, 242–43
Johnson, Angela (pseud.), 186–87, 188
Johnson, Melanie (pseud.), 121

Karan, Donna, 56
King, Larry, 97
Kinler, Deborah (pseud.), 169
Kirk, Marge (pseud.), 130–31

L. A. Law (TV show), 38
Landsman, Rachel (pseud.), 126
Leach, Penelope, 210, 214
Lese, Joe, 32
London, Tess (pseud.), 97

McClendon, James, 13
MacDonald, Cecilia (pseud.), 121
McDonald, Tony (pseud.), 84
McKinney, Dora (pseud.), 146–47
MacKinnon, Catharine, 99
Maldonado, Linda (pseud.), 13, 100–101, 179–80, 182, 192
Male brutality, 145, 147–49, 161–65
Male strength, image of, 165–66
Marchand, Jim (pseud.), 85
Margolies-Mezvinsky, Marjorie, 51
Marriage, 151, 197, 229
    appeal of, 166–70, 178–81
    and sexual liberation, 95–96
    strains in, 182–86
    and virginity, 66–67
    See also Companionate marriages; Open marriages
Masloski, Nancy, 207
Mason, Brooke (pseud.), 17, 19, 20, 28–29, 35, 192–93, 194
Maternity leave, 251–52
Matthews, Marcy (pseud.), 119–20
Medicare, 102
Memoirs of an Ex-Prom Queen (Shulman), 16
Men
    communication of, 157
    and economic revolution, 128–34, 237
    and household chores, 220–25
    and marriage, 182–86
    and sexual differences, 145–46, 155–60, 229
    and sexual relations, 160–65
    See also Fathers; Male brutality; Male strength
Menace II Society (film), 154

Michaels, Alison (pseud.), 222
Middle class, 237
  families, 135, 236
  morality, 65
  women, 25, 61, 101
Miller, Martha (pseud.), 112–13,
    155–56
Miller, Sharon (pseud.), 162
"Mommy track" debate, 213–16,
    224, 225, 247
Moore, David (pseud.), 181–82
Moore, Demi, 60
Morality
  and abortion, 29, 76–77, 89–90,
    232, 244
  middle class, 65
  and motherhood, 92–94
  and premarital sex, 64, 69, 75,
    94–95, 106
  of reproduction, 90, 91, 93,
    104–7
  and sexual liberation, 86–94,
    98–100
  and sexual revolution, 62–65,
    69, 72, 233
Moral Majority, 227
Morrison, Janelle (pseud.), 125–26
Motherhood, 106, 128, 151
  and bonding with child, 210–11
  conflicts in, 205–9
  demeaning of, 202–3
  good-enough, 213
  importance of, to women, 188–
    89, 214
  joys of, 256–58
  and morality, 92–94
  as responsibility, 254–55
  saintly version of, 212
  See also Single mothers;

Welfare mothers; Working
    mothers
Ms. Foundation, 12
Murphy Brown (TV series), 18,
    172–73, 176–78
Musat, James G., 32

Nannies, 124
National Abortion Rights Action
    League (NARAL), 12
National Women's Political
    Caucus, 12, 214–15
Natural rights, 79–80
New Jack City (film), 25
New Woman, 53
NOW (National Organization for
    Women), 12, 19, 29, 31, 32,
    214–15
Nudity, 75, 82

Obscenity, 99
Older women, 115, 129
Open marriages, 96
Orenstein, Peggy, 187
Orphanages, 257–58
Ortiz, Gabriella (pseud.), 13, 76,
    101, 167–68, 180, 221
Our Bodies, Ourselves (health
    guide), 148

Parker, Margot, 51–52
Part-time work, 224, 246–50, 252
Patterson, Gloria (pseud.), 13, 22–
    24, 35, 62, 66, 97–98, 153–
    54, 158, 161, 167, 174–76,
    180, 209, 241, 244
Pill, the, 66–68, 70, 85, 94

Planned Parenthood, 65

Planned Parenthood v. *Casey,*
  103–6

Polakow, Valerie, 243

Polasky, Cheryl (pseud.), 162,
  199–200

Poor black people, 66

Poor women
  abortion for, 102–7, 231–32,
    234
  and day care, 240–41
  and economic revolution, 117,
    124, 130, 135
  goals of, 204
  hardships of, 190, 191, 244
  needs of, 28–29
  pregnancy of, 61, 65, 114
  as single mothers, 176, 177,
    234, 237
  See also Welfare; Working-class
    women

Pornography, 99, 108

Poverty, of children, 201–2

Pregnancy
  and abortion, 103–4
  and contraception, 63, 70
  of poor women, 65
  teenage, 100, 114
  as trauma, 61–62

Premarital sex, 66, 71, 78, 81, 96,
    98, 102, 177
  and morality, 64, 69, 75, 94–95,
    106

Private Benjamin (film), 147

Pro-choice, on abortion, 11, 12,
    16, 25, 61, 73–74, 87, 91, 92,
    103

Professional women
  conflicts of, 192–93

  and economic revolution, 116,
    126, 135
  and femininity, 54
  and part-time work, 224
  See also Career women; College
    women, elite; Upscale
    women

Pro-life, on abortion, 25, 73–74,
    87, 91, 94, 103

Promiscuity, 98, 99

Prothrow-Stith, Deborah, 235

"Quality" time, 213

Quayle, Dan, 176

Radical feminists
  and child care, 224
  and complexity of problems,
    160
  and femininity, 56
  and independence of women,
    176
  and needs of women, 227–28
  on power, 99
  and rape, 148

Ramirez, Maria (pseud.), 9, 76,
    166–67, 181, 191, 220, 221,
    222

Ramo, Roberta Cooper, 257

Rape, 10, 18, 99, 148, 160
  See also Acquaintance rape

Ravenel, Aprill (pseud.), 13, 62,
    66, 154–55, 168, 174–76,
    202, 206, 241

Reagan, Ronald, 131, 204

Reasonable Doubts (TV series), 18

Redbook, 53

Rehnquist, William, 104
Religion, 65, 252–53
Religious right, 30, 94, 160, 176, 232
See also Conservatives
Remarriage, 95, 96, 116, 201
Reproduction, morality of, 90, 91, 93, 104–7
Republicans, 103, 232, 239, 245
Richards, Maggie (pseud.), 22
Right-to-life. See Pro-life
Rivers, Dawn (pseud.), 93
Robertson, Pat, 232
Roe v. Wade, 71–73, 76, 78–82, 85, 90–92, 103, 231
Roiphe, Anne, 16
Roiphe, Katie, 30, 31, 164, 165
Romance, 165, 170
Romano, Terry (pseud.), 205–6, 216, 219, 220
Rose, Julie, 213–14
Russell, Rosalind, 111
Rust v. Sullivan, 102

Sanders, Patricia (pseud.), 18–20, 28, 120, 180
Saxon, Bill (pseud.), 68
Scalia, Antonin, 109
Schoolgirls (Orenstein), 187
Schwartz, Felice, 213–15, 224, 226
Schwartz, Professor (pseud.), 86
Scorsese, Martin, 51
Second Sex, The (Beauvoir), 39
Second Stage, The (Friedan), 30, 227
Senate (U.S.), 32
Seventeen magazine, 44
Sex education, 99–100

Sexism, 188
in reverse, 133–34
Sexual abuse, 16
Sexual differences, 145–46, 155–60, 229
Sexual harassment, 10, 17, 18, 51, 132, 147
Sexuality
displays of, 41–43
as moral issue, 62–63
relations, 160–65
Sexual liberation, 25, 28
and marriage, 95–96
and morality, 86–94, 98–100
Sexually transmitted diseases, 100
Sexual revolution, 58–81
and abortion, 72–78
and clothes, 51
and economic revolution, 110–11
and morality, 62–65, 69, 72, 233
results of, 94–96
Sexual violence, 16, 108, 161–65
Shalala, Donna, 235
Shirelles, the, 150
Shulman, Alix Kates, 16
Silvestri, Andrea (pseud.), 156
Simon, Lisa, 207
Single mothers, 28, 240, 244
African-Americans as, 78, 201
and economic revolution, 124, 126, 127
growth of, 96, 151, 236, 241–42
hardships of, 124, 185, 186–89, 202
poor women as, 176, 177, 234, 237
upscale, 177–78
working, 191

Single women, 29, 169
and abortion, 75–76
and economic revolution, 114–15, 116, 120
upscale, 172–73
Skube, Michael, 21–22
Slavery, 233
Small businesses, 251–52, 253
Smith, Susan, 200–201
Social Security, 243, 249
Spousal abuse, 170
Stern, Pauline (pseud.), 70–71, 83, 84, 110
Stewart, Nicole (pseud.), 140–43
Stimpson, Catherine, 228
Stories, importance of, 149–52
Story, Joseph, 233
Style. *See* Clothes
Superwoman, myth of, 114
Supreme Court (U.S.), 102–4, 106, 109, 231
Sweden, 243–44
Swift, Judy (pseud.), 105, 110

Tannen, Deborah, 157, 158–59
Tax policies, 225, 239, 246, 247–48, 250, 251, 253, 254–55
Taylor, Veronica (pseud.), 153
Technological revolution, 112
Teenagers, 76
and abortion, 104
pregnancies of, 99–100, 114
thirtysomething (TV series), 18
Thomas, Amanda (pseud.), 101, 191
Thomas, Clarence, 32
Thomas, Tracey (pseud.), 84–86, 110

Trescott, Ruth (pseud.), 216–20
Two-parent families, encouragement of, 251
Two-person households, income in, 137

United Kingdom, 244
See also British
Upscale women, 82, 255
and day care, 240–43, 251–53
and economic revolution, 127–28
and feminism, 185
goals of, 204
influence of, 224–25
single, 172–73
single mothers as, 177–78
young, 127–28
Up the Sand Box (Roiphe), 16
Uribe, Carla (pseud.), 179, 180
USA Today, 32
U.S. Department of Labor and Commerce, 237

Values, war of, 151–52
Vanity Fair, 60
Victimization, 149, 170
Violence
family, 257
sexual, 16, 108, 161–65
Virginity, 60, 63, 66–67
Vogue, 51, 150
Vojdik, Valorie, 37, 38
Vulnerability, female, 143–49

"Wake Up Little Susie" (song), 61

Walker, Geraldine, 130
Washington, Courtney (pseud.), 61
Watson, Carolina (pseud.), 191, 193–94
Weaver, Sigourney, 52
Webster v. *Reproductive Services*, 102
Welch, April, 187, 188
Welfare, 202
  in Europe, 243
  and feminism, 27–28
  for single mothers, 124
  split over, 241
Welfare mothers, 189
  burden of, 177, 238
  and economic revolution, 128–29
  problem of, 234–35
Wharton, Edith, 51
White, Burton, 190
Wilder, Laura Ingalls, 150
Willis, Ellen, 30, 227, 228
"Will You Love Me Tomorrow?" (song), 150
Wilson, Andrew (pseud.), 182
Wilson, Nancy, 11, 19, 21, 47
Wilson, William Julius, 176, 235
Winnicott, D. W., 213
Wolf, Naomi, 24, 29, 30, 39, 132
Wollstonecraft, Mary, 39
Woman's Room, The (French), 115–16
Women
  bodies of, 148
  common ground for, 152–53
  communication of, 157
  earnings of, 129–31
  vs. fetus, 231

independence vs. responsibility, 189–90
  and sexual differences, 145–46, 155–60, 229
  and sexual relations, 160–65
  stories of, 149–53
  See also Feminism; Marriage; Motherhood; Poor women; Professional women; Single women; Working women
Woodruff, Judy, 223–24
Work
  vs. children, 186–90
  vs. family, 118, 172–98
Working-class women, 65
Working fathers, 183, 189
Working Girl (film), 52
Working Mother, 207
Working mothers
  children of, 123–26, 204
  conflicts of, work vs. family, 183
  and day care, 216–20, 240
  and economic revolution, 113–14, 123–28
  and family values, 250
  and feminism, mistrust of, 11
  and jobs with benefits, 247
  married, 191
  and maternity leave, 251–52
  and "mommy track" debate, 213–16
  needs of, with young children, 189–90
  and simplistic solutions, 11
  single, 191
  and tax policies, 239
  work schedules of, 215
  worries of, 16–17

Working wives, 134, 137
Working Woman, 53
Working women
  creation of new, 112
  and economic revolution, 112,
    114–23
  vs. housewives, 121–22
  numbers of, 114
  participation in labor force of,
    117–18

Wright, Deena (pseud.), 162

You Just Don't Understand
  (Tannen), 157
Young women, 130
  upscale, 127–28

ABOUT THE AUTHOR

Elizabeth Fox-Genovese is the Eleonore Raoul Professor of the Humanities and Professor of History at Emory University, where she is also a member of the English, Comparative Literature, and Women's Studies faculties. Her books include *Within the Plantation Household: Black and White Women of the Old South* and *Feminism Without Illusions.* She has published widely on women's issues and culture in many magazines and newspapers, and lives in Atlanta.

1558